ILLEGAL IMMIGRATION AND COMMERCIAL SEX

The New Slave Trade

Edited by

PHIL WILLIAMS

University of Pittsburgh

FRANK CASS
LONDON • PORTLAND, OR

First published in 1999 in Great Britain by
FRANK CASS PUBLISHERS
Newbury House, 900 Eastern Avenue
London, IG2 7HH

and in the United States of America by
FRANK CASS PUBLISHERS
c/o ISBS 5804 N.E. Hassalo Street
Portland, Oregon 97213-3644

Copyright © 1999 Frank Cass Publishers

Website: www.frankcass.com

British Library Cataloguing in Publication Data

Illegal Immigration and Commercial Sex: The New Slave Trade
  1. Illegal aliens 2. Illegal aliens – Transportation
  3. Illegal aliens – Social conditions
  I. Williams, Phil, 1948–
  323.6'31

ISBN 0-7146-4832-9 (cloth)
ISBN 0-7146-4384-X (paper)

Library of Congress Cataloging-in-Publication Data

Illegal Immigration and Commercial Sex: The New Slave Trade /
edited by Phil Williams
      p. cm.
  Includes bibliographical references.
  ISBN 0-7146-4832-9 (cloth). – ISBN -7416-4384-X (pbk.)
  1. Transnational crime. 2. Organized crime. 3 Illegal aliens.
  4. Sex crimes. 5. Smuggling. 6. Emigration and immigration.
  I. Williams, Phil, 1948–   .
  HV6252.H85   1999
  364.1'35–dc21   99-25237
                                                      CIP

This group of studies first appeared as a special issue of
Transnational Organized Crime, Vol.3, No.4,
Winter 1997 (ISSN 1357-7387), published by Frank Cass.

Printed in Great Britain by Antony Rowe Ltd.

Contents

DOCUMENTATION

Human Commodity Trafficking: An Overview[1]

PHIL WILLIAMS

Many of the activities of transnational criminal organizations are designed to provide illicit goods and services for which there is a large and flourishing demand. Because of this, organized crime is sometimes portrayed as relatively harmless, a form of borderline entrepreneurship that feeds on opportunities provided by various forms of prohibition. The criminals, and those who defend their activities, contend that they are simply meeting the demands of consumers willing to pay for certain kinds of commodities and services that are not regarded as socially acceptable. Drug trafficking is perhaps the most obvious activity that fits into this category, but similar arguments are made about illegal gambling and prostitution. In a similar vein, the smuggling of illegal aliens is sometimes portrayed as simply a means of circumventing immigration restrictions and, therefore, as a victimless crime. Such an innocuous portrayal of alien smuggling ignores many of the unpleasant realities of a business that reduces people to the level of commodities. In fact, many of those who are trafficked are not only treated appallingly *en route* but are sometimes indentured or forced into crime or prostitution on their arrival into the destination state. When examined closely, illegal alien trafficking frequently involves significant violations of human rights, with all too many cases of would be migrants being drowned on sub-standard ships, suffocated in containers, or left stranded by traffickers who take their money and fail to deliver them to the promised destination. Chinese snakeheads who organize much of the smuggling of Chinese citizens to the United States not only hire enforcers for the duration of the sea voyage, but also place the new immigrants in the hands of enforcers until final payment is made. Illegal aliens from China who arrive in New York, for example, are kept in basements in appalling conditions, are often shackled or handcuffed, and are subjected to considerable violence.[2] In some cases, the men are indentured for years, while women are forced into prostitution. The

1

illegal migrants have little recourse: their very illegality inhibits them from going to the authorities, a reluctance that is turned into a prohibition by the threat of violent retribution against informants.

For all this, illegal migrant trafficking is a large and growing industry, facilitated by the ease of travel, corruption or laxity of immigration officials in a significant number of countries, and driven by the asymmetry between the number of people wanting to migrate (for whatever reason) and the restrictions imposed by governments on the number of immigrants legally allowed to enter their countries. Although China is one of the major source countries, others include India, Sri Lanka, Albania, and Turkey (with the Kurdish minority providing a large outflow). In Africa the flow of illegal immigrants has been to the south with South Africa becoming either the final destination or a major transit point for those seeking to go to the United States or elsewhere. In fact, most developing countries have a flow of both legal and illegal immigrants seeking to escape from poverty or repression or to obtain greater freedom and economic opportunities elsewhere. In other cases, war, ethnic cleansing, environmental degradation, or political persecution are the driving forces for the exodus. Whatever the driving factors, however, in many cases criminal organizations have established themselves very effectively as the "travel agents" for illegal migrants. In some cases the entrepreneurs are not heavily involved in other forms of crime and have formed small organizations specifically to meet the migration demand. In other cases, well-established criminal groups have simply diversified their activities into one more profitable area of activity.

A sub-set of trafficking in migrants that highlights even more starkly the notion of treating people as commodities is the trafficking of women and children either for the commercial sex industry or for forced labor, or in some instances for use as beggars. One report by the International Organization for Migration has noted that prostitution in Asia increasingly involves women and children who have been trafficked across national borders. Explained in part by economic disparities among countries – as well as the failure of economic benefits to filter down to women – this phenomenon is likely to be intensified by the Asian economic crisis.[4] It also extends well beyond Asia with women from Thailand, the Philippines, and elsewhere in the region ending up in Western Europe and the United States. It has been estimated, for example, that 3,000 of the approximately 7,000 prostitutes in Berlin are from Thailand.[5]

In some cases, of course, women knowingly enter the world of commercial sex, albeit as an act of economic desperation and propelled by concern for their family. In other cases, women seeking better conditions and remuneration overseas are deceived by attractive package deals and offers of well-paying jobs, only to be forced into prostitution on their arrival. This happens not only to women from developing countries, but also to women from eastern Europe and the former Soviet Union who are trafficked to western Europe, Israel, and the United States.

In the world of human commodity trafficking, exploitation of children is, if anything, even more pronounced than that of women. It has been reported, for example, that handicapped children are being used as beggars in Cambodia and other developing countries. In some instances, unscrupulous traffickers are deliberately injuring or mutilating children in order to extract maximum sympathy and cash – all of which goes into the pockets of the traffickers.[6] In other cases, children are sold to agents by their parents and then taken to another country or region where they are forced into prostitution. Recruiters from India, for example, visit villages in Nepal and buy young girls who are subsequently taken to India for work in the commercial sex trade – especially in Bombay, which has a particularly large concentration of brothels, and is particularly notorious not only for its child prostitutes but also for the protection that is provided by politicians to the criminal organizations who control the sex trade.[7] Something similar happens with Burmese girls who are taken to Thailand for work as prostitutes. The economic dynamics are clear. "The transaction can substantially improve the economic situation of the family in two ways: firstly, it provides much needed income, and secondly, it takes away a potential economic burden on the family, that is, there will be no need to provide a dowry".[8] Nevertheless, trafficking in children for commercial sex remains the most pernicious aspect of the trafficking business and one in which there are very clear victims.

The exploitation of children in the sex trade, however, goes well beyond their movement from one country to another, and includes other forms such as sex tourism in which the consumers visit countries such as Thailand or Sri Lanka where there is a permissive attitude towards sex with children. Rather than the children being brought to the consumer market, the customers visit the markets that are promoted as part of the tourism industry. Another form of exploitation is the abuse of children for pornography, which is increasingly circulated among pedophiles using the Internet and the World Wide Web. Although these variations of the exploitation of children for commercial sex do not involve trafficking in the strict sense of the term they do involve treating children as commodities and consequently are considered here as part of the phenomenon of human commodity trafficking.

As well as the direct consequences for the victims, human commodity trafficking, like other forms of transnational criminal activity, is closely linked to corruption. Indeed, in this area of criminal activity, as in others, corruption provides the lubricant which allows criminal organizations to operate with maximum effectiveness and minimum interference. In human commodity trafficking, this might simply involve payoffs to immigration officers. Alternatively, the complicity of officials sometimes becomes more direct, involving the acquisition of false passports and visas. Perhaps the most notable case of official involvement was that of Jerry Stuchiner, an agent for the United States Immigration and Naturalization Service who was arrested in 1996 for providing Honduran passports to Chinese immigrant smugglers.[9] In other instances, of course, the corrupt officials adopt a lower profile and are not detected.

In spite of the payoffs that have to be made to protect human commodity trafficking, it remains a lucrative activity. From the perspective of the criminal organizations and others who control the trade in human commodities, it has several advantages:

- the initial investment or start-up costs for recruitment and transportation are small compared with the profits that can be made;

- the women and children are relatively durable and can be used and re-used for as long as it is profitable;

- women and children can also be sold or transferred to others in the same business who can then present them to their customers as "new";

- the exploitation of women and children for pornography has become much easier and less costly with the capacity to reproduce and distribute digital images at very low cost;

- most of these activities can be carried out with very little risk as penalties for trafficking in many countries are very low, while enforcement activities are often lax, sporadic, or nonexistent.

Against this background, the analyses in this volume attempt to shed light on various dimensions of human commodity trafficking. In assessing criminal activities, of course, precision is highly elusive since successful activities remain covert and undetected. Nevertheless, it is possible to highlight certain aspects of the business and to identify measures that could be taken to make it less profitable and more costly for the traffickers. With this in mind the volume seeks to illuminate the following questions:

- what are the dimensions of the global trade in illegal migrants and in the trafficking of women and children for commercial sex?

- what are the dynamics of the various aspects of human commodity trafficking?

- what is the precise role of organized crime in this business and how organized is it?

- what has been done about such activities and what initiatives are governments and international agencies currently taking to prevent, control, or mitigate human commodity trafficking?

No single volume can hope to provide definite answers to these questions. Nevertheless, the essays here shed considerable light on them. In the first study Margaret E. Beare looks at the trafficking of illegal migrants. Although Beare appropriately casts doubt on the proposition that this is a national security problem amenable to traditional military or even law enforcement solutions, she acknowledges very clearly that it is a "human security" problem. As such, it requires responses that do not simply extend beyond law enforcement but are truly comprehensive in scope. Her analysis also highlights the dynamics of the market for illegal migration, identifies several categories of migrants, and examines the support systems for illegal migrants. In addition, it examines the characteristics of sophisticated smuggling operations, the particular attractions of human smuggling by ocean-going cargo ships, and the often neglected but critically important role played by the "legitimate" society in facilitating illegal migration.

In the next study, Gillian Caldwell, Steve Galster, Jyothi Kanics, and Nadia Steinzor of Global Survival Network (GSN) examine the trafficking of Russian women for the commercial sex trade. The analysis is based on an investigation by GSN between April 1995 and Autumn 1997 which included the creation of a dummy company that ostensibly was involved in importing foreign women as escorts and entertainers. It focuses on the growing trade in Russian women for forced prostitution. The authors highlight the variety of destinations of these women, destinations that include Germany, the United States, Switzerland, Japan, and Macau. As part of an examination of who controls this trade, they also explore the role of Russian criminal organizations. The conclusion is that Russian mafia involvement in the sex trade and trafficking business is substantial, with most businesses owned or protected by criminal groups. At the same time, it is contended that the involvement of high-level groups which also pursue a variety of other criminal enterprises has declined, but that the vacuum has been filled by mid-level and lower-level groups. The analysis contains some very compelling case studies while also highlighting the role of collusion and corruption.

Trafficking in women from the former Soviet bloc has received considerable attention in the late 1990s. So too has trafficking in Asia, much of which revolves around Thailand which has had a pivotal role in the global sex trade since the early days of the Vietnam war. In the third essay in this collection, Pasuk Phongpaichit looks primarily at the role of Thailand as both a source country and a destination country, while also acknowledging that it is an important transshipment country in a variety of human commodity flows. The main focus is on the inward flow of women, especially from Burma, and the outward flow of workers and sex workers from Thailand to Japan, Taiwan, Germany, and other destinations. The author argues that human trafficking is linked to other illicit activities such as arms trading, illegal gambling, and drug trafficking and is facilitated by links to powerful figures in the bureaucracy, military, police, and politics. The analysis, which is rich in data, assesses the economic value of Thai out-migrants to the Thai economy as well as the value to the recipient countries. It also notes that during the expansion of Thai prostitution in Japan in the 1980s, around 90 percent of the women were tricked or forced into the commercial sex trade. In addition, the paper focuses on illegal immigrant workers in Thailand, about two-thirds of whom are Burmese. It emphasizes that Burmese women and girls who become involved in the sex trade are particularly vulnerable because they are illegal immigrants. For the agents and police in Thailand who control much of the trafficking, the benefits from four major inbound and outbound flows is estimated at somewhere between 200 and 280 million U.S. dollars. The social costs, however, are significant and the author identifies several ways of alleviating these. An appendix provides some vivid case studies of Thai prostitutes in Japan.

In the next study, Gerben J.N. Bruinsma and Guus Meershoek examine the role of organized crime in trafficking in women for prostitution in Holland. Using extensive empirical data from police sources, the authors look at the characteristics of prostitution in Belgium that attract trafficking in women. They identify the kinds of criminal organizations that engage in trafficking of women from eastern and central Europe to Holland and explore the *modus operandi* of these groups, including recruitment patterns, the trafficking process itself, and the nature of work in the prostitution sector of the economy. Significantly, they identify two categories of organizations involved in the trafficking business – loosely organized cliques of professionals and larger organized crime groups (with an average of 11 persons) with a clear division of labor among their members. The latter groups are also active in smuggling drugs, arms, and stolen cars in a reverse flow from that of the women.

The following piece by Sarah Shannon moves from the national level to the global and focuses on the role of organized crime in the global sex trade. Shannon suggests that the market is driven by demand but crucially supported both by widespread poverty and by cultural attitudes which discriminate against women and children. She highlights both global trends and regional peculiarities offering a broad survey that complements the more specifically national studies of Thailand and Holland as well as the analysis of women from Russia and other parts of the former Soviet Union. The conclusion is that the role of organized crime is multifaceted. The criminal groups are sometimes directly involved in trafficking women for prostitution while in other cases they provide security, support, and liaison services to pimps and brothel owners.

The essay by Phil Williams also offers a macro level analysis but focuses less on the organizations than on the market dynamics of trafficking in women and children for commercial sex. It contends that the markets in women and children are similar in essentials to other illicit markets, that there are many participants in these markets, and that criminal organizations, although important players, are not invariably the dominating force that is sometimes suggested. In addition, the paper argues that a better understanding of market dynamics facilitates the development of more effective counter-measures that not only create market barriers but also introduce greater risks and costs into market transactions. It looks at some of the measures taken by governments in response to trafficking in women and children and considers additional measures that could usefully be introduced and implemented. Important initiatives to counter trafficking in children were identified in a report presented to the UN General Assembly in October 1996, excerpts from which are included in the documentation section. Williams discusses this report and also highlights the importance of the World Congress Against Commercial Sexual Exploitation of Children held in Stockholm in August 1996 which produced a Declaration and Agenda for Action. Excerpts from the interim report of this Congress are also included in the documentation section.

In the following piece by Anna Grant, Fiona David, and Peter Grabosky, the emphasis shifts from trafficking in children as such to trafficking in child pornography. The authors examine how the transmission of child pornography has been revolutionized by digital technology and the World Wide Web which have facilitated cheap and easy communications and the reproduction and distribution of pornographic images of children. They suggest that although there might be some participants in the market for commercial reasons, this illicit activity differs from most others in that it is predominantly about personal gratification for pedophiles rather than profit as such. The authors identify different levels of organizations among pedophiles but suggest that there are quite sophisticated networks which use encryption as a security measure. Writing from an Australian perspective, they also look at the steps that have been taken in response to the rapid growth of child pornography and identify what they see as the most appropriate configuration of counter-measures in both the domestic and transnational context.

The study by Penelope Turnbull also focuses on counter-measures, but in this case on counter-measures developed by the European Union in response to trafficking in women and children. Echoing concerns voiced in a different context by Margaret Beare in her contribution, Turnbull contends that immigration and crime issues have been fused together in ways that obscure the human rights dimensions of many immigration issues. Nevertheless, she suggests, the EU has made considerable progress not only in placing the issue on the agenda but also in developing a cooperative approach among the member states. The leadership of Anita Gradin, Commissioner for Justice and Home Affairs, has been critical in devising a program which has included assistance to some of the supplier states located in eastern Europe, the development of more effective legislation to deal with the phenomenon, and greater transatlantic cooperation especially in relation to the trafficking of women from Ukraine.

Developing an information campaign for Ukraine has been a focus of cooperation between the United States and Western Europe. At the same time, the United States has gradually moved toward the development of a more comprehensive response This process was given considerable impetus on March 11, 1998 when President Clinton issued a memorandum (a copy of which can be found in the documentation section) directing the Secretary of State, the Attorney General, the Administrator of the Agency for International Development, and the Director of the United States Information Agency to give the issue greater attention. The Attorney General was required to take steps to ensure the safety of victims and witnesses and ensure their safe return to their country of origin. Temporary or permanent legal status for victims of trafficking was also to be considered as were legal changes to ensure that trafficking is criminalized and that prosecution efforts are more effective. The Secretary of State was required to cooperate with source, transit, and destination countries to develop strategies for protecting and assisting victims of trafficking. Preventive efforts based on public awareness campaigns were to be accompanied by assistance in devising and implementing legislation to combat trafficking and to provide assistance to its victims. In fact, the United States has initiated cooperative programs not only with Ukraine, but also Italy and Israel. Such initiatives are useful. Nevertheless, much more needs to be done at the international level before human commodity trafficking – a phenomenon that is sometimes described as the most modern form of slavery – is seriously inhibited. The phenomenon is widespread; the results often tragic; and the counter-measures, for all the recent flurry of initiatives, still far short of what is required to make a real dent in the problem.

NOTES

1. The term "human commodity trafficking" was suggested by Lina Calderon, Sheryl Pinelli, and Erin Crowe, three members of the author's Capstone Seminar on Transnational Organized Crime, held in the Graduate School of Public and International Affairs, University of Pittsburgh in 1994. See "Transnational Organized Crime: a Capstone Report" (University of Pittsburgh: Matthew B. Ridgway Center for International Security Studies, April 20, 1994), pp.14–21.
2. Peter Kwong, *Forbidden Workers: Illegal Chinese Immigrants and American Labor* (New York: New Press, 1997), p.82.
3. The United States has posted an INS officer to South Africa.
4. "Prostitution in Asia Increasingly Involves Trafficking", *Trafficking in Migrants*, No.15 (Geneva: International Organization for Migration, June 1997), p.1.
5. See "Germany", *Migration News Sheet* (Belgium, May 1997), reported in *Ibid.*, p.3.
6. "Children Recruited as Beggars", *IOM News*, No.2 (Geneva: International Organization for Migration, 1998), p.1.
7. Robert I. Friedman, "India's Shame: Sexual Slavery and Political Corruption are Leading to an AIDS Catastrophe", *The Nation* (April 8, 1996), Vol.262, No.14, p.11 and following.
8. "Prostitution in Asia Increasingly Involves Trafficking", *op.cit.*, p.2.
9. Brook Larmer and Melinda Liu, "Smuggling People", *Newsweek* (March 17, 1997), pp.34–36.

Illegal Migration:
Personal Tragedies, Social Problems, or National Security Threats?

MARGARET E. BEARE

INTRODUCTION

This study surveys the issue areas and policy dilemmas related broadly to illegal migration. Like all complex issues, to understand illegal migration one must understand the context: political, economic, and social environments; motivations of the illegal migrating populations and other non-illegal migrant groups; the identity of those who exploit and/or are serviced by the illegal migrants. This paper discusses illegal migration within the wider debate over "security threats" which result as a consequence of transnational crimes. The paper questions whether illegal migration should be seen, and responded to, as a security threat. Transnational crimes are increasingly being viewed from the perspective of threats to nation-states.[1] British Prime Minister, Tony Blair, in a speech prior to the May 1998 G8 Summit, identified issues such as poverty, the environment, unemployment, and organized crime as areas of great concern within the global economy.[2] Likewise in May 1998, President Clinton announced that the United States would be unveiling a comprehensive plan to combat organized crime including the trafficking in women and children. As stated by the White House policy adviser, "This is where the threats are now, and what we must focus on because transnational crime threatens us both politically and economically".[3]

"Threats" of many sorts are vulnerable to manipulation by the media and by governments – this appears to be particularly true of "security threats". There is no single criteron that determines what social conditions will be labeled a threat, or a security issue. For example, following the running aground of the Golden Venture off New York on June 1, 1993, the attention given to illegal migration soared in the United States from being a near non-issue, to a national

11

policy topic and an issue for the National Security Council. This catalytic event, of course, makes illegal migration neither more nor less serious than it was prior to the widely publicized incident. However, the media/political response illustrates the need for rational debate. The haphazardness (or more accurately, the politicization) of this process must be part of our discussion. In the same manner that "threats" must be evaluated, the broader consequences of certain definitions of risk must also be acknowledged.

In addition to the *opportunistic* uses of immigration and immigration threats by governments, media, etc., immigration issues can be exploited for more direct policy objectives. In a paper that claims to document the national security implications of illegal migration, Alan Dupont documents the deliberate manipulation of populations by government policies for specific objectives:

- diluting the influence and activities of indigenous communities considered to be hostile or troublesome (Chinese policy of settling ethnic Han people in Tibet and Hanoi's encouragement of the Vietnamese to settle in Eastern Cambodia);

- internal movement of citizens to remote outposts in order to secure sovereignty over the region (Inuit movement by the Government in Canada and the movement of Javanese migrants to sparsely populated archipelago regions);

- use of the "threat" of a wave of refugees to get countries to change their policies or offer aid (Chinese response to President Carter when pressured to loosen the restrictions on Chinese emigration – "How many million Chinese immigrants does the U.S. want?").[4]

Dupont notes that government policies can directly affect the *outflow* of prospective migrants – compare the lack of an exodus during the Pol Pot massacre era to the movement of refugees into Thailand when the regime fell. Likewise, Vietnam did little to curtail the early exodus of people during the late 1970s and early 1980s when those leaving were mainly ethnic Chinese. Later, Hanoi successfully stemmed the flow of immigrants out of Vietnam. At least in part, this was a politically motivated effort to give the appearance of being engaged in the larger economic community.

Dupont states:

Governments themselves have become part of the problem in the sense that they are more often than not the direct or indirect cause of the illegal migration and refugee movements. Not only can they compel, encourage, or prevent international population flows as a deliberate instrument of policy, they are usually the final arbiters of whether people will be allowed to leave or enter ... such decisions are frequently based on security considerations and broad calculations of national interest, rather than humanitarianism or purely economic factors.[5]

These examples illustrate that governments can manipulate populations for security reasons – with the possibility that these movements may later be deemed a security threat. This paper attempts to identify the complicity of diverse interest groups in the immigration "problem". Efforts to "correct" these problems must acknowledge the complicity of others and will call in most cases for a humanitarian rather than a military response.

National Security vs. Human Security

In this post cold-war environment, phrases such as "new security issues", "non-traditional security threats", "transnational crime threats", "regional security issues", and "human security" are used to express a broadening of the notion of insecurities. If writers had chosen different terminology, there might have been less of a tendency for cynics and critics to see the wider use of "security" rhetoric as an attempt by national security agencies (CIA, CSIS, MI5, etc.) to secure their organizational futures. While there may be some truth to this interpretation, the broader notion of human security deserves serious study.

The "security" word is weighted under a tremendous amount of baggage that serves to distort attempts to apply it in the broader "human" context. The word security is customarily located beside the word "threat". The traditional response in the west to a "security threat" is a military response. Certain countries have relied on a "war rhetoric" for so long that no election or budget process can seemingly proceed without a call to "war" – literally or figuratively. The process of studying "new" and important categories of human security issues requires "new" responses that are equally broad and which look to root causes and social solutions. This, I believe, was the point that the Honorable Lloyd Axworthy, the Canadian Minister for Foreign

Affairs, was making in a much quoted speech at York University in 1996. Axworthy called for: "... a response that links security, economic, social development and governance and that addresses the real problems of particular regions and states".[6]

"National security" and "human security" are distinct concepts. While these terms might overlap, they must not be thought of as forms or degrees of the same concept. The image of a continuum that is presented in some of the literature is not only incorrect, but may lead to inappropriate policy responses. For example, while there are aspects of illegal migration that constitute a significant *human security* issue and must be addressed with appropriate policies, in most jurisdictions the *national security* issues, if present, result from the root causes behind the illegal migration – not the illegal migration itself.

A danger of the common use of security rhetoric is in the response that is encouraged by the terminology. It is not good enough to assume that "of course" the response will be different for human security issues than for national security issues, that is, we intend to seek social, economic, and political policy responses to human security issues. There is too much pressure from powerful lobbying agencies, governments, and the military to respond with a known, traditional, highly visible military or "policing" effort. Experiences within the United States, as documented by authors such as Timothy Dunn, illustrate the piecemeal but accumulative move towards an institutionalized acceptance of a military response to immigration.[7]

In the area of illegal migration, the slippery-slope toward a military-type response is what one must resist. In contrast, increasingly we see the militarizing of social problems in the U.S. and elsewhere. A growing body of research has documented this trend.[8] As Kraska stated:

> The most ideologically compatible, and thus most popular battle-front for the new military has been social problems amenable to actual security strategies and tactics, such as urban violence, illegal drugs, and illegal immigration. Not surprisingly, these new military targets are touted by security specialists as emerging trends necessitating the military involvement. Clearly these problems existed previous to the end of the cold-war, hence, what we have are not problems in search of a solution but a solution in search of problems.[9]

Unfocused war rhetoric will not positively advance the issues or lead to policies that are defensible in a democratic/rational/legal justice system.[10] War rhetoric is just that – words to replace the Cold War.[11] This discourse argues that the criminal activity incidental to the end of the Cold War is international, extraordinary, and new, and hence, requires the shifting of existing resources to those organizations left starving for a mandate and resources: the military, security services, and intelligence agencies. Swept up in this grab for additional powers or to maintain their existing resources are the usual suspects: law enforcement, politicians, and the media.

However, once "human security" is separated from the automatic military assumptions of "national security" the term can legitimately be applied quite broadly – including aspects of illegal migration. This paper attempts to illustrate the human security aspects of this phenomenon and also to suggest why a predominantly law enforcement or military response is seldom appropriate for this issue. This concern is not unique to illegal migration; however the human face to immigration and the complexity of the issues involved make the specific responses particularly critical.

Traditional and Alternative Approaches to Immigration

Traditional views tend to see illegal immigration, including alien smuggling, as problematic only in terms of its "control" rather than in wider issues regarding the flow of people across borders. The response was traditionally one of supply, demands, and "costs". The underlying question is, "how can the state tilt the scales so that the risks of being involved in criminal activity are greater than the gains"? The size of the problem becomes a question of numbers – likewise, enforcement successes are also measured in numbers of aliens stopped at the border or arrested.

An extension of this control-oriented perspective takes a broader look at the threats associated with illegal migration and considers the illegal movement and smuggling of people as a security issue (national and/or human). The ebb and flow of people into or through countries is seen to have an impact on the social and economic fabric of a jurisdiction. From this perspective the size of the problem is measured as an increase in crime (real or perceived), incidents of visible violence involving immigrants, and economic labor issues.

A slightly different perspective focuses on the nature of the border and the symbolic and/or real reasons for maintaining the border and the consequences of adhering to what has been called the "territorial trap".[12]

From this broader perspective an understanding of notions of state, sovereignty, racism, employment, and markets is essential to understand the illegal movement of people – and therefore in understanding and developing appropriate policies and enforcement strategies to combat the accompanying criminal activity that turns migration and migrants into an illegal commodity. It is necessary to be continually sensitive to the political environments that help define immigration and illegal migration, and to provide the voice to expressions of what is or is not considered to be a national "threat".

All three perspectives – in an appropriate balance – may be required in order to understand and to respond to illegal migration, particularly if a desired outcome is the ability to make informed policy recommendations. It is only when one sees the illegal migrant and illegal migration within this broader context, that the options – both from an individual and from a policy perspective – become clearer.

Globalization and Issues of Sovereignty

Spontaneous migration (legal or illegal), whereby people move without coercion or the promise of a job, is relatively new. Societies within a global environment are aware of opportunities elsewhere and a "double" process occurs which facilitates migration, that is, this awareness of alternatives combines with international networks that offer support, advice, and enable mobility in ways that make the alternatives seem possible. As Portes states:

> The fulfillment of normative consumption expectations imported from the advanced countries becomes increasingly difficult under conditions of economic scarcity, while growing cross-national ties make it easier to seek a solution through migration.[13]

The issues *and* the solutions are therefore global ones. The large amount of media coverage and the apparent tightening of immigration processes in some jurisdictions require serious study and debate. Increasingly, as all forms of commodities cross borders or move across where borders no longer exist, people will also move – pulled by the hope of better opportunities or pushed by violence and deprivations. Sovereignty issues will increasingly arise in many areas. Business and criminal activity operates now within the global community. Regulation and enforcement-type activity is increasingly the responsibility of non-state agencies and agreements (conventions, treaties, etc). Countries feel pressure to conform with law enforcement and legislative standards set "elsewhere". This paper reaches no conclusion regarding this issue except to suggest that how we have traditionally thought about our borders may have to change. Globalization relates to migration and more specifically to illegal migration in three ways: it creates a *shared world view* as to the threats and risks that countries (developed and less developed) face; to the extent that the risks are real/actual, the *risks themselves are shared*; and globalization encourages and facilitates a *shared response* to these risks.

Current international debate on immigration has seemingly "agreed" that illegal migration and refugees are the foremost issues.[14] Globally, countries are defining illegal alien smuggling as a serious criminal enterprise. The findings of an Australian Federal Police assessment corroborate this conclusion. The large amount of media coverage and the apparent tightening of immigration processes in some jurisdictions requires serious study and debate.

In addition to labor market issues and sovereignty issues, there are linkages between alien smuggling and organized crime. Mixed with "real" issues is the sense that some of the concern may be out of proportion to the actual size of the illegal alien problem. The diverse issues blur and blend – from the issues of concrete realities of organized crime involvement to the more symbolic state sovereignty and the role of borders. While real concerns surround migration, the issue of immigration can incite strong resistance from a country.

The following are samplings of the recent declarations of "the threat" and responses to illegal migration.

- In February 1997, President Clinton declared that: "... an immigration emergency was in existence with respect to the smuggling into the United States of illegal aliens".[15]

- In May 1998 the Clinton administration announced an additional 280 million dollars to help intercept drugs and illegal immigrants along the border.

- The 1997 OECD "Working Paper on Migration" stressed that rather than a domestic issue, illegal migration was a new global reality.[16]

- Indonesian officials have agreed to upgrade police intelligence, defense, and customs links with Australia in order to stop illegal migration by stopping boat people from leaving Indonesia.[17]

- The South Korean government has decided to "crack down" on illegal entry of foreign workers by imposing stricter jail terms, payments to informants, and negotiations with China for an early signing of a criminal suspect repatriation treaty.[18]

- Japan, April 1, 1997, the ruling bloc approved a draft amendment to Japan's Immigration Law with a view to curbing a surge of illegal migrants being smuggled into the country in groups.

- Malaysia, June 11, 1997: Crackdown Continues ... massive one-day immigration inspection ... . About 1,000 illegal workers ... .

- "Austria is the European Centre of Traffickers in Human Beings", reads the headlines announcing the "skyrocketing" trade in illegal immigrants from the former Soviet Union through Austria to other European states.[19]

- Thailand: "Crackdown Planned on Illegal Immigrants" reads the headlines. Plans include the building of six holding centers for illegal aliens awaiting deportation and the doubling of efforts to stop migrants at the borders and to identify those living in Thailand.[20]

- "Immigration is the largest and most contentious problem facing the European Union", "Brussels proposes more help for people settling in the EU but tougher measures against illegal entrants".[21]

Powerful countries have powerful voices. In a global environment it is therefore even more important that the loudest voices are the wisest – which is not always the case. Illegal migrants – especially as they are portrayed by the media, politicians, and the police – are ideal objects for these get-tough quick fixes. The imagery is often of floodgates giving way in front of a sea of criminals, as waves of immigrants enter the country. As Schmid observed, aquatic images are popular![22] For example, the 1997 Canadian report, "Not Just Numbers: Canadian Framework for Future Immigration", addressed a number of the myths about immigration.[23] One such myth is the fear that hordes of foreigners are on their way to Canada. The report makes the point that, in fact, Canada must compete with other industrialized countries to attract the best human capital and that it does not always win in this competition.

Immigrants are "alien" in both a literal and a figurative sense – they are seen to be alien in the sense of being different from the "legitimate" public and any exceptional legislation or police powers adopted to counter their activities are argued to be justified due to the uniqueness of their threat. The demand is made to tighten up borders that no longer exist and to protect the sovereignty rights that have already been eroded, either by the reality of a new economic order that no longer pays heed to "state" or by the extraterritorial reach of neighboring governments. This territorial ambiguity may feed the anxiety that publicized crimes evoke.

"Foreign" threats are easier to target rhetorically in get-tough policies than home-grown criminals. In reality, however, the criminal activities are very much a part of the institutions within the various host, transit, and source countries. Like all other highly sophisticated criminal operations, the trafficking in humans is facilitated by networks of corruption. Travel documentation and border control areas are particularly vulnerable. Often the trafficking does not occur between neighboring countries but rather over vast distances and through numerous countries. Depending on the circumstances, officials in both the transit countries and in the destination country may be implicated.

We must see the real issues as the overlap and intermingling of markets facilitated by corruption and shades of corruption, that is, the sophisticated methods, facilitated by technology, whereby criminal operations give the appearance of legitimacy, leaving at best remnants of a trail. While political rhetoric can serve a positive role to heighten awareness of the links between some aspects of illegal migration and organized crime and corruption, in contrast, hyperbolic fear-mongering may lead to the opposite – a cynicism about even the real issues or a paralytic sense of powerlessness.

SEPARATING THE WHEAT FROM THE CHAFF

With so many issues woven through the illegal migration environment, it is impossible adequately to capture even the main characteristics. However, some key issues include:

- significant regional and unregulated movements of large populations within East Asia, into and through Eastern Europe, into and through South and Central America and up into North America.

- significant labor issues that arise both from situations where illegal migrants are welcomed as a source of labor and in situations where labor is fleeing in search of work.

- the ethnic tensions that arise when the immigrants are perceived to be a threat to "traditional" community values. These tensions and potential violence may cause internal population movements that can result in other consequences associated with displaced populations.

- the numerous political locations around the world that are wrecked by violence and ethno-nationalist strife. While the Cold War may be at an end, other wars have not ceased. The immigration environment is dotted with refugees and displaced persons fleeing from states of unrest and atrocities.

- significant threats to the environment and natural disasters that help to generate the immigration flow.

- the sophisticated transnational crime groups which profit from the illicit immigrant commodity. Because government immigration policies limit legal immigration, there is significant profit in the smuggling of humans.

While there is nothing new about migration in general, the rate of migration has accelerated and more countries are being affected by global migration patterns. The "everyday" of international business, therefore, demands negotiations between countries that previously might have been required between companies holding the same corner within communities. The mechanisms by which these negotiations are conducted, however, have changed. As Karl Polanyi noted as early as 1957, trade has become linked to peace, while historically it was linked with war and the military:

> it was an adjunct of the pirate, the rover, the armed caravan, the hunter and trapper, the sword-bearing merchant, the armed burgesses of the towns, the adventurers and explorers, the planters and conquistadors, the manhunters and slave traders, the colonial armies of the chartered companies.[24]

Sociologists who study migration have noted that international labor migration largely originates at an intermediate level of development not at the lowest level. The very poor and the unemployed are not the first to migrate.[25] Limited information suggests that the same model holds for the illegal migrant as for the legal immigrant. It is argued, for example, that Chinese migrants are leaving a country that is becoming increasingly affluent. Many arrive in Central and Eastern Europe with considerable sums of money. The bribes for documents and for an "invitation letter" to facilitate obtaining a Chinese passport, accommodation, and travel are sufficiently expensive as to limit those who can attempt either legal or illegal migration.[26]

PUSH-PULL FACTORS

Reasons for migration have changed in significant ways that will affect and are affecting the integration of the migrants into their host societies. Current research supports the claim that "push" factors are more instrumental in encouraging migration than are "pull" factors[27] – although even this conclusion varies between countries. Some countries, and parts of specific countries, have a tradition of emigrating, while other do not. Within China for example, the Fujian region has many links abroad and foreigners have come and settled in that province. The northern parts of China have less of an emigrating history. Chinese emigration into Central and Eastern Europe appears to be "pulled" by business opportunities, ease of entry, and access to the west. The key factors that push or/and pull migration include:

- economic disequilibrium between societies at different levels of development. As a result of communications, increased travel and international business, differences between rich and poor or safe and unsafe societies, are far more "visible" than ever.

- asylum seekers and refugees, including undocumented aliens, escaping from war or political persecution.

- the historic changes in eastern Europe and the former Soviet Union which involved unprecedented changes to borders and systems of sovereignty.

- the removal of internal border controls in the European Union, the ethnic war in Yugoslavia, and civil wars or invasions in other parts of the world.

- women being sold and/or otherwise deceived into a state of indentured prostitution and the wider sex-trade industry.

- demographic shifts that require segments of the population to move for employment.

- available "cross-national networks" that facilitate future migration from one area to another – including the growth of criminally assisted illegal migration.

- environmental degradation from which people must flee.

- deliberate governmental policies that manipulate populations for "larger" policy related interests.

There are few employment niches for many of the new immigrants. Hence, there is not an aggressive search to attract new human resources into many countries. The existing labor demand is for a highly skilled or unique population. While cheap labor remains the source of corporate profits in the developed world, corporations themselves move around the globe in search of this labor, accompanied by advantageous environmental protection laws (or lack of protections) and trade agreements. The free movement of industry serves to highlight the conspicuous inequalities, while at the same time reducing the need for legal migration to fill the lower level positions within the most developed countries.

The eras of government sponsored "multiculturalism" have ended. While the rights of new immigrants are still to be protected, the extra spending and "social movement" aspect to programs designed to safeguard the new migrant has ended – along with the end to other government outreach spending. "Pull" factors, therefore, take the form of kinship networks, creating an alternative industry illegally to service potential immigrants.

As government tightens its immigration policies, migrants become a commodity and those who can facilitate the migration of others find themselves in an extremely lucrative business. In addition, like many other areas of law enforcement, there are unintended or unanticipated consequences to many rational enforcement strategies. As law enforcement tightens its control on the illegal alien smuggling trade, it helps to create a monopoly for the particularly sophisticated alien smuggler. The more sophisticated the law enforcement response, the more sophisticated the smuggling operations. As a consequence, we must also look at the roles of organized crime and law enforcement in this illegal trade.

Specific to *illegal* migration, the illegal market is driven by the following supply and demand factors:

- push factors rather than pull factors;

- the number of workers wanting to go abroad exceeds legal opportunities, resulting in a clandestine movement;

- market forces at work – greater demand than can legally be met, resulting in a "value" attached to smuggling services (the larger the surplus of willing migrants, the larger the profits);

- as a government tightens its immigration policy, it helps to create a monopoly for the particularly sophisticated alien smuggler.

BUYING AND SELLING CITIZENSHIP

Who is buying and who is selling "citizenship" – or *de facto* residence chances? Thomas Straubhaar suggests that countries should sell citizenship rights under a system that would equalize these prices worldwide.[28] Critics argue that this raises moral problems due to the sense of "unfairness" created if the right to migrate is tied to the ability to pay. However, this ignores the fact that the unfairness already exists within the legitimate as well as in the illegitimate market.

Entrepreneurial categories for official immigration provide entry for the migrant with economic resources and *organized crime smugglers* offer a service for the remaining client-base of would-be immigrants "on credit". Organized crime tends to take over ill-regulated markets where, for moral or political reasons, the market is not satisfied by legitimate options.[29] In between these two models are the "recruiters". In the labor-producing countries (such as the Philippines) governments often charge their own citizens a fee for the privilege of emigrating. These fees are supposedly for migration-related services. Abella argues that this builds a toleration among migrants for private recruiter fees and that this may encourage illegitimate emigration.[30]

Like many illicit activities, there are various "shadings" that allow criminals who traffic in humans to see their work in more altruistic terms. For example, having residency rights to a country such as Canada or the United States is simply viewed as a commodity that can be turned to economic advantage. Pseudo-marriage schemes, study groups with letters of invitation from a citizen, and various passport manipulations – all done for cash – allow the smuggler and the smuggled to speak as if they are merely operating within a special type of tourist agency.[31] As one smuggler said: "First of all, I never go out to look for clients. Invariably it is the client who comes to me for help ... . Second, I do not traffic in drugs or ammunition. My work hurts nobody. In fact, it helps people".[32]

While our main concern might be the involvement of organized crime in the smuggling of aliens, there are many other abuses to the system aside from organized crime *and* the organized crime groups are not equally exploitive to the migrant nor as criminogenic in the collection of debts. While many operations are sophisticated and violent, other smuggling operations are more "local" and in some cases are not always perceived as criminal, but rather as being streetwise or even providing a valuable service. "Smugglers" or "brokers" may be more entrepreneurial and less gang oriented.

CATEGORIES OF MIGRANTS

Just as smugglers are not a uniform group, likewise, people who migrate are not a uniform population. Policies and practices must address this diversity. This paper acknowledges seven distinct categories of migrants based on their entry status and their status over the longer term: legal-legal (the "norm"); illegal-legal (converted/amnesty/cases/refugee claims); legal-illegal (over-stayers); illegal-illegal (independent); illegal-illegal (indentured); and legal-legal (indentured); and internal "migration".

- *Legal-Legal (the "norm")*
  One assumes that this is the normal route. The person applies for immigrant status, eventually gains legal entry and remains in the country as a legal immigrant. Formal procedures and protections are offered to the immigrant who complies with the rules and is fortunate enough to qualify. While adjustments to the new society may be difficult, this category is "visible". The immigrant lives physically within the communities and is able to be employed in a legitimate job with regular pay and taxes.

- *Illegal-Legal*
  This category may include the illegal alien or refugee who enters a country under false or undocumented methods and seeks to change his or her status after arrival. In some cases these people are vulnerable to unscrupulous lawyers and other advisers. The

"transition" period either into the new host society or back to the country of origin is often long and harsh.

- *Legal – Illegal*
  This group is claimed to comprise the largest percentage of the "illegal" migrant population. They enter the countries legally with time-specific visas and then fail to return to their countries of origin.

- *Illegal – Illegal (independent)*
  This group enters the country illegally and remains illegal. This category is different from the next as the person has financed or orchestrated his/her own arrival into the country or has been able to use friends rather than organized crime contacts. Work may consist of low paid, informal underground employment or work within various ethnic communities. Similar to the other categories of immigrants, there is great diversity within this category. Some independent illegal immigrants have merely moved across "borders" which had not previously been there. In some cases the movement is more like a *"rite de passage"* for young men and women. In other cases, it involves the illegal movement of unskilled labor from one Asian country to another. Immigrants, hoping to improve their life-chances may go into great debt during the process and fail to improve their living conditions.

- *Illegal-Illegal (indentured)*
  This category is perhaps the most vulnerable – vulnerable to the law and vulnerable to the criminals who assisted in the smuggling activity. When we study the links between the illegal alien and criminal activity, the link is usually through organized crime. At 30,000 U.S. dollars plus per person to be smuggled into Canada from Asia, the debt is only paid after a life-time. Depending on the smuggling group, in some cases even if the entry is not successful the debt remains and family members must share in the repayment process.

- *Legal-Legal (indentured)*
  Legal entry into a country does not ensure easy entry. Being legal does not immunize one from being under the control of those people who helped to finance the arrival. While it may facilitate greater job prospects, the amount of money required to pay back the debts owed may still mean that crime is an attractive or necessary option.

- *Internal "Migration"*
  People in this category are not true migrants in the sense of having crossed political borders. However, the processes of intermediary status prior to integration and in some cases a permanent state of marginalization and discrimination are similar. Many of the same economic and cultural characteristics of migration are shared by these migrants, depending on the nature of the mobility within the single national jurisdiction. In many cases the movement will be from the rural or less developed to the urban or developed centers. Shafir argues that including this group allows one to see broader aspects of immigrant-host relations of which political citizenship is only one form.[33] The same "security" concerns arise within countries when large internal population shifts occur.

The above categories are not mutually exclusive. The large-scale illegal or legal entry of immigrants can encourage internal migration to occur. For example, in the U.S., some writers speak of the "balkanization" within some states as seasonal *and* unauthorized workers move into states such as California and cities such as Los Angeles and unskilled whites move out. This "migration" has consequences for the schools and social services agencies.[34]

SUPPORT SYSTEMS FOR ILLEGAL MIGRANTS

If successful integration of new immigrants is an objective – especially if there is a belief that inadequate integration, denial of jobs, and inadequate services are factors that are partially responsible for criminal behavior – then it is important to determine what support structures are in place to assist both the legal and the illegal migrant.

Government Services and the Rights of Illegal Aliens

Different countries grant different protections to illegal aliens. In most cases however, the "protection", once the person is identified as being illegally in the country, is only in the form of physical restraint (holding facilities) while decisions are made regarding the person's status. Much debate has occurred within the United States regarding schooling, health, and subsistence benefits for undocumented citizens. Illegal status usually means that the normal benefits are not available to the aliens and their vulnerable status means that they will usually not ask. Unless there

26

are family members who can vouch for the person and support him/her upon arrival, the necessary support must come from other sources, that is, crime, underground systems.

"Guanxi" Networks (and guanxi-type networks)

Depending on the perspective of the writer, *guanxi* can be portrayed as criminogenic or a positive aspect of Asian life. At its simplest, *guanxi* refers to the loyalty and obligation ties that bind families, kin, and lineage villages throughout China. It is, however, more than this. It shapes social relationships and allows for global interactions along these network lines. Part of the impact of globalization that encourages illegal smuggling relates directly to these Asian *guanxi* ties.[35] Economic differences are emphasized through these networks. First, Chinese living abroad return to their home communities bearing generous gifts from countries such as North America – the comparison in life styles becomes very clear. Second, because *guanxi* members are in North America (and literally around the world) the potential migrant knows that he/she can expect assistance. Third, due to the importance of "saving face" within the Chinese culture, even when the passage is terrible and life in the new host country is awful, the illegal immigrants will write home very positively – thus encouraging other *guanxi* members to make the trip.[36]

The *guanxi* obligations are strictly adhered to and enforced, if necessary by criminal organizations engaged by the aggrieved party.[37] Those people who are united in a *guanxi* relationship have a right to request assistance and in return are obliged to repay the debt. The bond is strengthened by the kin, community, and cultural ties that ensure that these become "moral" obligations as well as social ones. In addition to ordinary exchanges, these global *guanxi* networks also facilitate the smuggling of drugs, aliens, weapons, and basically any legitimate or illegitimate commodity for which there is a market.

In addition to alien smuggling, these networks can also assist in the settling in process, employment, and eventually integration into the wider society. While the networks may involve criminal activity, it would be ethnocentric to view it strictly in this manner. It is a strength to the community members and it is not synonymous with criminal activity. Thus when Kerry states that "This system of *guanxi* corruption is eating away at the structures that provide stability in China today", he may have missed the point of the strength – both positive and negative – of this social bonding system.[38]

Organized Crime Support Systems

Depending on where the immigrant is coming from and the circumstances of the migration, the sole "support" – obtained at an exorbitant price – may come from criminals who traffic in human cargo. The difficulty arises in the pay-back. Police estimate that the cost of gaining illegal entry to North America from Asia is between 30,000 and 40,000 U.S. dollars. For women this may mean a lifetime in the sex trade. For men it may mean a career as a criminal. All criminal smuggling operations are not identical and are not equally exploitive to migrants. Some criminal groups who operate through word of mouth and community ties provide services and assistance similar to *guanxi* networks. Likewise, the reverse may also be true.

GENDER ISSUES

The transport of women is part of a broader picture of illegal human migration but it is different because it is also part of a picture of the exploitation of women. It becomes an immigration issue *plus* social problem/human rights problem/economic issue.[39] There are specific gender issues that must be acknowledged separately from the wider migrant (illegal and legal) community. While going abroad can be an opportunity for women, it may also be exploitive and abusive. For centuries women have been bought, sold, and sexually abused (war time and other times). These conditions continue into the 21st century, but now in a highly organized and systematic manner. A report by the Global Survival Network titled, *Crime and Servitude: An Exposé of the Traffic in Women for Prostitution from the Newly Independent States*, as well as the essay in this volume, catalogs the widespread indifference, lack of enforcement resources, lack of appropriate laws and capabilities in many regions, government corruption, and debt bondage conditions under which women must work.

Trafficking in women is said to be growing, although no true numbers are available because this offense has a significant hidden dimension. In addition to Asian networks, recent trends indicate that traffickers are moving women from central and eastern Europe to the west. Since profit is the objective, preferred routes reflect the greatest amount of profit. It is cheaper to bring women from central or eastern Europe than from developing countries further east. Therefore, these countries become source countries.

As a group, the women tend to be very young (age varies across source countries) and unemployed. Cases indicate that women are often offered jobs as entertainers or unskilled laboring positions but are then forced into prostitution. In some cases a woman will be knowingly entering the sex trade industry but will be naive as to the conditions under which she will have to work. A characteristic of this market that speaks to the role of women in many societies, is that recruitment often is done between family, friends, or acquaintances who approach the woman from these positions of trust. Betrayal coupled with exploitation and abuse characterizes this illicit trade.

According to Paul Pacor of the Australian Federal Police, the illegal immigrants in Australia's sex industry are perhaps the best example of exploitation. Cases that they have investigated indicate, as elsewhere, that women have little say over choice of customers, safe-sex practices, or after-hours activities. First victimized by the smugglers and pimps, the police may then subject the women to enforcement actions ranging from fines to prison terms and possibly deportation.

Cases involving the trafficking in illegal females and children reveal that shipment routes are vast and do not merely involve neighboring towns. These routes often involve women being transported around the world in search of safer or cheaper entry and also to service markets along the way. The numerous transshipment countries and the border crossings involved speak to corruption and/or benign neglect. While some of the biggest and highest profile cases have involved Asian women, the commodification of women is not just an Asian issue. For example, as EU states relax visa requirements they are experiencing trafficking in women from central and eastern Europe. Some of the women may be legal but still exploited and indentured. Categories of legal entertainers/dancers/hostesses, etc. may mean that the woman is legally in the country but still vulnerable to those who have paid her way and she may be forced into prostitution to recoup the costs. Therefore, it may be a human rights issue even if the women are legal but indentured.

In 1996, the Director General of the International Organization for Migration, Mr. James Purcell, made the point that no longer is the movement of women confined to women from developing countries but rather a more recent trend involves women from central and eastern European countries. An additional confusing factor is that some of the women will have entered the countries of destination as "entertainers" with legal papers, but the coercion and control by criminals are in place regardless. Economic manipulation makes it necessary that these women become prostitutes in order to survive.

There are also gender implications specific to the refugee issue. Some countries are accepting female sterilization and genital mutilations as grounds for emigrating. In 1994, a Federal judge in the U.S. ruled that one of the Chinese asylum seekers on the Golden Venture ship that went aground in New York in 1993 was eligible for asylum because he and his wife were resisting Chinese sterilization orders.

ORGANIZED CRIME AND ILLEGAL MIGRATION

Groups and Activities

Most countries have organized crime groups that are involved in the smuggling of illegal commodities. One of the most profitable commodities with the lowest risk is the trafficking in aliens. Groups that are not detected are perhaps the most sophisticated rather than the least guilty.

A complete service is offered: transport, documentation, transit accommodation, often even guided crossings. The image is powerful – border politics played out by criminal operators. Commodities of all types are run through, under, and over these "lines". As part of this criminal process, officials are compromised, business persons collaborate in criminal enterprises, and most significantly the illegitimate activities intertwine with the legitimate society.

Some alien smuggling operations epitomize the sophisticated end of criminal operations. In addition to the illegal act of smuggling, there is the exploitation of those who pay or are indentured in exchange for being transported and smuggled into a foreign country. Among all other groups, Chinese "snake-heads" (smugglers) have perhaps the most notorious reputation as human smugglers. The characteristics of sophisticated operations include:

- well equipped forgery workshops to create the essential documents, visas, and stamp marks;

- the ability to modify their operations to adapt to changing risks: different routes, entry schemes, and conveyances;

- operation centers, accommodations, and hideouts in transit countries and potential transit countries;

- the economic wealth for substantial bribes and the best in technology;

- the contacts and networks required to secure the assistance of corrupted officials;

- diversification of criminal activities – smuggling is combined with other organized crime activities involving illegal commodities and services;[40]

- an ability to use violence to obtain payments or services from illegal migrants within the destination country (or country of origin if smuggling is unsuccessful);

- the skill and experience to exploit the willing/knowing/complicit/ features of "legitimate" society.

A few of the above points deserve elaboration. The choice of conveyance used in the smuggling operations results in very different smuggling activities. If air travel is used, smugglers have to be adept at obtaining/creating false, stolen, or bought passports and other documents. The number that can be smuggled at any one time is somewhat limited and the "client" has to be briefed on how to act and what to say – or (and more likely) networks of officials have to be bribed. As one snake-head said: "The documents I prepare are authentic, but the people are not real". The sense was that genuine documents would be a waste because the "clients", out of their own environment and not able to speak the language, would not be convincing regardless of the documentation. Hence, bribery is the solution.

The main steps in human cargo smuggling are: recruitment, escaping, smuggling voyage, off-loading, and debt collection. Each of these steps involves less uncertainty than land or air travel. The following conditions make human smuggling by ocean-going cargo ships attractive to the smuggler:

- lower overheads (few documents and little bribery);

- smuggler is less reliant on the client to be convincing and to "perform;"

- easier logistics;

- approximately 150 clients can be moved at one time;

- amount charged remains about the same – 30,000 U.S. dollars per head.

31

However even these "easier logistics" are complicated. Evidence from Australia illustrates this point. The smugglers of the 139 PRC nationals on the *Min Pu Yu* had to:

- find, assess, and fit out a suitable ship;
- find a suitable crew – particularly a trustworthy captain;
- select suitable berthing prior to embarkation;
- carry out the covert loading of a large number of passengers;
- organize communications with the vessel during the voyage;
- deal with frequent mechanical problems;
- carry out pre-visits to the transit countries along the route to obtain supplies and fuel;
- arrange for a suitable covert landing point in the destination country.

Law enforcement officials speak of the ruthlessness of some of the smugglers who are prepared to sink boatloads of would-be migrants rather than get caught during the smuggling process. The conditions and dangers inflicted upon the human cargo are unmatched. During off-loading off the coast of the United States, the master ship will remain outside the 12-mile limit.[41] Ferries and small boats are hired to meet the cargo ship and transport the illegal aliens to shore. Cases that have come to the attention of officials reveal that if the small boats fail to appear, the aliens may be forced off the ship into the water. When land or air travel is used, one cannot over-emphasize the sophistication of the fraudulent document operations – not only in terms of the technology but also the expertise of knowing which countries require what documents and how various combinations of documents and countries can be used for maximum profit.

After documents have been used to gain entry to planes or boats, depending on the circumstances, the documents are often destroyed prior to arrival at their destinations so that the person arrives as an undocumented arrival seeking asylum.

Hence:

- passports can be produced in less time than it takes to obtain a legitimate passport;
- "used" passports are re-cycled for the next batch of clients;

- multi-visas give a passport credibility and are easily forged; in some areas legitimate visas are easily obtained via bribery;

- complicated schemes such as plane-switching occur whereby the client clears customs and once inside the boarding area, switches boarding passes with another person and boards for the U.S. with a doctored passport.

Debt Collection

Although it may vary, in some operations the client pays the smuggler only after he or she arrives. "Safe" passage may be a misleading term but the passage is usually guaranteed in the sense that if the smuggling operation is not successful the first time, they will try again.

When illegal aliens enter the destination country, either the relatives or friends pay and the clients are released immediately into the community, or the clients are met by local Asian gangs and taken to a "safe house" where they are tortured, beaten, or raped until the debt is paid. The solution is often for the client to work for the gangs.[42] In Australia it is estimated that an illegal prostitute may need to service 300 to 500 customers before beginning to earn money for herself.

Local gangs in destination countries are used instead of the home based smugglers – smuggling groups out of Hong Kong do not have the legal status, connections, or English language ability to operate within the destination countries. If relatives (or the clients) are late with the money, 10 to 20 percent in interest is charged each week. The point is made clear to the client both in the home and host countries that if the client attempts to cheat the smugglers – whoever they are, and at which ever end of the route – there will be an enforcement gang to back up the original agreement.

Money is shipped between the home and host countries to cover these debts in many non-traditional ways. The use of Fujianese travel agencies is one way to transfer money.

Clients: Victims or Criminals

Seemingly no scheme is too bizarre for the smugglers of illegal aliens if a high enough profit is involved. During August 1997, newspapers were reporting a bizarre scheme that involved criminal gangs smuggling deaf Mexicans into New York City, North Carolina, and Chicago. These vulnerable populations were forced to sell trinkets for food and lodging.

This operation was estimated to earn the criminal gang a gross revenue of more than one million U.S. dollars per year. Vulnerable illegal migrants can be forced to become criminals by the criminals who bring then into countries illegally. These organized crime traffickers exploit the phenomenon of illegal migration for massive profits. However, the illicit profits alone are not the sole consideration. Exploitation and abuse of humanity are also significant considerations.

Men and women succumb to these schemes and end up owing massive debts to the smugglers that in many cases can never be fully repaid. This is the critical link between illegal smuggling and other forms of criminal activity. The illegal alien must engage in whatever crimes will provide the required installment payments to the smuggling rings. For men, this may involve diverse criminal activities for profit, such as theft and fraud operations. For women, the sex trade is one of the few available profit generating activities. Some of the publicity that has drawn attention to the smuggling rings has focused on the stories of exploitive schemes involving the trafficking of women for prostitution and for use in other forms of the sex industry.

Trafficking in women involves several distinct and unresolved enforcement and policy issues. Are the women criminals or victims? Governments in some cases arrest the women and/or simply deport them with little apparent concern for what happens to them upon their return. In cases where women are formally processed and sanctioned, there may well be the sense that justice has hardly been served by the punishment given to these "victims". These same arguments can be made for the migrant male who agrees to enter the country illegally with dreams of the profits that can be legitimately made, only to find that the debt is beyond what can be legally earned, particularly by an illegal alien.

THE ROLE OF THE "LEGITIMATE" SOCIETY IN FACILITATING ILLEGAL MIGRATION

Corruption Issues

In many ways the entire illegal migration framework is about corruption. Corruption is a companion in most of the smuggling schemes generated by organized criminals and one can say with certainty it is an aspect of *every* sophisticated operation that has been responsible for the ongoing smuggling of illegal aliens. When smuggled aliens pass through numerous countries, one can be sure corruption is involved. Usually it is in the form of a bribe or service. However, there is the passive complicity of the transit countries who choose, as informal policy, to do nothing about the illegal aliens passing through their countries. The argument is that whoever blows the whistle on the aliens ends up having the expense and effort of processing them and taking some form of often costly action. Conversely, the laws may prohibit the transit country from taking further action. Therefore, they are allowed to pass through.

Corruption is an issue regardless of what parts of the world are being involved in this illegal trade. Among those officials (particularly at the borders and other ports of entry) who might resist the temptation to be involved in drug trafficking, there is a sense that alien smuggling is somewhat less of a risk and possibly less serious – and the profits are large for what may be a "passive" neglect of duty rather than more direct "active" participation in the criminal activity. Just as the smugglers can "neutralize" their criminal activity with rhetoric that they are only helping people, officials use similar justifications. Some of the corruption involves people from the same *guanxi* or community network. Sometimes it is strictly in exchange for money.

This is not "an Asian" problem. It occurs everywhere because of the illicit profits that can be made:

- Guatemala (August 1997) – a complete shift of immigration employees responsible for guarding the entry area to La Aurora International Airport was suspended following a dispute over illegal payments obtained from Ecuadorians bearing fake documents;

- Hong Kong – an investigation was underway into consulates suspected of taking bribes for granting visas to multi-million dollar immigrant smuggling rings (estimated to be worth 20,000 dollars for a U.S. or Canadian visa and 10,000 dollars for a British visa);

- In Hong Kong, in the mid 1990s the Independent Commission against Corruption (ICAC) was concerned about the high number of illegal aliens going through Kai Tak airport. In 1996 organized crime gangs were detected using Chinese officials' passports to smuggle mainland immigrants through Kai Tak airport to the United States and Australia.[45] It was thought that the green official passports would be less scrutinized, especially when accompanied with forged letters of invitation from legitimate businesses;

- During the past several years Thailand has become a springboard for illegal entry into other countries, including Canada. Burmese, Chinese, Bangladesh's, and others enter Thailand through Burma with the help of racketeers. The Immigration Bureau has taken disciplinary actions against many immigration officers found guilty of abetting the smuggling of aliens. Research from Chulalongkorn University into Thailand's illegal economy some of which appears elsewhere in this volume, points at the corruption of the police.

The Demand

Our ambivalence toward organized crime has been well noted. If there was no demand for the services offered by organized criminals, their profits would vanish and the monopolies would weaken. A significant proportion of illegal migration and illegal smuggling exists or is facilitated because there is a demand for either the labor, the bribes, or the existence of a sex trade. The demand issue has two aspects. First, the illegal aliens themselves often are desired, either for their labor (often cheap labor), the bribes that are paid, the political platforming that their presence can generate, or for their participation in the sex trade. Second, as we have discussed, there is a large demand for smugglers to assist people who want to move but fail to either qualify or who exceed the quota for legal migration. Hence, this is a very lucrative industry that will not "go away" as long as the market remains.

In addition to these direct "benefits", there are the other illegal "indirect" commodities that are often part of the same smuggling operations through which the immigrant travels, for example, drugs or pornography. These commodities form the basis of extremely profitable enterprises because again the demand is great. The demand simply is for smuggled commodities. The form of commodity is only the variation. Society evaluates differently, however, each commodity in what could be seen as a chain of illegal commodities. The same distribution networks, the same corrupt officials, the same routes can serve the trafficking in different illicit commodities.

CONCLUSION:
AREAS IN NEED OF DEBATE, RESEARCH, AND ACTION

This paper concludes that while limiting the movement of illegal aliens is an essential concern and must be part of a policy and enforcement approach, there are other issues that need to be addressed and which might produce more positive results. Three areas, in particular, must be addressed:

Migrants – Legal and Illegal – as a Commodity

Crisp distinctions between worthy refugees and economically motivated illegal aliens may be somewhat artificial in an environment where corporations relocate around the world, and seek out or abandon adverse labor and environmental conditions at their will. Legal barriers to trade and investment abroad are falling while countries are increasing their expenditures on migration control. From the migrants point of view, it may seem as though everything and everyone can move except "labor". Once illegal movement of people becomes an issue, it quickly becomes a sovereignty issue. When people are moving uncontrolled across borders, the state appears to feel particularly threatened.

However, illegal migration is typically not viewed as a "national" issue (nor a sovereignty issue) when the migration is "good for the country", that is, when the illegal laborer is seen to be necessary or beneficial. For example, in East Flores, Indonesia, payments from illegal migration are the mainstay of the local economy (comments in correspondence from Graeme Hugo). Accordingly, local police and labor officials ignore the practices. Even without direct bribes, they see it as a part of the local economy. Once conditions change, the traditional tolerance could be replaced with targeted enforcement practices. These contradictions are highly conducive to the creation of illegal markets.

Sanctioning the "Demand:"
The Profiteers, Policies of States, and the Public

People who drive the illegal migration market are those who benefit directly and corruptly or indirectly from this activity. The greatest impact will be to target those who have made an illegal commodity out of the transport of humans: the smugglers, those who use the illegal labor and services, the corrupt officials, the "legitimate" businesses who are negligent by ignoring and profiting from the trade, the state policies that manipulate immigrant populations for short-term objectives, and the members of the public who pay for illicit services. However, there are dangers or futility associated with targeting each of these groups. Corruption is hard to eliminate and tends not to stay "eliminated". Sophisticated smugglers are part of organized crime operations, the dismantling of which requires a greater level of cross-jurisdictional law enforcement capability than we have acquired to date. Holding business accountable is an excellent idea but, again, not without hazard.

For example, Canada and other countries fine airlines or ships for each illegal person on board. Although the amount of the fine varies, it is significant. The intention is excellent – to ensure that these companies do everything they can to prevent the transport of illegal aliens. The less ideal consequence is that unscrupulous or violent smugglers are prepared to kill their stowaways or passengers in order to avoid detection and the fines. A case in Canada involved Romanian stowaways on a container ship from Dubai. The ship was Taiwanese-owned with Taiwanese officers and a Filipino crew. In this case, the allegations were that two stowaways were forced onto an oil-drum raft off the coast of Spain and a third was tossed into the Atlantic. While in this case the stowaways may have been on board without the knowledge of the crew, smuggling operations are no less callous.

Limiting the Flow of Illegal Migration

As the "crackdown" rhetoric indicates, controlling the number of illegal aliens who successfully enter a country is largely a law enforcement function. However, there may be negative consequences associated with greater law enforcement in this area. As the literature suggests, more law enforcement means that the smuggling activity becomes dominated by the sophisticated and possibly more violent organized crime groups rather than independent entrepreneurs.

Illegal smuggling, by its cross-border nature, requires two different jurisdictions. As law enforcement agencies "crack-down" on illegal immigration, this illegal market becomes the domain of the sophisticated organized crime operator. The result is two-fold: huge profits for organized crime groups and new forms of collaboration between and across previously competitive organized crime groups. For example, a smuggling ring in China involved Triad members working together as partners with Japanese Yakuza. Similarly, Chinese Triad members have teamed up with Italian Mafia members to smuggle foreigners into Italy and Europe.

Quick deportation for illegal aliens is seen by some countries as being a good deterrent for other would-be illegal aliens. Policy decisions, however, must address the real issues of who is the victim versus the criminal in some of these smuggling schemes. Women deported back into poverty and abuse, and possibly disowned during this process, may not equate to social justice. As Schmid (and Savona) conclude:

> The problem of immigration cannot be solved satisfactorily at the border ... . The real frontiers are elsewhere. The problem of migration has to be solved at the frontiers of a cleaner environment, more economic development and good governance.[44]

Likewise, "declaring war on illegal immigration" is, according to Demetrios Papademetriou, a "good applause line, but wars lest we forget impose terrible sacrifices":

> Unintended but predictable border incidents, vigilantism, racially motivated violence, and discrimination in the workplace are the types of consequences that ethnically diverse societies can ill-afford – and all rich countries are now ethnically diverse.[45]

ILLEGAL MIGRATION AS SECURITY ISSUE?

Yes. If one is sincere in the belief that *human security issues* must be addressed very differently from traditional national security threats, then illegal migration can and should be seen as a human security issue. The long-term focus, resources, and commitment must be directed toward peace building activities, environmental restoration projects, employment, training, and investment programs. The gender issues involved in the trafficking of women and children will be profiled as a major threat to the women and children who are directly involved and to the power imbalances between the sexes within societies.

While the flow of illegal immigrants into specific countries, and particularly into certain border towns, may be a threat to the economic stability of those communities, the issues that must be addressed are most likely issues relating to the destruction of the environment, poverty, unemployment, or the aftermath of wars and other forms of violence. The related crimes that may accompany some forms of illegal migration are most likely linked to the involvement of organized crime in the human trafficking market and can be dealt with by traditional "policing". To label "illegal migration" as a generic form of national security threat would be an equivalent of blaming the victims *and* will prove to be futile.

NOTES

The original version of this paper was prepared for the CSCAP Study Group Transnational Crime and presented in Manila, May 1998.

1. See Micheal Sherry, *In the Shadows of War* (New Haven: Yale University Press, 1995); Phil Williams, "Transnational Criminal Organizations and International Security", *Survival*, Vol. 36 (1) (1994), pp.96–113; Uday C. Bhaskar, "Post Cold War Security", draft paper given as a lecture at Skidmore College, Saratoga Springs, NY, U.S.A. (1997), and Uday C. Bhaskar, "Strategic Impact of Transnational Crime", paper presented to CSCAP Study Group on Transnational Crime, Bangkok, Thailand (1997). John McFarlane, "Transnational Crime as a Security Issue", paper presented at the (1997) meeting of CSCAP in Bangkok, Thailand; and Peter Lupsha, "Transnational Organized Crime versus the Nation-State", *Transnational Organized Crime*, Vol.2, No.1 (Spring 1996), pp.21–48.
2. *Globe and Mail,* May 12, 1998, p.A17.
3. *Washington Post,* Foreign Service, May 11, 1998, p.A18.
4. Alan Dupont, "Unregulated Population Flows in East Asia: A New Security Dilemma?", *Pacific Review*, Vol.9, No.1 (1997), pp.1–22.
5. *Ibid.,* p.22.
6. Timothy Dunn, *The Militarization of the US-Mexico Border, 1978–1992: Low-Intensity Conflict Doctrine Comes Home*, (Austin: CMAS Books, University of Texas at Austin, 1996).
7. Lloyd Axworthy, *Building Peace to Last: Establishing a Canadian Peacebuilding Initiative*, (Ottawa, Canada: Department of Foreign and International Trade, May 5, 1998).
8. Dunn, *Ibid,* Peter B. Kraska, "Militarizing American Police: The Rise and Normalization of Paramilitary Units", *Social Problems*, Vol.44, No.1 (Feb. 1997); Michael Sherry, *op.cit*, 1995; Michael Klare, *World Security: Trends and Challenges at Century's End* (Daniel C. Thomas, 1991); Thomas Naylor, "From Cold-War to Crime War: The Search for a New 'National Security Threat'", *Transnational Organized Crime*, Vol.1, No. 4 (Winter 1995).
9. Peter B. Kraska, "Militarizing Social Problems: High-Modern Tendencies in the Crime and Drug Wars" (draft presentation paper, 1997).
10. *The New War*, by Senator John Kerry is particularly strident. While much of the information is factual and speaks clearly to a changing global criminal activity, it is only on the final page that Kerry acknowledges that "demand" for drugs fuels 70 percent of U.S. crime and that tackling drug education, health care, and the school system will be essential before there will be any real impact on criminal operations – global or domestic. John Kerry's description of billions of dollars "hemorrhaging out of our economy", *The New War*, p.193, is dramatic but false – not that billions of dollars are not involved in the criminal markets and/or are laundered, but rather is false in that it paints an old simplistic picture of two distinct markets – one legitimate and the other illegitimate while in fact the reality might even be more serious.
11. Naylor, *op.cit.*
12. Roxanne Lynn Doty, "The Double-Writing of Statecraft: Exploring State Responses to Illegal Immigration", *Alternatives*, Vol.21 (1996), pp.171–189.
13. Alejandro Portes, *The Economic Sociology of Immigration* (New York: Russell Sage Foundation, 1995), p.21.
14. Roxanne Lynn Doty, *op.cit.*; Philip L. Martin, "Comparative Migration Policies", *International Migration Review*, Vol.28, No.1 (1993), pp.164-170; and Doris Meissner, R.D. Hormats, A. Garrigues Walker, and Shijuro Ogata, *International Migration Challenges in a New Era: A Report to the Trilateral Commission*, Vol.44 (1993).
15. Presidential Determination, No. 97–16 (Feb. 12, 1997).
16. Nermin Abadan-Unat, "Summary of Main Results of Conference of OECD Working Paper on Migration", *The Future of Migration* (Paris: OECD, 1987), pp.19–27, and Roxanne Lynn Doty, *op. cit.*
17. *China News Agency*, Taiwan, Sept. 8, 1997.

18. Seoul, *The Korea Herald*, Sept. 3, 1997.
19. Report by Gerhart Walter.
20. Bangkok, *The Sunday Nation*, Feb. 18, 1996.
21. *The Independent*, Jan. 28, 1994.
22. A.P. Schmid (with the cooperation of E. Savona), "Migration and Crime: A Framework for Discussion", *Migration and Crime*, International Scientific and Professional Advisory Council of the United Nations Crime Prevention and Criminal Justice Programme. Proceedings of an Ancillary Meeting held May 3, 1995 in Cairo, Egypt, pp.5-42.
23. *Canada, Not Just Numbers: A Canadian Framework for Future Immigration, Immigration Legislative Review*, Ministry of Public Works and Government Services (1997), p.2-3.
24. As quoted in Virginia Haufler, *Dangerous Commerce: Insurance and the Management of International Risk* (Ithica, New York: Cornell University Press, 1997), p.141.
25. Alejandro Portes, *op.cit.*
26. *Chinese Migrants in Central and Eastern Europe: The Cases of the Czech Republic, Hungary and Romania* (Geneva: International Organization for Migration, Sept. 1995).
27. Ineke Haen Marshall, *Minorities, Migrants, and Crime: Diversity and Similarity Across Europe and the United States* (London: Sage Publications, 1997) and G.O.W. Mueller, "The General Report", paper presented at the International Conference on Migration and Crime, International Scientific and Professional Advisory Council of the United Nations Crime Prevention and Criminal Justice Program (ISPAC), Courmayeur Mont Blanc, Italy (1996).
28. Thomas Straubhaar", Migration Pressure", *International Migration*, Vol.31, No.1 (1993).
29. A.P. Schmid, *op.cit.*, p.29.
30. Manolo Abella, *Sending Workers Abroad* (Geneva: International Labor Office, 1997).
31. Xin Jing Yi Er San, "Smuggling Fuzhou People to United States", *National Affaires* (July 1995).
32. *Ibid.*
33. Gershon Shafir, *Immigrants and Nationalists: Ethnic Conflict and Accommodation in Catalonia, the Basque Country, Latvia, and Estonia* (Albany, New York: State University of New York Press, 1995), p.3.
34. *Wall Street Journal* (Jan. 19, 1994).
35. Willard, Myers, "Orb Weavers – Global Webs: The Structure and Activities of Transnational Ethnic Chinese Criminal Groups", *Transnational Organized Crime*, Vol.1, No.4 (Winter, 1995), pp.1-36.
36. Zheng Wang, "Ocean-Going Smuggling of Illegal Chinese Immigrants: Operation, Causation and Policy Implications", *Transnational Organized Crime*, Vol.2, No.1 (Spring, 1996), pp. 49-65.
37. Willard Myers, *op.cit.*
38. John Kerry, The New War: The Web of Crime That Threatens America's Security (New York: Simon and Schuster, 1997).
39. International Organization for Migration, European Conference on Trafficking in Women Organized by the European Commission and the IOM, Vienna, June 10-11, 1996.
40. Chinese Migrants in Central and Eastern Europe, *op.cit.*
41. Zheng Wang, *op.cit.*
42. *Ibid.*
43. Hong Kong, *South China Morning Post*, Aug. 21, 1996
44. Schmid, *op.cit.*, p.30.
45. Demetrios G. Papademetriou, "Migration: Think Again", *Foreign Policy* (Winter, 1997-98), pp.15-31.

Capitalizing on Transition Economies: The Role of the Russian Mafiya in Trafficking Women for Forced Prostitution

GILLIAN CALDWELL
STEVE GALSTER
JYOTHI KANICS
NADIA STEINZOR

INTRODUCTION

The United Nations estimates that four million people are trafficked throughout the world each year, resulting in annual illicit profits to criminal syndicates of up to seven billion dollars. One of the fastest growing trafficking businesses is the sex trade.

For purposes of this analysis, trafficking is defined as all acts involving the recruitment or transportation of persons within or across borders. This recruitment involves deception, coercion or force, abuse of authority, debt bondage, or fraud for the purpose of placing persons in situations of abuse or exploitation such as forced prostitution, sweatshop labor, or exploitative domestic servitude.[1]

Every year the trafficking of human beings for the commercial sex trade places hundreds of thousands of women at risk of losing their personal freedom. They suffer physical and emotional harm, work in degrading and sometimes life-threatening situations, and are cheated of their earnings. An increasing number of females trafficked for the sex trade are from Russia and the Newly Independent States because of various economic pressures and greater mobility they now have since the break-up of the former Soviet Union.[2]

During the chaos of massive political, social, and economic change in Russia and the Newly Independent States, criminal elements have been able to establish themselves in the international business of trafficking women by placing them in abusive situations of debt-bondage and sexual slavery. Operating through nominally reputable employment agencies, entertainment companies, or marriage agencies, these criminals mislead and manipulate women, who become pawns in an illegal worldwide trade. In many cases, women and children are traded from one pimp to another several times over.

RESEARCH METHODOLOGY

Law enforcement agencies in countries of destination often minimize the extent of trafficking. Governments usually respond to trafficking as a problem of illegal migration, an approach that redefines victimized women as criminals. To learn why and how this form of modern slavery persists, and to propose solutions, the Global Survival Network (GSN) conducted an investigation from April 1995 through the Autumn of 1997 to uncover the rapidly growing trade in Russian women for purposes of forced prostitution.

Due to the underground nature of the trade, the study combined conventional and unconventional research techniques. GSN conducted open interviews with numerous non-governmental organizations, more than 50 women who had been trafficked overseas, and police and government officials in Russia, Western Europe, Asia, and the United States.

In order to learn more about the world of organized crime and its role in Russian sex trafficking, GSN also conducted some unconventional research by establishing a dummy company that purportedly specialized in importing foreign women as escorts and entertainers. The company was "based" in the United States and claimed to specialize in "Foreign Models, Escorts, and Entertainers". Company "employees" represented the business while brochures, business cards, and telephone and fax lines gave the operation a look of authenticity. Under the guise of this company, GSN successfully gained *entree* to the operations of international trafficking networks based in Russia and beyond. Many of the interviews were recorded with hidden cameras and provide unparalleled insight into the trafficking underworld in action.

While conducting investigations through this front, GSN met Russian pimps and traffickers who revealed their *modus operandi*, as well as the identities of their financial investors and overseas partners. GSN combined these findings with other information collected through conventional research. Together this information provided GSN with enough detail to target several countries including Germany, Switzerland, Japan, Macau, and the United States where Russian women and girls work as prostitutes in substantial numbers.[3] Wherever legal, interviews were recorded by hidden camera directly inside the establishments where prostitution was occurring. Whenever possible the investigators revealed the nature of their work. In some cases, security conditions for both the investigator and the persons interviewed prevented disclosure. In order to preserve the safety and privacy of all parties involved, pseudonyms have been given to the persons interviewed during GSN's covert investigations, and to others who have requested them.

THE FORMER SOVIET BLOC AND GLOBAL SEX TRAFFICKING: AN OVERVIEW

Since the break-up of the Soviet Union, sex trafficking between Russia and the former Eastern Bloc on the one hand, and Asia, Western Europe, and the United States on the other, has continued to increase. Russian women are in high demand in many countries because of their "exotic" nature and relative novelty in the sex market. Russia and the Newly Independent States, including Ukraine and Latvia, have become primary countries of origin, supplementing and sometimes replacing previously significant sources of women from Asia and Latin America. In a study in the Netherlands, 75 percent of the trafficked women interviewed were from central and eastern Europe, compared to relatively minimal numbers before 1989.[4]

Clearly, the number of Russian women working in international sex industries is large and growing. According to official records, 50,000 women leave Russia permanently every year.[5] Unofficial estimates by non-governmental organizations and researchers indicate that perhaps hundreds of thousands of other women leave Russia annually in search of temporary work, with plans to return.[6] Few Russian women who are willing to travel abroad for work have the cash to purchase airline or train tickets, consequently, most arrive via trafficking networks.

Germany

Today, between 60 and 80 percent of the women trafficked into Germany come from Eastern Europe, Russia, and the Newly Independent States.[7] An estimated 15,000 Russian and Eastern European women work in Germany's red light districts.[8] Although many brothels, sex clubs, massage parlors, and saunas are owned and operated by Germans, they are frequently under the financial control of foreign organized crime groups from Russia, Turkey, and the former Yugoslavia.

Switzerland

According to recent figures, the number of women from Russia entering Switzerland has increased steadily during Russia's transition to a market economy. The Federal Ministry for Foreigners maintains detailed citizenship records of each person who receives a dancer's visa. The visa allows the recipient to work in bars and cabarets for up to eight months and has become a primary instrument used by traffickers to move women into the country legally.[9] Between December 1989 and August 1990 the Swiss granted 933 such visas to foreigners: 217 to residents of the Dominican Republic, 167 to Brazilians, 88 to Thais, 323 to individuals from European countries, and none to Russians.[10] Of the 1,439 dancer visas issued by the Swiss government between December 1991 and August 1992, 72 were issued to Russian citizens.[11] From August to December 1995, the number of dancer visas issued to Russians reached 303 of the 1,616 issued.[12]

Japan

As part of a general rise in communication and trade between Russia and Japan, China, and other Pacific Rim nations in recent years, increasing numbers of Russian women have also appeared in Asia as waitresses, dancers, and prostitutes. In undercover meetings with traffickers, GSN found that Russian women and girls are frequently brought to Japan via Moscow, Kiev, and Vladivostok by air, or from Vladivostok by ship. They may also be routed through a third country, such as Thailand or Brunei. Many Russian women are forced to work illegally as prostitutes, often in exclusive clubs which are open only to Japanese men, and sometimes only to club members. They may also be found in many of Japan's "snack clubs", popular nightclubs that offer drinking, dancing, and women whom Japanese men can take to nearby "love hotels", which are linked to the clubs.[13] In addition, GSN investigators found that Russian prostitutes are openly advertised in Japanese pornographic magazines, with their photograph and telephone number included for clients who prefer a house or hotel visit.

To circumvent Japan's laws which prohibit migrant women from working as prostitutes, traffickers have increasingly used "entertainer" visas to transit women into the country. As early as 1992, a series of reports issued by the Tokyo Bureau of TASS, the Russian news agency, revealed that Russian women entering Japan to work in the entertainment industry were often forced into prostitution. According to the Japanese Ministry of Justice, of the 17,513 persons from the Soviet Union who entered Japan in 1989, 378 came with entertainer visas.[14] The numbers have increased steadily each year and reached a record-high in 1995, when 4,763 of the 22,060 Russians who came to Japan entered as entertainers.[15] From 1990–95 entertainment visas accounted for approximately 1 in 5 of all visas granted to Russians entering Japan. Furthermore, the proportion of young (15-29 years old) women entering Japan has also steadily increased during Russia's transition to a market economy – from 15 percent in 1990 to 40 percent in 1995.[16]

GSN found that many foreign women are trafficked to Japan on "temporary permits" or tourist visas, which they may be forced to overstay while working as prostitutes. According to the Japanese Immigration Bureau, the number of foreign women who overstay their tourist visas has increased significantly. During 1994, for example, approximately 3,000 more women overstayed their visas than in 1993.[17] The Japanese Ministry of Justice reports that from 1989 to 1995 between 15,500 and 25,600 Russians entered Japan each year on "temporary visitor" or tourist visas – an average of 70 percent of all visas issued to Russians.[18] It is impossible to know how many of the tourist visas were issued to Russian women trafficked into the country, but local non-governmental organizations that work with illegally exploited migrant women in Japan believe the numbers to be significant.

In meetings with GSN, the Japanese National Police insisted that the trafficking of Russian women into Japan was not a major problem and that it had only investigated a few cases.[19] One of these cases was in Hiratsuka, Kanagawa Prefecture, where police arrested a bar owner for employing nine Russian women working as prostitutes.[20] The Japanese owner hailed from Sakhalin Island and had his own contacts in Russia, with whom he created an employment agency to recruit Russian women. In the Russian Far East, they advertised contests for women to work as waitresses in Japan, and boasted an attendance of at least 100 women for each event. According to the Japanese police, the bar owner earned 85,000 U.S. dollars monthly from his Russian workers.

Macau

Another focal point of the trade is Macau, located 40 nautical miles from Hong Kong. Macau has become a popular weekend getaway for Chinese and Hong Kong citizens as well as a vacation destination for tourists from all over the world. GSN identified several clubs in Macau where Russian women are employed as prostitutes. One source informed GSN, however, that the Macau government began cracking down on Russian prostitutes in 1996 by refusing to issue visas to Russian women, largely in an effort to exclude Russian criminal elements.[21] Recent GSN surveys in Macau (1997-1998) indicated another upsurge in Russian sex workers, mainly from the Russian Far East. In nearby Hong Kong approximately 50 local organized crime groups control places of public entertainment and illegal gambling, such as casinos (which often employ foreign women), and pornography and prostitution rings.[22]

United States

The United States is another popular destination for Russian women, who are drawn by advertisements for marriage agencies or jobs as domestic servants, models, and entertainers. While no precise figures exist on the number of foreign women who enter the United States via trafficking networks, press reports of the exploitation of migrant women as domestic servants, laborers, and prostitutes have become increasingly widespread. Non-governmental organizations, such as Children of the Night and Promise in California, and the Paul and Lisa Program in New York City, report a rising number of women working in the U.S. sex industry who are from Russia, the Newly Independent States, and eastern Europe.

Statistics from the U.S. Immigration and Naturalization Service (INS) reveal dramatic increases in the number of visa applications from Russia and the Newly Independent States. For example, overall applications from Russia, Belarus, and Ukraine increased from 3,000 in 1988 to 129,500 in 1992.[23] According to officials at the U.S. Department of State, in 1996 more than 124,000 visas were granted to Russian citizens alone.[24]

Some women are trafficked into the United States on fiancé, student, or business visas. Most, however, enter the country with tourist visas, which they then overstay. This is a common immigration problem in the United States as 50 percent of illegal immigration in the country involves visa overstays.[25]

TRAFFICKING IN CHILDREN

The growing number of young women and children who are trafficked illustrates a disturbing trend. For various reasons, including the AIDS epidemic, virgins are increasingly in demand and can fetch some of the highest prices in the international sex market. A telling statistic comes from the Netherlands, where the Foundation Against Traffic in Women reports that, of the women it assisted in 1995 and 1996 who came from the central and eastern European Countries and the Newly Independent States, more than 75 percent were under the age of 25 and 57 percent were under 21.[26]

The German Federal Department of Criminal Investigation estimates that five percent of the women trafficked from eastern Europe are younger than 18 years of age.[27] Solwodi (Solidarity with Women in Distress), a German non-governmental organization working with migrant prostitutes, estimates that the actual number of underage migrant women working in German sex clubs is much higher.[28] Many of their clients seeking legal assistance are between 15 and 21 years old.[29] Traffickers lure girls with promises of work as *au-pairs*, waitresses, or dancers, then transport them abroad to work as prostitutes with false passports which hide their actual age.[30]

"Natasha", a Moscow-based Russian citizen who traffics women and girls to Japan to work as prostitutes, informed GSN that she could obtain foreign passports for underage girls. "According to our rules", she said, "you must obtain an international passport. But, to go abroad, if she is only 16, she must get approval from her parents. If you want to avoid it, we can make her a passport where it will be indicated that she is 18, so she doesn't need to have any approvals".[31] Natasha said such a passport could be obtained through contacts working for the Ministry of Foreign Affairs and would cost about 800 dollars, which she said should be reimbursed from the salary of the girl once she begins working.

In Germany, pimps employ young girls as prostitutes to service truck drivers and travelers along the borders with Poland and the Czech Republic.[32] In addition, several German citizens have been arrested for sexually exploiting children by producing pornographic films in Romania and Hungary.[33] When German citizen "Peter R." was arrested in 1996 on 36 charges of trafficking in human beings, pimping, and bribery, he had at least 23 Russian and Ukrainian women working for him in his brothels. He allegedly recruited by placing ads for "babysitters" in Polish newspapers. Police suspected he was responsible for trafficking up to 500 women and girls into Germany under false pretenses. One of Peter R.'s victims was a 16-year-old girl, who stated that she was brought into Germany by 2 men who confiscated her passport, raped and beat her, and took her to Hamburg, where she was forced to have sex with 10 clients per day.[34]

WHY WOMEN GO:
ECONOMIES AND SOCIETIES IN TRANSITION

Modern-day servitude usually begins with the best of motives – hope for a better life. A recent Russian study analyzed interviews with women standing in line at embassies in Moscow and at the few state-registered firms that offer employment opportunities abroad, regarding their reasons for emigrating. Eighty-six percent of respondents said they were seeking higher earnings.[35]

Women have special incentives to leave Russia and other Newly Independent States, stemming from their rapid socio-economic decline in the chaotic post-communist transition that ensued after 1991. This transition brought massive social dislocation and uncertainty – as well as new political freedoms for all and emerging economic opportunities for a few. Between 1991 and 1995 Russia's real gross domestic product fell 34 percent, while per capita annual income is currently a mere 3,400 U.S. dollars.[36] Almost one-quarter of the population lives below the poverty line.[37] Women account for nearly two-thirds of the unemployed nationwide and as much as 85 or 90 percent in some regions of the Russian Federation.[38] In 1996, 87 percent of Russia's employed urban residents whose monthly income was less than 21 U.S. dollars were women.[39] According to Zoya Khotkina, a specialist in women and employment at the Moscow Center for Gender Studies, "Seventy percent of the women graduating from institutes of higher learning and from schools declare that they cannot find gainful employment".[40]

In a society where the female literacy rate is approximately 98 percent and where many women are university educated, Human Rights Watch concluded in a 1995 report that: "Women in Russia face widespread employment discrimination that is practiced, condoned, and tolerated by the government".[41] Jobs are often secured through personal connections to high-level managers, directors, or members of a mafiya group.[42] Few women have such connections, forcing many highly trained female engineers, doctors, lawyers, teachers, and other professionals to look for jobs outside their profession.

Sexual harassment often accompanies job discrimination. In many Russian businesses it is not unusual for a male boss to demand that his female secretary have sexual relations with him. There are no civil or labor laws relating to sexual harassment in Russia. The relevant criminal provision for sexual coercion is rarely applied, and cases brought under it seldom reach a court. Syostri, a support center for survivors of domestic violence, rape, and sexual assault in Moscow, reports receiving over 2,500 calls on its single crisis telephone hotline in the first 3 years of operation.[43] Only 1 in 5 reports made to police are accepted and investigated, which may explain at least in part why only 5 to 10 percent of the women subjected to domestic violence or sexual assault report their experience to police.[44]

For women confronting unemployment, sexual harassment, and domestic violence, an offer of good pay for work abroad often seems a magical escape to a better world. According to Elena Tiuriukanova of the Institute for Population Studies in Moscow, "although women's migration has great public resonance, there is practically no official policy aimed at stopping violence, sexual harassment, trafficking in women and other forms of human rights' violations in the field of female labor migration".[45] Some women and girls conclude that they might as well take their chances abroad. Victims of their own hopes and illusions, most trafficked women, leave their home country willingly to pursue a seemingly legitimate opportunity, and even those who know they may have to engage in the sex business assume that they will be treated humanely. However they often fall victim to the skilled deceptions of the traffickers and their agents, who force them into lives far worse than they ever imagined.

WHO CONTROLS THE TRADE: THE MAFIYA CONNECTION

The lucrative human trafficking business in Russia and throughout the world has attracted the attention of organized criminal groups, also known as "mafiya". This analysis considers an organized criminal group in Russia as "mafiya" if it is "characterized by profit-oriented criminal activity, uses violence or threat of violence, expends resources to discourage cooperation of its members with police, and corrupts legitimate government authority".[46] Unlike the Italian Mafiya, which is organized hierarchically and often within families around a single "godfather", the Russian Mafiya, or "bratva" (brotherhood) is generally divided into networks arranged along regional or ethnic lines.

The collapse of the Soviet Union seriously weakened governmental control over the economy and law enforcement. This void has quickly been filled by organized criminal groups, which have capitalized on a legacy of corruption and underground networks. According to the Russian Ministry of Internal Affairs (MVD), in 1993 there were at least 5,000 organized crime groups in Russia, with an estimated leadership of 18,000 and a membership of 100,000. By 1994, the number of criminal gangs in Russia grew to approximately 8,000.[47] More recent estimates have put the number even higher.[48]

Many mafiya members are former employees of the military and national security agency, the KGB, which was replaced after 1991 by the FSB (the state intelligence bureau). As security police often have political connections, access to weapons, and knowledge of the banking and business worlds, they are well-positioned to participate in domestic and international criminal activities.

The economic impact of the mafiya is significant and growing. By late 1996, criminal groups controlled an estimated 40,000 Russian businesses, including 500 joint ventures with foreign investors and 550 banks.[48] The amount of money paid for protection by a mafiya group can be as high as half a company's profits.[49] An estimated 70 to 80 percent of all businessmen in major Russian cities pay protection money to the mafiya.[50] Organized crime financial activity accounts for an estimated 40 percent of Russia's gross domestic product,[51] generating more than 10 billion U.S. dollars annually.[52]

Russian mafiya commerce includes the usual criminal activities: extortion, money laundering, and the trafficking of weapons, drugs, vehicles, and raw materials.[53] White collar crime – credit card fraud, computer hacking, etc. – is increasingly the domain of the more sophisticated mafiya organizations.

All levels of the Russian/NIS criminal world are involved at some level in the profitable and rapidly growing sex industry. In 1995, more than 200 illegal sex businesses existed in Moscow alone, providing services ranging from escorts and prostitutes for Russian or foreign businessmen, to sending groups of women to other countries to work as prostitutes. Some companies also make inexpensive pornographic films which are sold in Russia or exported to European countries.

GSN probed criminal connections with the sex business through interviews with Russian pimps, law-enforcement personnel, traffickers, and others, and found that:

- overall mafiya involvement in the Russian/NIS sex trade is substantial, with most sex businesses either owned or protected by organized crime groups.

- the sex business attracts mafiya investors (as owners or security providers) because the profit margin are high, the risk factor is low, and association brings added social status in mafiya circles.

- mafiya "roofs" are primarily sought to protect against extortion from other criminal groups and corrupt authorities. A roof will cost the protected business at least 10 percent of its visible profits.

- international trafficking operations based in Russia/NIS are generally controlled by smaller mafiya groups as they are less visible to competing organizations and authorities, and require less "protection" to sustain.

- control over domestic prostitution varies. It is controlled by larger mafiya organizations in clubs and hotels, while street prostitution is illegally regulated by police in collaboration with individual pimps. Escort services are the most independently run, paying a small percentage to criminal groups for protection against largely non-existent threats.

To understand the specific roles played by the mafiya in the sex trafficking business, one must look at each mafiya group as a company and coldly view its involvement as it does – as a wise financial investment. No matter how small or large the investment, the risk factor is low because most laws and law enforcement efforts target the sex worker, rather than the trafficker. Profit margins are high and consistent as overhead is low and a single sex worker can service multiple clients every day. Finally, there is the added fringe benefit that instant access to prostitutes increases one's status in mafiya circles.

Profit margins are especially important to Russian mafiya groups, not only because they increase the group's holdings, but because they secure and increase their position in what may be the world's toughest and most competitive crime society. The Russian mafiya has grown out of, as much as it has contributed to, post-perestroika instability, and has adapted to it better than any sector of the post-Soviet business world. This instability breeds anxiety and opportunity for all businesses, legal and illegal, which are pressured quickly to create profits. "Credit" is unpopular in Russia. Hard currency reserves and cash flow is critical to running any successful business – legal or illegal.

Extortion, practiced under the guise of providing security, is a fast way to produce income. Successful investments, however, generate more profit. Money markets that invest in off-the-books commercial operations have been a long-time favorite of mafiya groups. Since 1991 Russian organized crime groups have created scores of banks to launder and invest their foreign currency. These banks are legally registered, but generally conceal actual levels of deposits so as to avoid tax inspection payments. Bank deposits may be used to finance illegal commercial activities, which can generate rates of return as high as 50 to 100 percent.

The fastest money making investment opportunities are in the black market. Running guns and drugs continues to be profitable, but both have associated high risks because of the stiff criminal penalties they carry. The human trafficking business offers investors less risk and a significant rate of return. Although total net earnings may not compare with profits from white collar criminal activity, it is a stable industry that endures through good and bad economic times. For example, a mafiya group can "buy" a women to work as a prostitute in a hotel that it "protects". They may pay her as little as 500 dollars a month to work the hotel, while she earns from 2,000 to 10,000 dollars a month for the mafiya controlling her. Even where criminal groups offer the woman a portion of her earnings as commission on top of her 500 dollars, they will still secure a minimum return of 100 percent and often more than 1,000 percent on their investment, or 1,000 to 10,000 dollars a month. Of course, net earnings multiply with each additional sex worker; one mafiya group that controlled one Moscow hotel in 1996 employed no less than 35 sex workers on any given night.[54] Escort services provide similar earnings, as they involve minimal overhead and can operate more covertly. Sex-related profits from mafiya-controlled night clubs and brothels is more difficult to estimate. Yet clearly, cash flow is consistent and brisk; profits accumulate and are collected daily.

GSN found that some "high-level" mafiya groups that control businesses, such as oil operations or banks, are also investors in, or security providers to, sex trafficking operations. Investigators were unable to learn what level of return these groups are getting on their investments, although a "roof" generally extorts from 10 to 30 percent of net profits. Nonetheless, high level organized crime groups appear less involved in the sex business in terms of control and investment levels than they did during the early 1990s. Mid to lower level mafiya groups have filled most of the vacuum, as have entrepreneurial individuals and corrupt officials.

While domestic prostitutes may have the freedom to operate more independently, women and girls trafficked for forced prostitution do not. Few sex workers from Russia and the NIS reach the receiving country without assistance and/or coercion from a criminal group or network. Since the fall of the Berlin Wall, trade and travel controls in most of the former Soviet Union are significantly relaxed, but in order to leave Russia and find work in another country, a woman needs money to travel, a visa, and a contact in the country to which she is traveling, where she will be unfamiliar with the local language and culture. A minor will also need a falsified passport which shows her age to be at least 18 so that she can travel without her parents' consent.

Thus, the two central prerequisites to becoming a trafficker are connections to market providers in countries of destination and cash. Other necessities are secured relatively easily: women and girls desperate to earn money, visa invitation letters, and plane tickets. Traffickers secure the down payment for the costs of trafficking across borders in several different ways. Some enlist the support and investment of a mafiya group to provide the down payment; others use their own money and deduct the costs from the earnings of the women and girls they are trafficking. With round-trip flights from Moscow or Kiev to Tokyo costing as little as 800 U.S. dollars, many industrious traffickers choose to spend their own money instead of sharing their profits. Today, almost anyone can be a trafficker.

The specific types of traffickers and their connections to the mafiya vary widely, case by case, and country by country. However, if the woman or girl is forcibly deported or returns to her country of origin and is unable or unwilling to pay her "debt", the trafficker may require the services of a mafiya group later – if he is not a member of one already.

Case Studies

In Moscow GSN investigators made contact with "Sergey", a former surgeon and current pimp.[55] Posing as members of a fake model and escort company, investigators told Sergey they were interested in him as a possible Moscow-based agent, as a recruiter for the company, and as someone who could help secure a "roof", or protection, for the operation. Sergey expressed interest in working together and in meetings with investigators over the course of eight months revealed various facets of his and other people's links to the sex trade.

Sergey explained that in Moscow most pimps have approximately 5 to 10 women and girls working for them and that they "buy" their employees from one another. Sergey started his business as a pimp when he was hired by a representative of an American marriage agency to recruit women to work for "consummation" with American clients while they are in Moscow looking for wives. Consummation refers to the act of sitting with men in bars and encouraging them to buy and consume drinks. The bar makes money from the purchase of alcohol, and if the man elects to take the woman out of the bar for sex, the fee is split between the woman and the pimp or bar owner. When the American marriage agency representative failed to pay Sergey for his recruiting activities, he retaliated by using the women he had gathered to supply his own escort business.

When investigators asked Sergey if he could secure police protection for his sex-trade business, he clearly demonstrated his inclination toward working with the mafiya instead of with police. However, his preference had nothing to do with concerns about the illegality of his operations. "We won't tell them (police) anything ... they will want a lot of money. They will not help, but each one of them will come and demand money ... I can lie to the police and to the government, but I'm not going to lie to the mafiya". GSN later found that Sergey's respect for the mafiya was not completely fear-driven: "Whatever people say about the Russian mafiya, I got from them more than I gave".

GSN investigators saw the mafiya's influence first-hand at a marriage agency event at the Hotel Ukraine in Moscow, organized by a California-based "mail-order bride" company. GSN filmed the proceedings as a mafiya pimp, who controlled prostitution in the hotel, walked into the invitation-only party and, much to the consternation of the U.S. company representatives, sat with the prospective wives, presumably making them other offers. After the meeting, the pimp and three other men demanded money from the assistant organizer of the event and strip-searched her when she insisted that she had none. The organizer related the story to GSN:

On Saturday we rented a room in the Ukraine Hotel for the event, and on Saturday everything was quiet. Sunday everything went smoothly until later on when we had about 50 girls in the hall and about 5 guys came in and one guy wanted to come into the hall where the social took place. I told him no because we were doing video and the noise would interfere. He said it was his restaurant, his hotel, et cetera. Twenty minutes later three guys came to me, asked me if I knew Asman, said he is a member of the Solntsevo mafiya and that I must pay five thousand dollars, otherwise, he said "people will come and start shooting here and the end of the evening will be not so good".

The organizer noted that if that could happen in the Hotel Ukraine, across from the offices of the federal government in Moscow, "imagine what is happening in some province where there is no control"!

Mafiya activities are increasingly international in scope. Approximately one-quarter of the organized crime groups in Russia are thought to have international ties, supported in part by large-scale emigration to Europe, the United States, and Israel after the dissolution of the Soviet Union.[56] The United Nations estimates that at least 200 of the several thousand Russian mafiya groups are sophisticated networks, with operations in 50 countries.[57]

Germany

Today, Berlin is a central base for mafiya operations in Germany. In Germany, members of the Russian mafiya control the traffic of Russian women and children for prostitution, together with pimps from Turkey and the former Yugoslavia. In 1998 the German police estimated that traffickers earned 35-50 million U.S. dollars annually in interest on loans to foreign women and girls entering Germany to work as prostitutes.[58] According to German police, more than 50 percent of Russian business owners in Berlin have been involved in criminal cases.[59]

According to Dagobert Lindlau, who has written extensively about the growth of organized crime in Germany, the Russian mafiya "not only kill violently and often, but without much thought. They don't wait until all other means of pressure are exhausted. They just kill as soon as someone gives them the slightest bit of trouble".[60] Many police officials saw the mafiya's hand in the murder of 4 Ukrainian women, ages 18 to 28, who had entered Germany on visitor visas and were working illegally as prostitutes. They were killed on August 14, 1994, in the Edel Brothel in Frankfurt, probably because they had witnessed the simultaneous strangulation of the club's Hungarian owner, Gabor Bartos, and his wife Ingrid Bartos.

Although the police report listed robbery as the likely motive, the brutal efficiency of the killings led many police to suspect it was the work of the Russian mafiya. Women who had worked in the Bartos' brothel indicated that Bartos may have been punished for refusing to involve the mafiya when he recruited women in Russia. They also said that Bartos was abusive and kept their passports in his safe. In an interview with GSN, a specialist in the German Organized Crime Bureau, reported that the Russian man accused of murder in the Bartos case was sentenced in July 1996 to life in prison. Although the judge stated for the record that he saw no signs of organized crime involvement, the specialist told GSN he was not so sure.[61]

Macau to Vladivostok

Mafiya violence is suspected in another murder case, involving a trafficked Russian woman and a prominent Hong Kong lawyer. On June 24, 1994, Russian police in Vladivostok discovered the mutilated corpses of a man and a woman in a hotel. Both had been fatally wounded with shots to the head, and forensics reports indicated signs of torture.[62] Investigations revealed that the woman, 20-year-old Natasha Samofalova, and the man, 49-year-old Gary Alderdice, had met in April in Macau, where Natasha was working as a prostitute. She was under contract with the night club, which had a business agreement with a Vladivostok-based mafiya group.

Alderdice arranged to see Samofalova outside of the club on several occasions and even took her to parties with him in Hong Kong.[63] In May, Samofalova left Macau and returned to Vladivostok where she rented an apartment. She reportedly told her friends and mafiya sponsors that she would not be working for them much longer. Alderdice flew to Vladivostok. His friends said that he intended to "buy" Samofalova's freedom from her pimps.[64] The next time anyone saw them was when the police found their bodies.

When Jeff Bond, a reporter for the Vladivostok News, interviewed District Prosecutor Aleksandr Shcherbakov about the investigation, Shcherbakov denied reports that the couple had been tortured and said that he believed Alderdice was only carrying 2,700 dollars.[65] Some speculated it was a simple robbery, and Alderdice's partner, Michael Lunn, stated that Alderdice had entered Russia with less than 3,000 dollars in cash.[66] Robbery is cited as a plausible explanation as many Russian customs officials are on the payroll of crime groups, and information regarding the cash Alderdice carried into the country could have been conveyed immediately.[67]

However, police arrested Sergei Sukhanov because he was seen in the area on the night of the murders and his fingerprints were found in the apartment. Sukhanov had been Samofalova's boss at a travel agency specializing in cruise ships to Japan for wealthy Russians who want to buy cars.[68] Following the murders, Sukhanov was rumored to be in the business of trafficking Russian women to work as prostitutes in Macau and China. Sukhanov denies all such rumors, and claims he was a close friend of Samofalova's and helped her purchase her apartment when she returned to Vladivostok. Sukhanov was released several weeks after his arrest, and three other suspects were subsequently murdered. In the end, not unlike many murders in Vladivostok, the Alderdice-Samofalova murder remains unsolved.

As Gary Alderdice was a distant relative of the British royal family, what would have been a routine check into a murdered prostitute in Russia turned into a professional, well-coordinated investigation of high importance between police in Vladivostok, Hong Kong, and Macau. Police activity against brothels and local pimps in Hong Kong has existed for years, but as a result of the Alderdice scandal and investigation Russian prostitutes are now more difficult to find in Hong Kong and Macau. In 1996, a GSN investigator found "Club Fortuna", the Macau club where Natasha had originally worked, and met the main pimp as well as several prostitutes who had known Natasha. No one was willing to talk about the murder, but they all confirmed that it was more difficult to find Russian women in Macau as a result of some "political difficulties". As stated earlier, Russian sex workers have increased again in number in 1997–98.

The United States

The U.S. Federal Bureau of Investigation (FBI) estimates that at least 15 organized crime groups with former Soviet ethnic origins were operating in the United States in 1993.[69] FBI Director Louis Freeh estimates that at least 200 of Russia's crime groups maintain connections with U.S. counterparts in 17 cities and in 14 states nationwide.[70] Russian organized crime is concentrated in New York City, northern New Jersey, Philadelphia, Boston, Chicago, Miami, Cleveland, and California.[71] Criminal activities among Russian mafiya groups in the United States include extortion, auto theft, fuel tax fraud, insurance and medical fraud, money laundering, counterfeiting, credit card forgery, narcotics trafficking, and prostitution.

In 1994, the United States Department of Justice assigned "highest investigative priority" status to the Russian mafiya, placing it in the same category as La Cosa Nostra, the infamous Italian mafiya family, and the Colombian cocaine cartel known as Cali. The FBI established Russian Organized Crime (ROC) squads in New York City, Los Angeles, and Moscow, and many state and local governments have formed task forces to address the problem.

Concern about organized crime has increased in tandem with immigration from Russia and the Newly Independent States. A 1990 Census report indicates that 2.9 million people of Russian and Eurasian descent live in the United States. While ethnic affinity by no means implies complicity, the tight-knit nature of immigrant communities often contributes to a criminal ring's ability to operate covertly.

In one of the few nationally publicized incidents involving the traffic of Russian women into the United States, the *Washington Post* ran a March 1996 story in the Metro section reporting that agents of the Immigration and Naturalization Service (INS), the FBI, and the Montgomery Country Police had raided "Russian Touch Massage", a downtown Bethesda massage parlor, and detained six Russian female employees on suspicion of being undocumented workers.

Gregory Baytler, a native of St. Petersburg, Russia, and the head of Russian Touch, was arrested and subsequently indicted on misdemeanor charges, including maintaining a bawdy house for lewdness, keeping a bawdy house, and maintaining a disorderly house. Undercover police investigators established that the women working at Russian Touch offered sexual services, including "hand releases", but were unable to prove that prostitution was taking place. Baytler was also charged and indicted for audio interception without consent – a felony – for filming customers with a hidden camera. Six of the eight mafiya Russian women working in the establishment were taken into custody by the INS and transported to Baltimore for processing. While none of the women was charged by the police, four were deported and two left the United States voluntarily.

GSN met with Montgomery County Police to discuss the details of the case. According to Detective Rob Musser, the 8 Russian women discovered working at Russian Touch Massage were all between the ages of 28 and 35. Two had work visas and the rest had tourist visas. They had all answered advertisements in Moscow and St. Petersburg newspapers offering positions in the United States as *au pairs*, sales clerks, and waitresses. Their tickets to the United States had been arranged by two travel agencies, one located in Brooklyn, and another in Rego Park, New York. The women were charged approximately 1,800 dollars by the agencies for "facilitating" the trip, and their passports were confiscated while they worked off their debt. Both procedures are characteristic of trafficking operations. The police suspected high level government connections because of the ease with which Russian Touch Massage had obtained tourist visas for single Russian women, but were unable to verify their suspicions.

According to Detective Musser, the women working at Russian Touch were living at the massage parlor, sleeping on the massage tables at night. They were charged 150 dollars a week for their housing and were not paid any salary. One of the women interviewed indicated that she had earned 1,500 dollars in the last month in tips, before her "expenses" were deducted. They were also responsible for doing all the cleaning and laundry in the massage parlor. Meanwhile, Mr. Baytler received 100 dollars per hour for each massage, with an estimated 6 to 8 clients per hour, 24 hours a day. Because Baytler had failed to pay his taxes, the IRS seized more than 100,000 dollars from his bank account through civil procedures. Baytler organized a plea bargain with prosecutors and charges were dropped in July 1996, with the restriction that he be prohibited from operating any other businesses in Montgomery County. However, another massage parlor opened recently in Silver Spring, Maryland. Though it has been licensed in the name of another Russian man, the massage tables and equipment are identical to those in the Russian Touch Massage Parlor.

In March 1997, a GSN investigator visited the spa which advertises "Body Massage" and "Aroma Steam", located inconspicuously above a day care center. Although a sign in the massage room from the management clearly stated "Massage and body shampoo. Please do not ask for sexual favors", the Ukrainian masseuse made it clear that she expected to be asked to perform sexual services. When the investigator declined, and asked about the sign, she informed him that "We must have this, it is the law. So you cannot ask for this favor, you just point. Clients know this". She also informed the investigator that there are 6 to 7 Russian and Ukrainian women working at the spa, which is open from 10 a.m. to 10 p.m., with 2 to 4 women working at a time. The Russian owner of the spa keeps 60 dollars of the total (90 U.S. dollars charged per hour), so that the women make most of their money from tips for sexual services.

GSN research revealed that the case was partly pursued by local and federal authorities because, several months earlier in November 1995, a Russian woman had been murdered in her apartment. Her throat was slit from ear to ear. She had reportedly been working as a prostitute at the time in Reiserstown, Maryland. Authorities suspected mafiya involvement in the murder, and were investigating possible connections to Baytler's operation in Bethesda, which they were ultimately unable to substantiate. The murder remains unsolved.

MECHANISMS OF CONTROL

A woman who decides to travel abroad for work faces many obstacles, especially the lack of travel and living expenses and the need for assistance to find a job. As she may have limited funds and no contacts overseas, she is likely to turn to one of the seemingly reputable firms that specialize in placing women with foreign employers. According to Elena Tiuriukanova, in 1996 in all of Russia only 61 companies were officially licensed to act as intermediaries for Russians seeking jobs abroad. Furthermore, of the 61 licensed companies, none addressed women's employment specifically, even though women dominate contemporary labor migration out of Russia.

Agents, who are often friends or acquaintances, strike a deal, sometimes with a written contract, and promise to advance the cost of the airline ticket and arrange for the international documentation, with the understanding that they will be reimbursed once the woman or girl begins working. GSN found that trafficking networks in Russia and the Newly Independent States charge women anywhere from 1,500 to 30,000 dollars for their "services" in facilitating documentation, jobs, and transportation. Modeling and marriage agencies, which draw inquiries from large numbers of women, often serve as hunting grounds for sex traffickers. One representative of a modeling firm told GSN investigators that he had access to a databank of over 20,000 girls who were interested in employment abroad.

61

Document Manipulation

To trade in women, traffickers must secure several documents, including visas or work permits from countries of destination. Although some papers can be purchased illegally, in most cases bribery is not necessary because legitimate means will work just as well. Traffickers may use tourist, entertainment, fiancé, student, and business visas.

According to Swiss police there have been instances in which cabaret owners or intermediary companies submitted false passports and other documentation when applying for the work permits of Russian women.[72] Women from a range of countries also enter Switzerland as tourists, either alone or through trafficking networks. A Swiss tourist visa allows them to stay for a maximum period of three months. After the expiration date, some women remain in Switzerland and work illegally as domestic workers in private homes, as striptease dancers in clubs, or as prostitutes.[73]

Most trafficked women enter Germany with a three-month tourist visa, and then overstay by working "undercover".[74] This is a risky practice as German law stipulates that migrants who enter the country or stay illegally may be punished with fines and/or imprisonment of one year.[75] Furthermore, although German nationals may work as prostitutes if they are registered, the practice of prostitution by foreigners is grounds for deportation.[76] In addition to tourist visas, trafficking operations in Germany often utilize entertainment visas. Some operations have even established language schools and vocational institutes that allow women to gain legal entry on short-term visas.[77]

It is generally easier to obtain legal documentation from countries bordering Germany than from Germany itself, where immigration is more strictly regulated. For example, GSN found that because citizens from Poland do not require a visa to enter Germany, many trafficked women carry false Polish passports. Not surprisingly, Poland itself has become a major source of trafficked women, as well as a central transit country for traffic to other points in Europe.

Coercion and Isolation

Traffickers control women by emotional and physical manipulation. They begin by isolating them from the surrounding local society. This is usually easily achieved due to the women's poor grasp of the local language and their illegal status in the host country. Many brothel operators prefer foreign women precisely because they are easy to control.[78] A typical isolation strategy is to trick or coerce a woman into surrendering her passport, making her a virtual "nonperson".

Another technique is to compel a woman to work and live in the same place, and to forbid her from leaving the premises without permission. Isolation makes a woman vulnerable to additional forms of control, such as withholding pay, physical intimidation, and drug or alcohol dependency. A recent study in the Netherlands revealed that among more than 250 trafficked women interviewed, there were 177 reported instances of violence and extreme pressure, including cases of rape, passport confiscation, withholding of salaries, and physical or psychological abuse by traffickers, pimps, and clients.[79] Using such actions, traffickers and brothel operators imprison women in a world of economic and sexual exploitation that imposes constant fear of arrest and deportation, as well as of reprisals by the traffickers themselves, to whom the women must pay off accrued debts.

DEBT BONDAGE:
CASE STUDIES OF JAPAN, GERMANY, AND SWITZERLAND

Traffickers often carry out their work behind a legal facade, behind which women are persuaded to sign contracts that stipulate each party's obligations and financial returns. Through these usually innocuous-looking documents, the women become ensnared in a financial arrangement that leaves them in debt and obligated indefinitely to their employers. Such deceptive accounting, long outlawed by the International Labor Organization and most national governments, is the norm in the world of traffickers and their victims.

A Moscow-based trafficking business that transports women from Moscow to Japan to work as prostitutes provided GSN with a sample of the contract that women must sign prior to departure.[80] The contract exemplifies the debt bondage schemes routinely used by traffickers, though they are disguised under the rubric of "service provider", a position that entails "entertaining and escort work for and with male customers at the premises of the principal (club owner) in Tokyo, Japan". Despite the euphemistic language of the contract, the Russian recruiter made it clear in her interview with GSN that the women trafficked to Japan were required to have sex with clients. "Every client has the right to demand that the girls sleep with them", the trafficker said. The contract lays out clear terms, including the following:

- the woman will work a minimum of eight hours per day, six days per week.

- the woman must "provide services" to a minimum of four clients per day.

- the woman will earn 200 dollars per client, but all money will be held in trust by the club owner until the contract is complete.

- the woman will receive a cash allowance of 50 dollars per day, which will be subtracted from the sum held in trust.

- the principal will retain 30 percent of all money earned and held in trust.

- the woman agrees to pay for all clothes, food, and beverages through her daily allowance, or by drawing on money held in trust.

Although the total anticipated earnings, excluding tips, for a three-month contract are 47,280 dollars to the "service provider" and 18,720 dollars to the principal (club owner), further provisions give the traffickers room to maneuver their way out of paying any money at all to the women they hire. For example, contract provisions specifically state that:

> In the event that the service provider engages in any activity which may bring embarrassment to the principal or which is illegal (purposes of this agreement excepted) or in the event that the service provider fails to follow reasonable direction given by the principal... (the principal) may immediately terminate this agreement without any requirement for formal notice. In such instances the principal and/or its authorized agent may retain all moneys held in trust for the service provider (...). If the service provider without reasonable cause breaches any part of this agreement then the principal may, at its discretion, terminate this agreement and all moneys held in trust by the principal or its authorized agent for and on behalf of the service provider may be retained.

Japan

In Japan, nightclub operators commonly control women by employing a penalty system, an incentive system, or both.[81] Under the penalty system operators deduct earnings from women who do not perform satisfactorily. Women working in "consummation" clubs in Japan told GSN that unsatisfactory performance includes failing to applaud during strip shows, not keeping ice in clients' drinks, not wearing provocative clothes, or failing to be "animated" (talking, touching, flirting, and drinking with patrons to encourage liquor sales). Under the incentive system a woman gains extra cash by performing well. For every drink that a client buys, she may receive a small percentage of the purchase; she may also receive a bonus for every client she brings into the club. At the end of the evening, the female employees have to sit with the managers to discuss their performance as well as any penalties. The manager then has his workers driven to their apartment and telephones later to make sure they are there.

These monetary penalties are added to the debt to traffickers that most women incur even before they start working in a sex-oriented business. In Japan, the average trafficked woman accumulates debts of about 35,000 U.S. dollars,[82] though some women may owe as much as 300,000 U.S. dollars. A 1992 article in the newspaper *Mainishi Shimbun* reported that most Russian women coming to Japan to work at bars and clubs earn only 500 U.S. dollars per month, well below minimum wage.[83]

Germany

In Germany, GSN found that women pay anywhere from 6,000–18,000 U.S. dollars to pimps and traffickers to cover their "costs", including a passport, visa, and transportation to Germany.[84] These costs become debt, often with interest expected. As a result, foreign prostitutes in Germany give at least 50 to 60 percent of their earnings directly to pimps or club and brothel owners.[85] The German Organized Crime Bureau (BKA) estimates that by the time a woman's three-month visa expires, brothel owners have usually pocketed approximately 21,000 U.S. dollars, after expenses, for her services as a prostitute.[86] According to a lawyer with a non-governmental organization that serves trafficked women, many of the youngest girls end up with no money at all.[87]

This exploitative situation is compounded by the high cost of living in Germany and the low fees charged for sex. A woman needs an estimated 600 U.S. dollars to cover basic expenses such as rent, food, transportation, medical costs and clothing.[88] After accounting for these costs, there is little if any money left to repay debts to traffickers (and the woman may be in further debt if her earnings have been low), let alone to facilitate an eventual return home. Additionally, she can charge relatively little for her services. One hour with a woman can be purchased at many sex clubs in Germany for as little as 70–90 U.S. dollars. For thirty minutes, or for meetings in apartments rather than in clubs and brothels, sex can cost as little as 18–36 U.S. dollars with a condom, and 42–60 U.S. dollars without a condom. One expert from the German Organized Crime Bureau calculated that the average migrant prostitute earns 300 U.S. dollars per day and keeps as little as 12 U.S. dollars.[89]

Switzerland

The situation is equally harsh in Switzerland. Foreign dancers who are working in Geneva are paid an average of 83–97 U.S. dollars per day, but are charged 970–1,386 U.S. dollars per month for housing, generally provided by the clubs or pimps. Additional money is needed for insurance and debt to the traffickers.[90] This leaves many women with 416 U.S. dollars or less per month to purchase food and any other incidentals.[91] Saving money to return home becomes virtually impossible.

The stresses of working as a prostitute often lead to dependence on alcohol or hard drugs, and some traffickers and brothel operators actually encourage dependence as a means of controlling the women. GSN found that pressure is placed on women working in entertainment clubs to provide "animation" in order to generate alcohol sales. A woman's salary is often contingent on the value and volume of drinks she helps sell. According to the Women's Information Center (FIZ) in Zurich, "the situation in the clubs is that they have to "animate" clients to drink alcohol, which makes them very quickly alcoholics, and they have to generate at least 10,000 dollars of alcohol sales a month".[92]

These psychologically debilitating conditions make it difficult for women's and health organizations to reach illegal sex workers with vital information regarding their legal rights, contraception, disease, and safe sex practices. In the words of a representative from the Berlin Health Department, "Normally, the women from Russia don't like to talk to us about their feelings; they are very shy and ashamed, and we are paid by the government ... they don't know if they can talk to us ... And they feel ashamed by the customers, and by what they want them to do".[93]

In Switzerland, too, this reticence to talk with government officials isolates trafficked women from potential help, not only in matters of health and welfare, but in prosecuting their pimps. Swiss police claim that the enforcement problem lies less in the legal code than in obtaining proof to convict. However, most governments have failed to offer stays of deportation to potential witnesses in trafficking cases, or the necessary witness protection and relocation programs. Under these circumstances and because of the dangers posed to her and her family at home, it is rare for a trafficked woman to agree to testify against the pimps or procurers who brought her into the country. According to a staff person at FIZ in Zurich: "Our experience has shown that none of the women concerned dare to charge against trafficking, because they are threatened with murder and reprisals, and protection during the trial is not guaranteed".[94]

COLLUSION AND CORRUPTION

A Moscow pimp explained the role of the police to GSN investigators: "Here, street prostitution is controlled on the level of the police station ... mafiya controls the moment when (a woman) goes abroad".[95] A 21-year-old woman who supervises a group of prostitutes on Tverskaya street in Moscow told GSN that she pays the police between 10–20 dollars per night for each girl in her group in order to avoid arrest or interrogation. When GSN asked if there is competition between the police and the mafiya, Sergey shook his head and said: "The police are the same as the mafiya, but with epaulets". Police officers interviewed for this report said that they "understood" such remarks, but insisted that many police officials are "clean" and try their best to fight organized crime. The control that recruiters, pimps, and mafiya have over the lives of women becomes stronger when government authorities choose to ignore trafficking or even help to foster it. GSN's interviews revealed serious allegations that some Russian police and FSB officials are involved in the sex trade because of high profits to be gained from facilitating illegal activities. Extortion of prostitutes by police within Russia was widely reported to investigators.

Widespread indifference to women's issues, a lack of resources, and a heavy workload have prevented even honest law enforcement officials from tackling the growing problem of sex trafficking. Russia's judicial and criminal system is plagued by a lack of fair procedures, a severe case backlog, and manipulation by political authorities.[96] In 1996, the Council of Judges passed a no-confidence resolution regarding Justice Minister Kovalev because the courts had received less than 20 percent of the funds needed for administrative costs and salaries; many courts had stopped hearing cases.[97] The government's inability to fund justice system operations has left many of Russia's 15,000 judges, as well as procurators who supervise criminal investigations, open to bribes and threats by executive, military, and security forces, as well as the mafiya.[98] President Yeltsin warned in a radio address on September 27, 1997, that judges "are defenseless against the pressure of criminal structures".[99]

Germany

As in Russia, some of the police in Germany have been complicit in the sex trade and protected traffickers. In May 1996, Sigfried S., the Chief of the Special Commission on Organized Crime in Frankfurt on Oder, on the German-Polish border, was arrested for working with a local German pimp, "Peter R.", to control a ring of Eastern European prostitutes. The pimp supplied the police chief with information on local brothels and other organized crime activities in the region. In exchange, the police chief informed Peter R. of planned raids on his own brothels, for which the police chief received money from Peter R. and sexual favors from the prostitutes.[100]

Japan

Cooperation between Japanese organized crime groups – the Yakuza – and Japanese law enforcement officials is more difficult to document. However, because the Yakuza performs the service of controlling many small-scale criminals and intervening in disputes among citizens, police reportedly ignore mob activities.[101] Evidence exists of Yakuza paying off police to rescind charges for illegal activities, including trafficking.[102] Police indifference to trafficking often has severe ramifications for individuals. A Thai woman seeking shelter with House in Emergency of Love and Peace (HELP), a Japanese non-governmental organization, told counselors that when she tried to escape from a club where she worked for a pimp, she approached a police officer. The officer demanded 250 U.S. dollars before agreeing to help, which she paid; then he sold her back to her pimp for an unknown amount.[103]

In one Japanese sex club, GSN interviewed a South American woman about connections between Yakuza and the police. "Maria" said that her club is owned by a Yakuza company and managed by an American man. Although it is advertised only as a strip club, clients can pay extra for sexual favors. Despite the presence of numerous illegal workers in the club, including herself, Maria said the police never cause problems. "Police and Yakuza are tight", she explained. "The police don't do anything around here. If we have a problem we don't bother talking to them".[104]

CONCLUSIONS AND RECOMMENDATIONS

Governments have traditionally framed trafficking as an immigration question, and have treated people who are trafficked as violators of immigration laws because they often cross borders illegally and may work without proper papers. However, by defining trafficked persons primarily as illegal migrants, a state ensures their powerlessness and lack of means for self-protection. In fact, as many of the stories recounted in this report show, tightening legal screws gives traffickers a more prominent role in the migration flow. When potential migrants are denied the means of entering and remaining in a country independently, they are forced to turn to apparently legitimate organizations that offer to handle visas and passports. Even worse, once a government has made entry more restrictive, it may assume that it has no other obligation to those persons who have been trafficked.

Moreover, increased scrutiny and prosecution of illegal migrants by countries of destination make women hesitant to report abuse to authorities; they know they will be treated as illegal migrants and summarily arrested, detained, and deported. This is particularly true for women working in the sex industry, as prostitutes or the associated activities of brothel-keeping and pimping are criminalized in most countries. An estimated 90 percent of the foreign women working illegally in German brothels, for example, are deported when discovered by authorities, while those who run illegal trafficking operations are rarely brought to justice. In contrast to individual women with illegal status, criminal networks are entrenched, organized, and well-connected economically and politically. Greater priority must be placed on weakening the scope and influence of organized crime, rather than on punishing the actions of victimized women. Enforcement actions aimed at sex workers whether they are working voluntarily or under coercive circumstances – only serve to increase organized crime control and profits.

However, prosecution of traffickers is complicated. Even when stays of deportation are granted to women who are willing to testify, the individual s(and her family) run the risk of suffering retaliation from thwarted traffickers. Witness protection and relocation programs are rarely offered for cases involving trafficking. Additionally, while the state may benefit from a woman's testimony because it can lead to a crackdown on organized crime, the benefits to the witness are minimal – perhaps, as in Belgium and the Netherlands, a stay of deportation for the duration of a trial, with no guarantee of residency after proceedings are completed.

What governments fail to understand, or choose to ignore, is that trafficking is a contravention of basic human rights condemned by an array of international conventions, treaties, and other instruments. Furthermore, practices routinely used by traffickers, such as debt bondage, threats, intimidation, and withholding of wages are illegal under national laws. A trafficked person must be treated not as a criminal but as a fully empowered human being. If each government focused on these human rights abuses when they are inflicted on foreign women residing within their national borders, they would be addressing fundamental human rights violations associated with trafficking operations. A broader, more consistent approach to stopping the traffic in women is clearly needed. State action is only part of the solution, since the profitable trade in women depends greatly on the naivetè and powerlessness of its victims. It is therefore important that any attempt to curb trafficking addresses not only law enforcement and immigration authorities, but the need to educate women – particularly young women and those who are economically vulnerable – about the patterns and dangers of trafficking. Finally, and perhaps most importantly, education and rights-based initiatives to address the problem must be coupled with economic initiatives that provide women and girls at risk with viable alternatives so that they can sustain themselves and their families.

NOTES

1. Senate Congressional Resolution 82 (Concurrent Resolution with H. Con. Res. 239), "105th Congress 2nd Session", *Congressional Record*, Tue., March 10, 1998.
2. Although this study focused on the trafficking of women out of Russia, we also interviewed women trafficked from Newly Independent States such as Latvia and Ukraine.
3. GSN focused its research on these countries because all had been identified through investigations as significant "receiving countries" for women trafficked from Russia and

the Newly Independent States. Additional investigations would undoubtedly document similar trafficking patterns and methods worldwide. Numerous other countries, including Israel, Belgium, Spain, Finland, Greece, Turkey, Italy, Australia Thailand, Vietnam, Cambodia, the Philippines, Saudi Arabia, Cyprus, Egypt, the United Arab Emirates, Tanzania, and South Africa have witnessed increases in the number of women trafficked from Central and Eastern European countries

4. "One Year La Strada: Results of the First Central and East European Program on Prevention of Trafficking in Women", The Dutch Foundation Against Trafficking in Women (STV)/La Strada Program (Sept. 1996), p.13.
5. The National Bureau of Statistics of Russia, cited in Elena Tiuriukanova, "Women in Search of Jobs Abroad: Female Labour Migration from Russia", *Valday-96, Proceedings of the First Summer School on Women's and Gender Studies in Russia* (Moscow: 1997).
6. *Ibid.*
7. Paul Hockenos, "I Had Moral Problems": East Europe Struggles with the Booking Sex-Trade Business", *Ft. Worth Star-Telegram*, May 19, 1996.
8. German Department of Criminal Investigation, *Solwodi/Newsletter,* No.26 (Mainz: Aug. 1994), p.2.
9. Interview with Silvia Steiner, Chief of Sittenpolizei (morals police) (Zurich, Switzerland: June 1996).
10. "Effectif Des Danseuses (artistes de varietes), par nationalite et cantonî (table of statistics)", Federal Ministry for Foreigners (Switzerland: Aug. 1990).
11. *Ibid*, Aug. (1992).
12. *Ibid*, Dec. (1995).
13. Interview, Shoji Rutsuko, Director, *HELP* (Tokyo: June 1996).
14. "Number of Russians Who Entered Japan 1989-1995" (*Statistical table*) (Japanese Ministry of Justice: 1996).
15. *Ibid.*
16. *Ibid.*
17. *HELP Network News*, No. 23, Dec. 1994, p.1.
18. "Number of Russians Who Entered Japan 1989-1995", *op.cit.*
19. Interview with members of the Japanese National Police (Tokyo: June 1996).
20. Interview with Hong Kong police (June 1996).
21. Hong Kong Police, "Triad Societies: General Briefing Paper", *Trends in Organized Crime*, Vol.2, No.2 (Winter 1996), pp.30–31.
22. Jennifer Gould, "The Russian Mob Takes Over", *The Village Voice*, March 4, 1997, p.36.
23. Victoria Pope, "Trafficking in Women: Procuring Russians for Sex Abroad – Even in America", *U.S. News and World Repor,* April 7, 1997, p.43.
24. Michael Fix and Jeffrey S. Passel, "Immigration and Immigrants: Setting the Record Straight, Urban Institute" (1994), p.25.
25. "One Year La Strada", *op.cit.*, p.13.
26. *Solwodi/Newsletter, op.cit.*, p.2
27. *Ibid.*
28. Interview with counselor for migrant and trafficked women (July 1996).
29. Helena Karlen and Christina Hagner, "*Commercial Sexual Exploitation of Children in Some Eastern European Countries*" (Bangkok, Thailand: ECPAT, The International Campaign to End Child Prostitution in Asian Tourism, 1996), p.32.
30. Interview with "Natasha", Russia (Feb. 1996).
31. Helena Karlen and Christina Hagner, *op.cit.*, p.33.
32. *Ibid.*, p.25.
33. "East European Women Fall into Widening Net of Human Trafficking; Western Officials Note Rise in Young Victims Tricked into Forced Prostitution", *The Wall Street Journal*, European Edition , March 1-2, 1996.
34. Elena Tiuriukanova, "Women in Search of Jobs Abroad: Female Labour Migration from Russia", *Valday-96, Proceedings of the First Summer School on Women's and Gender Studies in Russia* (Moscow: 1997).

35. "Human Rights Country Reports: Russia" (Washington D.C.: U.S. Department of State, 1997), p.3.
36. *Ibid.*, pp.3–4.
37. Fiona Fleck, "Russian Women Pushed Out of Job Market at Home", *Reuters News Service* (February 27, 1993), states that at least 75 percent of Russia's unemployed are women. In addition, a range of sources agree that official estimates of unemployment are considerably lower than actual numbers.
38. *Human Rights Country Reports: Russia. op.cit.*, p.30.
39. Zoya Khotkina, "Gender Aspects of Unemployment and the System of Social Security", *unpublished article* (Moscow, March 1994).
40. "Neither Jobs Nor Justice: Discrimination Against Women in Russia", *Human Rights Watch*, New York (March 1995), p.6.
41. Interview with Elena Gapova, Associate Professor, Byelorussian State University, Washington, DC (Dec.1995).
42. Annual Report, Center "SYOSTRI", Moscow (1996).
43. *Ibid.*
44. Elena Tiuriukanova, *op.cit.*
45. Annelise Anderson, "The Red Mafia: A Legacy of Communism", Edward P. Lazear, , ed., *Economic Transition in Eastern Europe and Russia: Realities of Reform* (Stanford: Hoover Institution Press, 1995), p.3.
46. Viktor Bulgakov, head of the department of the Moscow police for organized crime, cited in *ITAR-TASS News Agency* (World Service) (Moscow: Oct. 11, 1995).
47. "Crime: the World Ministerial Conference on Transnational Organized Crime", in *Crime Prevention and Criminal Justice Newsletter*, Nos. 26–27, the United Nation, Nov. 1995.
48. Stephen Handelman, "Can Russia's New Mafia Be Broken"?, *The New York Times*, Nov. 9, 1996.
49. Brian Duffy and Jeff Trimble, "The Wise Guys of Russia", *U.S. News and World Report*, March 7, 1994, p.45.
50. Information from a government report submitted to Russian President Boris Yeltsin, cited in Annelise Anderson, *op.cit.*, p.16.
51. S.C.Gwynne and Larry Gurwin, "Russia Connection", *Time*, July 8, 1996; and Louise I. Shelley, "The Price Tag of Russian Organized Crime", *Transition*, Feb. 1997, p.7.
52. Stephanie Bentura, "Russian Mob Emerges as U.S. Organized Crime Threat", *Agence France Presse*, Jan. 30, 1996.
53. L. Shelley, "Criminal Kaleidoscope: The Diversification and Adaptation of Criminal Activities in the Soviet Successor States", *European Journal of Crime, Criminal Law, and Criminal Justice*, Vol.3 (1996), p.252.
54. Interview with "Larisa", Moscow, Russia (1996).
55. Interviews with "Sergey", Russia (1996).
56. L. Shelley, "Criminal Kaleidoscope", *op.cit.*, p.255.
57. *Russian Organized Crime* (Washington D.C.: Center for Strategic and International Studies, 1997), p.10.
58. Agistra (Working Team Against International and Racial Exploitation), written summary of organization's work, Frankfurt, Germany, 1998, p.3.
59. Interview with Andreas Reinhardt, German Organized Crime Bureau, Berlin (July 1996).
60. Quoted in Stephen Kinzer, "Ivan in Berlin: The Long Shadow of the Russian Mob", the *New York Times* (Dec. 11, 1994).
61. Interview with Andreas Reinhardt, German Organized Crime Bureau, Berlin (July 1996).
62. Interview with Hong Kong Police Department (June 1996).
63. *Ibid.*
64. Interview with Jeff Bond, former staff writer for the *Vladivostok News* (Jan. 1997).
65. Jeff Bond, "Alderdice Suspect Asserts His Innocence", *Vladivostok News*, July 15, 1994.
66. Interview with Jeff Bond.

67. *Ibid.*
68. *Ibid.*
69. Daniel E. Lungren, "Russian Organized Crime: California's Newest Threat", California Department of Justice (March 1996), p.9.
70. *Ibid.*
71. *Ibid.*
72. Interview with Silvia Steiner, Chief of Sittenpolizei (morals police), Zurich, Switzerland (June 1996).
73. Regula Turtschi, "Legislation on Trafficking", *FIZ Newsletter* (Zurich: Switzerland, Jan. 1996).
74. Interview with Andreas Reinhardt, German Organized Crime Bureau, Berlin, Germany (July 1996).
75. *Trafficking in Women, Forced Labour and Slavery-Like Practices in Marriage, Domestic Labour and Prostitution*, Global Alliance Against Traffic in Women and Foundation Against Trafficking in Women, Preliminary Report, first draft (Utrecht, the Netherlands: 1996), p.105.
76. *Ibid.*, p.110.
77. Interview with Andreas Reinhardt, German Organized Crime Bureau, Berlin, Germany (July 1996).
78. Diana Hummel, "Si Piensas Viajar a Europa", *Informationstelle Latein Amerika*, No.146, Germany (June 1991).
79. "One Year La Strada", *op.cit*, p.21.
80. Interview with "Natasha", in Russia (Feb. 1996).
81. Interview with "Vera", in Japan (June 1996).
82. Interview with Shoji Rutsuko, Director of *HELP*, Tokyo (June 1996).
83. "Russian Women Prostituting at Below Minimum Wage: Yen 60,000 a Month in Tokyo", *Mainishi Shimbun*, Sept. 2, 1992.
84. Interviews with Amnesty for Women, Hamburg, Germany (July 1996) and Andreas Reinhardt, German Organized Crime Bureau, Berlin, Germany (July 1996).
85. Interview with counselor for migrant and trafficked women, Germany (July 1996).
86. "East European Women Fall into Widening Net of Human Trafficking; Western Officials Note Rise in Young Victims Tricked into Forced Prostitution", *Wall Street Journal*, European edition, March 1–2, 1996.
87. Interview with counselor for migrant and trafficked women, Germany (July 1996).
88. Information provided by Amnesty for Women, Hamburg, Germany, in correspondence with GSN (December 1996).
89. Interview with Andreas Reinhardt, German Organized Crime Bureau, Berlin, Germany (July 1996).
90. Interview with Sylvia Poirot, counselor, Aspasie, Geneva, Switzerland (June 1996).
91. *Ibid.*
92. Interview with Kuyo Kuoh, counselor, Frauen Informazion Zentrum (FIZ), Zurich, Switzerland (June 1996).
93. Interview with counselor for Berlin Health Department, Germany (July 1996).
94. Interview with Kuyo Kuoh (June 1996).
95. Interview with "Sergey", Russia (Feb. 1996).
96. "Human Rights Country Reports: Russia", *op.cit*, p.4.
97. *Ibid.*
98. *Ibid.*
99. "The Criminal Dons will Never Triumph", *Rossiskaya Gazeta*, Sept. 27, 1997.
100. Claudia Keikus, "Komissar verkaufte Tips an Bordell-Chef", *Berliner Kurier*, May 23, 1996.
101. "More Eyes on Yakuzaís Role in Japanese Economy", *Japanese Economic Institute* (1992), p.5.
102. *Ibid.*, p.5.
103. Interview with Shoji Rutsuko, Director of *HELP*, Tokyo, Japan (June 1996).
104. Interview with "Maria", Tokyo, Japan (June 1996).

Trafficking in People in Thailand

PASUK PHONGPAICHIT

INTRODUCTION

Between 1991 and 1994, 20,982 Thai females were deported from Japan as illegal workers.[1] Many had no proper travel documents as they had entered Japan using fake passports of other nationalities. About 80 percent had worked in sex services. Agents who helped them to enter Japan charged a fee of approximately 800,000 *baht* per person and then made them provide sex to clients to pay this "debt". Agents made an estimated net gain of over four billion *baht* a year from trafficking women.[2]

Thailand is a major center for trafficking in people. Thai workers and sex workers are trafficked to countries in Asia and elsewhere. Cheap labor is trafficked in from Burma and other neighboring countries. Thailand is also a convenient transit point for other flows: south Asians arrive in Bangkok and are smuggled across the land border into Malaysia; mainland Chinese arrive for onward shipment to third countries. Bangkok serves as a clearing house for sex workers from the Philippines, eastern Europe, and elsewhere.

This paper attempts to gauge the scale of this business and to describe its major characteristics. The treatment is not comprehensive, largely because the information is difficult to gather. Instead, the paper concentrates on the main inward and outward flows – especially Thai workers and sex workers to Japan, Taiwan, Germany and other destinations; and Burmese in-migrants – covering the period 1994–95.

This research is part of a larger project on Thailand's illegal economy.[3] In addition to human trafficking, the project looks at arms trading, prostitution, illegal gambling, oil smuggling, and drug trafficking. The project found that these six major illegal economic activities do not exist independently of each other. Rather, all are linked in a complex network of relationships. Some drug traders are linked to dealers in contraband arms. Some traffickers in women to Japan are connected to high military officers who provide protection to organized crime syndicates involved in gambling and other activities. Some smugglers in diesel oil are linked to traffickers of labor to foreign countries. And so on. There is also a regular pattern of linkages to powerful figures in the bureaucracy, military, police, and politics who provide protection to businessmen engaged in the illegal economy.

THE SETTING

Disparities of income, differing structures of labor demand, and differing conditions of supply provide the setting for labor migration across countries. Transnational migration is not new to the east and southeast Asian regions. In the eighteenth and nineteenth centuries, Chinese and South Asians migrated in large numbers from poverty-stricken areas of origin to labor-scarce but land-abundant countries like Siam, Singapore, Malaya, and Indonesia. Chinese migrated to Southeast Asia and to the U.S. under systems of indentured labor.[4] The flow of transnational migration into Southeast Asia was disrupted from the 1920s, first by local governments that feared the spread of communist ideology, and later by the Second World War and the tumult of decolonization. The flow revived again in the 1970s.[5]

The recent surge of transnational migration in the region involves both inbound and outbound moves, skilled and unskilled workers, males and females. Skilled and professional workers move relatively easily between countries within the framework of rules for visas, work permits, and citizenship. Unskilled workers have more difficulty as not all countries officially welcome them. Yet, rapid economic growth has generated high demand for unskilled workers and has induced a large flow of transnational unskilled migrants which operates both inside and outside the law.

This flow is propelled by employers in high-growth countries seeking cheap labor. The flood of temporary migration to the Middle East in the 1970s, for instance, was initiated by the Middle East countries themselves on a government-to-government basis. Labor migration to Brunei and Singapore is similar. In these countries, governments recognized the economic compulsion to admit foreign migrants. They quickly regularized the migration flow with rules and procedures. Lately Hong Kong, Malaysia, Taiwan, South Korea, and Thailand have begun to allow in-migration of manual labor within official limits on the types and numbers of migrants permitted. But as a result of high demand and significant wage differentials between sending and receiving countries, the movement of migrants tends to overflow these legal limits.

Japan remains the only country in the region that officially closes its labor market to unskilled labor, although the market for skilled and professional workers has opened a little. However, Japan ranks very high as a destination for transnational migrants in the region. High wage levels and the appreciation of the *yen* made it possible for migrants to Japan to save significant amounts when valued in the currency of the migrant's home country. Hence, Japan is the most attractive country for transnational migrants from poorer countries.

Illegal trafficking in labor arises because governments refuse to recognize the economic need for imported manual labor. Imperfect information about job availability, access, and mobility make these potential migrants prey to agents and labor recruiters.

Migrants are pushed to migrate by a lack of jobs and income in their own countries, and are pulled by stories of better opportunities overseas. They are motivated by the desire to improve themselves by whatever means possible. For many the feeling of *pai tai auo dapna* (go prepared to die in the next war/trip) is so strong that they risk even their lives. Many are also motivated by the spirit of "proving to themselves that they also can make it".

Thailand is both an exporter and importer of migrant workers. The inbound and outbound streams amount to approximately 1.5 million people, or about 5 percent of Thailand's total labor force of 32 million.

Most migrant workers are illegal. They travel with the help of agents and labor recruiters, sometimes under an indentured labor system. Agents include organized gangs controlled by the underworld, aided by corrupt police and other government officials in the immigration office, the airport authority, and other offices. Agents earn fees by smuggling illegal migrants but also by assisting legal migrants to places like Taiwan where the earnings can be very high.

This paper estimates the revenue generated by migration of unskilled labor in and out of Thailand, and its distribution among the migrants and the agents. Migrants are divided into two categories: unskilled manual labor and women in the sexual services trade. For out-migrants the calculations are focused on the largest markets for Thai unskilled labor and prostitutes in the 1990s, namely Japan, Taiwan, and

Germany. For the in-migrants to Thailand the focus is on Burmese citizens, who constitute the single largest inward stream.

Inevitably this is an attempt to estimate the inestimable. By definition, illegal income is not properly recorded. However, the scale of the business is so large that it deserves an effort at estimation even though the results can only be approximate.

TRANSNATIONAL MIGRANTS FROM THAILAND: AN OVERVIEW

A large number of Thai manual workers began migrating to work overseas temporarily in the 1970s. By the 1980s more than 100,000 workers traveled abroad each year. The major destinations at that time were Saudi Arabia and other Middle Eastern countries. In 1989 there were 264,600 Thai workers abroad, of whom 140,000 or 53 percent were in Saudi Arabia. The next largest market was Singapore with 30,000.

In the 1990s the major markets shifted to other Asian countries in the region. Based on the official records of the Ministry of Labor, the number of migrants working abroad from 1991-95 ranged from 63,000 to over 100,000 a year (Table 1). The total stock of Thai migrants working outside Thailand in 1995 was estimated to be about 450,000, both legal and illegal. The proportion of illegals was approximately 60 percent.

Out-migrants receive higher wages in recipient countries than they could expect in Thailand, but lower than wages of nationals. According to a 1985 sample survey of Thai migrants, workers in the Middle East received around 4,500 *baht* a month for manual work and between 5,490 and 9,937 *baht* for semi-skilled jobs in iron works, assembly shops, cleaning, cooking, typing, cement works, and bus conducting. Skilled and professional workers received higher wages of 11,000–32,000 *baht* a month. For manual and semi-skilled workers in Malaysia and Brunei the monthly wages were between 5,400 and 16,000 *baht*.[6] By comparison, the minimum wage for unskilled workers in Thailand at the time was 70 *baht* a day or 1,750 *baht* for a 25-day month.

In 1995 an unskilled worker in Taiwan received up to 14,880 Taiwan dollars a month or 14,434 *baht*. The comparable figure based on Thailand's minimum wage would be 3,625 *baht* a month. A manual worker working in construction in Japan in 1994 received 1,200–1,800 *baht* a day or 30,000-45,000 *baht* a month as compared to less than 4,000

TABLE 1

THAI LABOR OUT-MIGRATION (official), 1991-95

Country	1991	1992	1993	1994	1995
Middle East					
Saudi Arabia	5,613	8,701	5,035	4,152	1,625
Israel	874	1,064	1,797	7,641	6,364
Qatar	928	944	751	1,534	1,045
Bahrain	1,047	841	750	594	175
Jordan	46	14	8	7	4
Kuwait	3,121	3,313	1,859	1,212	571
Libya	7,651	5,407	4,597	160	264
Others	2,293	2,503	2,525	8,122	241
Sub-total	*21,482*	*23,092*	*17,019*	*17,614*	*11,172*
Asia					
Malaysia	2,473	6,608	11,358	12,232	5,853
Singapore	9,488	11,337	14,171	15,100	7,610
Brunei	8,840	12,729	14,750	16,553	8,275
Hong Kong	8,431	7,273	5,182	5,851	3,463
Japan	6,263	6,773	5,388	8,848	4,102
Taiwan	2,237	10,938	66,891	91,162	60,474
Others	745	507	660	741	629
Sub-total	*38,477*	*56,165*	*118,600*	*150,487*	*90,406*
North America, Europe and others					
USA	2,167	978	706	831	420
UK	247	60	64	96	45
Germany	363	171	185	242	138
Denmark	397	704	649	49	25
Australia	44	-	30	23	12
Others	672	611	697	422	156
Other Countries	*3,890*	*2,524*	*2,331*	*1,663*	*796*
Grand Total	*63,849*	*81,718*	*137,950*	*169,764*	*102,374*

Notes. The figures for 1995 relate to the period Jan–June. The figures in this table include only those migrants with official permits. The data underestimate the total as they do not include those who went abroad to work on tourist visas, those disguised as brides marrying nationals of recipient countries, and those smuggled into other foreign countries illegally or by using fake passports. Source: Ministry of Labor.

baht a month in Thailand. An equivalent Japanese worker would earn double the migrant wage and would also expect a year-end bonus of three to four months which is not available to the migrant. Thus, the migrant's earnings are around 40 percent of his Japanese counterpart but possibly 10 times what he would earn back in Thailand.[7]

Workers who go abroad legally on a contract basis often stay and work illegally after the contract expires. They have paid very high fees to agents for the contract in the first place. At the end of the contract period they have little or no clear profit after repaying the agent, and hence they are tempted to stay on. This is true in the case of Taiwan and South Korea as well as Japan.

THE ECONOMIC VALUE OF THAI OUT-MIGRANTS TO THE THAI ECONOMY

Since the early 1980s, remittances from Thai out-migrants have increased foreign exchange, helping to fill the trade gap and reduce the current account deficit.[8] In 1976 remittances totaled only 485 million *baht*. By 1995, they had risen ninety times to 45,700 million *baht* (Table 2). In the late 1980s total remittances from workers accounted for 17 percent of the trade deficit. In 1994, this ratio was 15 percent. According to the Bank of Thailand, until 1981 the highest amount of remittance through the banking channel came from the Middle East. The next highest came from the U.S. Japan's share has been important from the mid–1980s. However, official figures underestimate the value of remittances from Japan as part of the income is sent back to Thailand via human carriers and other unofficial channels.

THE ECONOMIC VALUE TO THE RECIPIENT COUNTRIES: JAPAN, GERMANY, AND TAIWAN

Recipient countries benefit a great deal from migrants as they gain their services without having to pay for their education or training. Some economists suggest, therefore, that recipient countries should compensate the sending countries.[9]

For skilled and professional workers, the value of education and training bundled with the worker can be very high. It is not insignificant even for manual laborers. Many unskilled Thai workers in Japan have completed primary education, several have secondary

TABLE 2

REMITTANCES SENT BACK TO THAILAND BY OUT-MIGRANTS
(MILLION BAHT)

Country	1983	1986	1990	1995
Brunei	24.6	40.9	104.3	
Indonesia	24.0	107.9	22.5	
Malaysia	53.0	107.9	51.9	
Singapore	382.4	370.6	549.1	
Middle East	15,667.6	10,521.0	5,837.6	
Japan	354.2	925.7	1,787.2	
North Europe	243.0	655.2	1,033.1	
USA	2,085.7	6,807.5	12,440.6	
Others**	622.8	1,443.7	3,128.8	
Total	19,457.3	20,899.8	24,906.6	45,700.0

** France, Germany, Italy

Source: Bank of Thailand. Figure for 1995 is estimate by Thai Farmers Research Centre, quoted in The Nation (May 1, 1997).

education, and a few have teacher's qualifications. Among prostitutes the education level ranges from primary to secondary.

Recipient countries also benefit from discounted wage costs. Migrant workers receive much lower wages than their local counterparts. The national minimum wage in Japan was 4,757 yen per day in 1994 and the national average wage for construction workers was 14,430 yen per day (figures from ILO, Bangkok). An illegal Thai male worker earned around half of the national average for construction workers. In addition, illegal migrants are not covered by any welfare provisions. Employers thus benefit a great deal by saving on wages and other labor costs. They may run the risk of being prosecuted under the immigration laws but so far no Japanese employer has been prosecuted harshly by the Japanese authorities for employing illegal migrants.[10]

Many times these workers become sick or suffer accidents. Thai prostitutes may get pregnant accidentally. Often hospitals refuse to accept them because they have no papers and cannot guarantee payment. If a hospital agrees to treat them for humanitarian reasons the cost of the treatment often rests with the hospital. Patients may run away as soon as they recover. Japanese NGOs, in collaboration with some Thai NGOs, have persuaded the Japanese local authorities to allow them to help illegal Thai migrants with health and other problems. The Japanese authorities agree in order to reduce the negative social repercussions of migrant workers.

THAI MIGRANTS TO JAPAN:
MANUAL WORKERS AND SEX WORKERS

Male Thai migrants in Japan work in factories, grocery stores as fruit and vegetable packers, hotels and restaurants as dishwashers and cooks, and other manual jobs. Some female Thai migrants also work in factories, but many more work as prostitutes or as hostesses, waitresses, and bar staff often doubling as prostitutes. This fact is disguised in the official data (Table 3), but sources who deal with repatriation at the Thai embassy in Japan confirm that most female Thai illegal migrants sent home in 1994 worked as prostitutes.

TABLE 3

OCCUPATION OF ILLEGAL THAI WORKERS IN JAPAN, 1994

	Total	Male	Female
Construction	15,869	15,691	178
Factory worker	13,793	10,654	3,139
Host/hostess	7,858	7,413	445
Other manual	4,456	3,656	800
Waitress/bar staff	4,107	1,865	2,242
Dish washer	2,937	1,407	1,530
Cook	2,413	1,787	626
Other services	1,738	1,051	687
Others	6,181	3,495	2,686
(transport workers)	480		
(prostitutes)	1,176		
(others)	3,438		

Source: Japanese Immigration Office

Between 1991 and 1995, the annual inflow of Thai workers to Japan is estimated at 10–15,000 persons, based on statistics of those found overstaying their visas. Of these, 60 percent, or 6,000 to 9,000, were women.

TRAFFICKING WOMEN TO JAPAN

Prostitution and migrant labor are illegal in Japan. Thus, Thai immigrants who enter Japan to work as sex workers are illegal on two counts. Nevertheless, Japanese and Thai agents play crucial roles in facilitating the imports of Thai women for sex services.

The large scale trafficking of southeast Asian women for sex services in Japan began in the 1970s. Previously, Japanese men came to other Asian countries on organized sex tours which began around 1960 and expanded rapidly in the 1970s. In the beginning, Taiwan was the major destination for sex tours. Later, it moved to the Philippines and Thailand. In 1981, it was estimated that a Japanese tourist spent on average 70 U.S. dollars for sex service in the Philippines. However the woman pocketed only five to seven dollars. In the 1970s and 1980s NGOs and feminist movements in Japan, the Philippines, and Thailand protested against Japanese sex tours. When the prime minister of Japan visited Southeast Asian countries in 1981, local women's groups demonstrated against him in protest of sex tours.

Around this time agents began importing southeast Asian women – many from the Philippines – to Japan for sex services. In the 1980s Philippine Prime Minister Aquino tried to stem this out-migration using stricter airport policing. Many corrupt immigration officials who co-operated with agents were charged with criminal offenses, making it difficult for agents to operate in the Philippines. So, agents then moved into Thailand and the trafficking of Thai women to Japan has increased rapidly since the 1970s. The trade peaked during the early-1990s when the number of Thai women overstaying their visas was running at 28,000 per year. It was estimated that there were about 100,000 foreign sex workers in Japan at this time, most of whom were from the Philippines and Thailand. As the Japanese economy slowed, the number of Thai women overstaying dropped back slightly to 24,926 in 1994 and 24,179 in 1995. According to a former Thai consular official in Japan who assisted women deported to Thailand, there were 23,000 Thai female sex workers in Japan in 1995 (based on the number of Thai women who overstayed their visas that year). Yet the real number would be higher as the 23,000 does not include those using a non-Thai passport.

About half of the Filipina women who migrate to work in Japan travel on a legal visa as artists or entertainers, but many work as sex workers. These Filipina migrants have some advantages over their Thai counterparts: better English skills and support from the large Filipino community in Japan. Most are Catholic and meet at church on Sundays. In contrast, a Thai community formed in Japan in the 1990s, but its members were primarily engaged in the trafficking of women or in businesses which prey on the women's income. They were not a supportive community.

The trafficking of Thai women to Japan for sex services is well organized under the control of Japanese and Thai agents linked to the criminal worlds of both countries. The agents in Thailand organize passports, visas, air tickets, and some training in Japanese language for the women. In the past, many women were brought into Japan using fake Malaysian passports as Malaysians could enter Japan without a visa. Between 1991 and 1994, 46,995 Thais were sent back to Thailand for illegally entering Japan. Of all the women returnees, more than 70 percent said they entered Japan using fake passports and most had worked as sex workers.

Presently it is more difficult to enter Japan using a Malaysian passport as Japanese immigration is stricter about policing. Women now travel with their agents as tourists to other countries and enter Japan from there. In 1997 a Japanese gang leader was arrested in Thailand for having smuggled over 40 women through the airport inside large suitcases.[11]

In the beginning most of the agents were Japanese and many of the bars where Thai women worked were controlled by Taiwanese mamasans. More recently, Thai women married to Japanese bar-owners, pimps, and Yakuza gangsters operate as mamasans and play a role in the trafficking of Thai women. There are other Thais who have invested in bars and Thai restaurants especially to serve Thai prostitutes on their off-days and evening outings.

During the expansion of Thai prostitution in Japan in the 1980s, around 90 percent of the women were forced or tricked into the trade. By 1995–96, based on information obtained from detainees or deportees from Japan, this percentage had fallen to approximately 20 percent. In other words, about 80 percent of the women going to Japan in the mid-1990s had the explicit intention of working in sex services. However, many did not know that once they arrived in Japan they would have to work under the control of an agent.[12]

A SYSTEM OF INDENTURED LABOR IN JAPAN

Virtually all Thai women entering Japan to work in sex services have to operate under the control of agents. Some may arrive on a tourist visa and then overstay and enter the trade, but they still have to operate under the control of a mamasan or bar owner. Agents will advance all travel, food, and lodging costs and make the woman pay the debt by working in Japan. In 1993–94 the debt from travel costs alone was around 3–4 million *yen* (700,000–800,000 *baht*).

The income earned from each male client ranges from 20–40,000 *yen* depending on the type of establishment, the location, and whether it is a short-term or full-night service. The rate of savings depends on the fees and tips received, and on the number of clients per day. The quickest record for paying this debt is three to four months; usually it takes nine to 12 months or more. If the bonded woman is unlucky she may be cheated and resold to another agent who starts the debt again. Generally however, Japanese agents honor their contracts. Once the debt is paid the woman may be able to operate as a freelance sex worker for a while. However this is risky and difficult. Often women who have worked off their debts get arrested and deported back to Thailand. Often the arrest happens around a year after their arrival in Japan. Such timing may not be accidental as establishments earn more from bonded prostitutes. There is, then, an incentive for agents and mamasans to inform the Japanese police about freelancers.

A Thai prostitute in Osaka in 1994–95 was estimated to generate an annual income of 1,560,000 *baht*. Of this 375,000 *baht* (24 percent of the total) went to the Thai agents who arranged the trip to Japan and the remainder (76 percent) to the mamasan. Of the mamasan's portion, 800,000 *baht* was repayment of the "debt" and the remainder was food and lodging charged at 80,000 *baht* a month.[13] Most Thai prostitutes in Osaka operate at the relatively low end of the market where the usual fee per session is 20,000 *yen*, or 5,000 *baht* at the going exchange rate (based on information from a former Thai consular official in Japan). To pay off the 800,000 *baht* debt plus the cost of housing and food within 12 months, a woman has to serve approximately 26 clients each month.

Once the debt is paid the woman will usually stay on with the mamasan. She will get half of the fees after deducting charges for food and lodging. If she averages one client every one or two days, her net income will be 22–45,000 *baht* per month. However, the supply of clients may be precarious. The mamasan earns more from a bonded woman and so will allocate clients to the non-bonded woman only after she has used up her bonded women.

A non-bonded sex worker can earn more by freelancing, but she needs accommodation. As a foreigner it is impossible for a Thai woman to rent an apartment on her own, so she must find a Japanese to help her. If she is able to average one client a day her earnings, net of her personal expenses, will be around 31,250 *baht* a month. Her potential income and saving will rise steeply if she can get more than one client a day and if she refrains from spending on bars and gambling.

TABLE 4

ESTIMATES OF MONTHLY INCOME AND SAVING POTENTIAL OF A FREELANCE THAI SEX WORKER IN OSAKA, 1994-95

	Baht/month
Gross income per month:	125,000
= 25 working days at 5,000 baht (one customer) a day	
Less expenses:	
Payment to Yakuza (25 days at 750)	18,750
Food and lodging	37,500
Recreation expenses (bars and night-clubs, gambling)	25,000
Clothing, tobacco, other personal expenses	12,500
Potential Savings	31,250

NGO worker Naiyana Suphapung interviewed approximately 100 Thai women in Japan who were facing deportation or repatriation. Each woman had at least 100,000 *baht* savings. This sample of women would represent the low end of earning and saving capacity. Most were brought to Japan as indentured labor. Most had stayed in Japan only one year or less and were caught just before or just after they paid their debt. Their savings came from client tips. In the interviews, they probably underestimated their savings. Thais who have frequented the districts where Thai prostitutes can be found think that a woman may be able to save more than a hundred thousand *baht* a year if she does not spend heavily on gambling and on Thai men.

From this rough estimation it appears that prostitution in Japan is quite lucrative. Even if a woman works only as indentured labor she can still save an amount which, when translated into *baht* from an appreciating yen, is a highly significant sum in the Thai context. For example, it can be compared to the gross yearly starting income of an overseas Ph.D graduate in economics at a leading Thai university of 132,000 *baht*.

The horrendous stories of exploitation and harsh treatment by pimps, mamasans, and agents is the other side of the coin. To prevent indentured women from running away, the mamasans and agents seize their passports, confine them to the establishment, and allow them out only when necessary. Beating and torture are common. In addition, the women are forced to provide sex for three or four male clients a day, even during menstruation. Women with previous experience in sex services elsewhere describe working conditions in Japan as highly oppressive.

Three Thai women who were lured into Japan as indentured labor and forced into prostitution banded together and murdered their (Thai) mamasan in order to recoup their passports so that they could escape. They were each sentenced to ten years in jail. Japanese NGOs helped them to appeal, and also to sue the bar owner to retrieve wages which had not been paid to them as agreed. The Japanese judge in the case awarded compensation, noting "These women suffered unspeakable psychological damage by being forced to provide sex".[14] Such murder cases are quite common. Between September 1991 and June 1992, Thai women were involved in nine cases of murder in Japan. Six of these involved the murder of a Thai mamasan. There have also been cases of suicide among Thai prostitutes and deaths due to AIDS and other health hazards.

The potential for saving makes many women overlook the negative side of the venture. Thus, despite all the stories about harsh treatment, exploitation, and risk, many women still flock to Japan. Some of those who go through the ordeal once wish to return as they believe that their experience will allow them to manage the situation better the second time around.

While women's earnings are substantial, especially viewed in the context of their earning power at home, revenues for agents and mamasans are much greater. This income plays a large role in perpetuating the trafficking. Gross income generated by Thai prostitutes for Japanese pimps and businessmen in 1995 was 3,105,000 *yen*, or 31,050 million U.S. dollars, or 776,250 million *baht* (at 1995 exchange rates). The sum is based on the estimate of 23,000 Thai sex workers working in Japan with an average fee-per-client of 30,000 *yen* (higher than the Osaka data cited above because prices in Tokyo are higher), and an average rate of 1.5 clients a day.

THAI PROSTITUTES IN GERMANY

Germany is the largest market for Thai prostitutes in Europe. According to unofficial figures from NGOs, 2,000 of the 6,000 prostitutes in Berlin are Thai. According to several NGOs there are around 10,000 Thais living in Berlin. Between 1991 and 1995, approximately 500 Thai women traveled to Germany to work as prostitutes.[15]

Most Thai prostitutes in Germany operate under a system of indentured labor similar to that in Japan. Prostitution is legal but foreigners cannot work without a permit. Agents must import Thai women on tourist visas or under the pretext of coming to be married. The illegality of their immigration status means that Thai women are subject to control by agents and pimps, who employ a system of imposed debt or indentured labor in order to control the women.

The rates charged by agents range upwards from 3,000 marks (42,000 *baht*). Women arrange their own air tickets and visa to Germany while the agency provides employment upon arrival. Alternatively, the agent organizes visa, air tickets, and job placement and charges between 10–40,000 marks, equivalent to 140,000–560,000 *baht* (information from Pataya Ruenkaew).

A freelance German prostitute in a large city earns a gross income of 2,000 marks per day. Her daily expenses are 150–200 marks and this leaves her with a net earnings of 1,750–1,800 marks or 24,500–25,200 *baht* per day. Working 25 days a month, net monthly earnings will be 612,500–630,000 *baht*. But a Thai prostitute under the control of a pimp is able to retain only 2.5 percent of the total client cost. She will average only 50 marks per client. If she has to service 3 to 4 clients a day, she will earn 150–200 marks or 2,100–2,800 *baht*.

THAI PROSTITUTES IN THE U.S.A.

There is no estimate of the number of Thai prostitutes in the U.S. However, reports of police raids on brothels suggest that the trafficking of Thai women into the U.S. for sex services is increasing. Agents and mamasans operate a system of indentured labor similar to the practice in Japan and Germany.

An underground brothel was raided by the New York police in 1994. A mamasan who turned state witness gave an account of the trade, claiming that she had bought 50 Thai women in 1994. Underground brothels using foreign women exist in big cities such as New York, Los Angeles, Seattle, and San Diego. They are often in Chinatown areas, run by gangs from the Asian underworld. Some brothels formerly received their regular supplies of women from Taiwan and Hong Kong. Around

1993 these supplies began to dwindle and agents started to trade in Thai women. The suppliers (who are Thai) sell women in their twenties at prices ranging from 6,000 to 15,000 U.S. dollars. The brothel owner/mamasan then expects to earn at least three times the purchase price from each girl. The girl will be told she is indebted for 18–45,000 dollars, depending on the cost to the mamasan. In most cases the "debt" is just a trick. According to the mamasan informer, the captors "have no intention of setting the women free until they are no longer usable".[16] This is different from the Japanese system as the U.S. case is really a slave trade.

At the rate of 130 U.S. dollars per client (100 dollars for sex service and 30 dollars for admission fee), an indentured woman will be made to serve 200 to 400 men in order to pay her debt. In addition, she will be charged 1,200 dollars a month for room and board, payable through sex with 12 more men.

The women work from 11 a.m. to 4 a.m. and have sex on average with two men a night. They receive nothing except tips and are confined to the establishment. After one woman jumped from a second-story window to escape a brothel in New York, the owner installed iron bars.

Based on these accounts, the gross annual income a Thai woman generates for her mamasan is as follows. She services two clients per day at an average fee per head of 3,250 *baht* for 25 days each month, earning a total annual income of *baht* 1,950,000. Of this, the agents in Thailand take 150,000 to 375,000 *baht* and the mamasan takes the remaining *baht* 1,575,000 to 1,800,000.

THAI UNSKILLED WORKERS IN TAIWAN

Taiwan, which began accepting legal migrants in 1992, is becoming Thailand"s largest market for unskilled labor (mostly male). The Ministry of Labor recorded an average of 72,842 Thais traveling to Taiwan in each year from 1993 to 1995, and the Ministry estimates that another 3,000 arrive illegally. However, based on the number of Thais who overstayed their visa between January and March 1995, about 100,000 Thais migrate to work in Taiwan annually, of which approximately 20 percent are women.

Taiwan is quickly becoming a large market for Thai prostitutes, spurred in great part by demand. As the Taiwanese economy prospers and education spreads among young men and women, fewer Taiwanese women are prepared to enter the prostitution trade. Yet the demand for young prostitutes remains high. Thus, agents seek out vulnerable recruits in nearby places like Thailand and the Philippines.

IMMIGRANT WORKERS INTO THAILAND

The economic boom in Thailand in the 1990s led to a rapid increase in demand for skilled and unskilled labor. Meanwhile Thailand's immediate neighbors were facing poor economic conditions and political problems. Burma's repressive military rule, an absence of democracy, and forced labor propelled migrants across the border into Thailand.[17] Illegal immigrants began trickling in to work in border towns. By 1995–96 they could be found throughout the country including Bangkok. By 1995 the Immigration Office estimated that just over half a million foreigners were working illegally in Thailand (Table 5).

TABLE 5

OFFICIAL ESTIMATES OF ILLEGAL WORKERS IN THAILAND
(AUGUST 1995)

Origin	Number
Burmese	334,123
Chinese	100,000
Laos, Cambodia	10,000
South Asians	81,357
Total	525,480

In early 1996 the Ministry of Labor assessed the number of illegal immigrant workers – 728,137 persons of whom two-thirds were Burmese – based on information obtained from local businessmen and labor officers. In May 1997 a research team at the Institute for Population and Social Research at Mahidol University concluded its study on transnational workers in Thailand. Based on a province by province survey, it estimated the figure at approximately one million (970,903).[18]

The inflow of Burmese contains a large but unknown number working in the sex services trade. According to an NGO, there are at least 20,000 Burmese women forced into sex services in Thai border towns and many others working elsewhere including Bangkok.[19] A government official working on immigrant labor estimates that 5 percent – or 35,000 – of Burmese immigrants are prostitutes.

Thailand itself has a large prostitution trade both for local clientele and tourists. Virtually all recruits were formerly local, but now young Thai women remain in school longer and fewer enter the sex trade. Those few who do, tend to start at an older age. To supply the continuing demand for very young women, agents increasingly seek *dek nok* (outside or foreign kids). In the early 1990s, recruiting agents shifted their attention to migrant women from Burma, Southern China, and Laos.[20]

Other migrants from Burma, Laos, and Cambodia work in manual jobs, including crewmen in fishing boats, tappers in rubber gardens, maids and servants in households, manual labor in construction, and workers in sweatshops and small factories. Among Chinese migrants there are skilled and professional workers in the formal sector and others who work in services. South Asian migrants often sell food and clothing and have links with other south Asians who previously settled in Thailand and are established as traders in food and textile products.

Unskilled immigrants work for wages lower than local Thais. Burmese migrants are prepared to receive rather low wages since the alternative in Burma may be unpaid forced labor. Minorities such as the Mon, Karen, and Shan people prefer to come to Thailand to escape forced labor and other repressive policies imposed on them by the Burmese government. Illegal immigrants cannot demand protection according to the labor laws. Burmese male migrants near the border areas may accept wages of 20–25 *baht* a day. In hinterland areas, wages rise to 40–70 *baht*, around half the wages for local Thais. Burmese crewmen in fishing boats earn around 700–750 *baht* a month while local Thais get 1,800–3,000 *baht*. Hence, employers of Burmese migrants save 50–70 percent of labor cost.

BURMESE PROSTITUTES IN THAILAND[21]

In 1993–94 the government under prime minister Chuan Leekpai tried to eradicate child prostitution. Raids on brothels where young Burmese women were being forced to offer sex services were initiated. Since then, establishments have become more discrete.

In Mae Sai, Chiang Rai, agents operate through local grocery stores.

Clients contact the store owners and choose women from picture books. Women are then brought to an appointed hotel. In Chiang Mai, the agents operate in restaurants which have upstairs rooms for sex service. In Ranong, agents rent houses to keep Burmese women and use motor-cyclists to deliver the women to clients. Restaurants may also act as fronts for sex services. Clients view the women while they wait on tables and then take them outside for service.

Before the government campaign against under-age prostitution, many recruits were extremely young. Now the age range in open establishments is 18–20 in Chiang Rai and 20–30 in the rented houses in Ranong. In restaurants however, some women are still as young as 15.

The fee per client varies. In Mae Sai it was 50–100 *baht* but in 1995 it rose to 2–300 *baht* short-time and 6–700 *baht* over-night. In Chiang Mai the over-night fee is 1,000 *baht* and above, while short-time is 300 to 400 *baht* for foreigners and 110–140 *baht* for local clients. In some places if the client keeps the girl too long for the short-time service (usually half an hour), the owner will fine the girl. In Ranong before 1993, there was only short-time service. Brothel-owners would not let clients take women out. The temporary fee was 80–100 *baht* per service. After a major police crackdown in 1993, brothels went underground and the short-time fee rose to 400 *baht*.

In Mae Sai brothel owners collect the fee from the client and give the girl a token. At the end of the month the owner will pay the girl her wage according to the number of tokens she has collected. The monthly earnings of a girl, net of the portion retained by the brothel owner, ranges between 3–4,000 *baht*. In Mae Sai a large number of clients are foreigners from Japan, Taiwan, and Hong Kong, while in Chiang Mai most clients are westerners. In Ranong clients are mostly migrant Burmese workers, especially fishermen.

As brothels become better concealed, women become more exploited. The protection fees paid to the police increase and women are made to work harder to defray the cost. Some local police officers are involved in the trafficking in Burmese women for prostitution. Interviews with rescued women reveal that some Thai policemen are prominent in the transport of women from the border into Thailand.

As they are illegal immigrants working in an illegal trade, Burmese prostitutes often work in underground brothels. They service low-paid males and have to provide many services a day. In such third and fourth rate places it is easy to contract sexually-transmitted diseases and AIDS.

Police raids on brothels with young (aged below eighteen) Burmese and hill women in the mid-1990s revealed a high incidence of HIV-positive (up to 40 percent). Many of the women had been abducted or forced into prostitution.

The women usually service two to six clients a day. But on festive seasons, such as Songkran, or when the fishing boats are in dock, a girl may have to service up to 20 clients a day, after which, many must see a doctor.

ESTIMATING THE EARNINGS FROM HUMAN TRAFFICKING

Data on fees earned by trafficking agents comes from interviews with Thais deported back to Thailand, case studies of known suicides, and interviews of women who seek assistance from an NGO in Japan. For the period 1991–94, the average sum paid by a male worker to be smuggled into Japan was around 150–200,000 *baht*. This sum must be paid before traveling. Workers usually borrow to make the payment.

Most women who go to work as prostitutes are subject to indentured labor. In the early 1990s the debt forced upon women was around 800,000 *baht* per head. The Thai agents spent up to 150,000 *baht* for the cost of travel, documents, providing some training to the women in Japanese language, and other expenses. They then sold the woman to a Japanese agent for 375,000 *baht*, realizing a profit of 225,000 *baht* per woman. The Japanese agent then imposed a debt of 800,000 *baht* on the woman, making a profit of 425,000 *baht*. In August 1995, a social worker from the NGO Friends of Women in Asia (FOWIA) found that the indenture amount had increased from 800,000 to between 1 and 1.2 million *baht*, partly as a result of the appreciation of the *yen*. The calculations here use the old fees as most Thai migrants who were in Japan in 1993-95 would have traveled before August 1995.

For workers going to Taiwan, the Thai government stipulated that agents can charge a fee of up to 56,000 *baht* to cover visa and other travel costs. However the Thai government cannot properly enforce this regulation. The Ministry of Foreign Affairs reports that Thai agents charge much higher fees of 70,000–100,000 *baht* even though workers have legal status.

There is no information available on the fees Thai women pay to go to Taiwan as sex workers. The Ministry of Foreign Affairs in Thailand reported that between June 1994 and June 1995 the problems of Thai women working as sex workers in Taiwan had become more serious. The organized syndicates which trade in Thai women include Taiwanese and Thai nationals. The trade involves some officers who came from Taipei to work in the Taiwanese economic and trade offices in Thailand. Some immigration officers both in Thailand and in Taiwan also facilitate the trade.

The trading of Thai women into Europe involves agents who are Thai, German, Belgian, and other European nationalities. Thai women who migrate temporarily to work as sex workers in Germany must work under a system of indentured labor as in Japan. They will be charged with a debt of 3,000–4,000 marks or more depending on whether the fee includes an air ticket and a marriage certificate with a German man. An NGO which assists Thai women migrants in Germany found that a fee of up to 10,000 marks or 140,000 *baht* is common. In total, the agent fees earned from trafficking people out to these three major markets amounted to some 4–6 billion *baht* a year (Table 6).

TABLE 6

ESTIMATED ANNUAL INCOME ACCRUING TO AGENTS FROM MIGRANT FEES IN MAJOR MARKETS FOR ILLEGAL THAI WORKERS, 1993–95

Country	Type of Worker	Persons/ year	Fee per person Baht	Total Fees m.Baht
Japan	Male	4–6,000	150–200,000	6–800
	Female sex worker	6–9,000	800,000	4,800–7,200
Taiwan	Male and Female	100,000	70–100,000	7–10,000
Germany	Female sex-worker	500	140,000	70
Total		110,500–115,500	12,400–17,070	4,168–5,988

Before June 1996 the Thai government allowed Thai employers legally to hire Burmese migrants if they registered the worker and paid a deposit, originally set at 50,000 *baht* but later reduced to 5,000. Only a few hundred Burmese workers registered under these rules as the procedure was complicated and cumbersome. The workers were reported to the police, detained, bailed out, and sent to court before they could officially be allowed to work temporarily in Thailand.

In June 1996 the Thai government relaxed the above rules. It permitted Burmese in 43 provinces who had entered Thailand before

June 1996 to work for two years in selected occupations, namely manual labor, agricultural wage work, crewing in sea fisheries and related works, wage labor in construction, mining, transport, and factories. Migrants must report to an immigration officer within a specified time in order to apply for a work permit and their employers must pay a fee of 1,000 *baht* per head plus a 5,000 *baht* deposit. Many employers prefer not to report but rather to pay an illegal fee to officials if necessary. When the deadline expired, 340,819 Burmese had reported themselves and 288,511 had registered for work permits.[22]

For most male migrants, employers preferred to pay a bribe to the police rather than undergo the cumbersome registration procedure. The usual fee was around 5,000 *baht*. Some police visit houses where Burmese are employed as maids and demand 600 *baht* a month as a protection fee. Burmese food vendors near border areas said they paid the local police 600 *baht* a month as a fee to work in Thailand. In their research on the process of importing young women from neighboring countries, Kritaya and Phornsuk interviewed a sample of 33 young female migrants, mostly from Burma. They found that 78 percent of the women who entered Thailand and worked as sex workers were helped by agents. The average fee charged was 4,022 *baht* per person, excluding the cost of traveling, which added an average 2,337 *baht* per person.[23] In addition, agents probably paid the police as well, but Kritaya and Phornsuk did not report this part of the fee. It is assumed that the payment per person to the police was the same as for migrant men, 5,000 *baht*. For simplicity the round figure of 10,000 *baht* is taken to cover the total of fees paid to agents and police.

The estimation of fees from Burmese in-migrants takes the conservative route of assuming an inflow of around 200,000 persons a year, with five percent coming as sex-workers. This gives an annual total of just over one billion *baht* (Table 7).

In sum, the total fees accruing to agents and police in Thailand from four major streams of outbound and inbound trafficking in people amounted to 5-7 billion *baht*, equivalent to 200–280 million U.S. dollars at the 1994-5 exchange rate.

THE SOCIAL COST OF TRANSNATIONAL MIGRATION

New systems of indentured labor generate large benefits for agents, procurers, customers, and for governments keen to earn foreign

TABLE 7

ESTIMATED FEES EARNED BY AGENTS FROM ILLEGAL BURMESE
MIGRANTS, 1993–95

Persons/ Year	Fee per person Baht		Total Fees Million Baht
Sex workers	10,000	10,000	100
Other workers	200,000	5,000	1,000
Total	210,000	–	1,100

exchange. Yet they also involve costs for victims, their families and other social support systems, and society.

Migrant workers rarely learn useful skills, and rarely earn enough to enable them and their families to improve their situation. Those who work in engineering or semi-skilled jobs in construction may return with some increase in ability. However most migrants go to work in manual jobs which offer little or no opportunity to acquire skills. A large proportion of the remittance is used for current consumption, housing, and debt service.[24] Most often, migration is just a short-term survival strategy with no sustainable and long-lasting beneficial impact on their families and community.

Young women who go to work as prostitutes learn the skill of luring others to follow them. Migration to work in sex services in Bangkok shows a similar pattern.[25] An elder sister goes first. Once she is too old to continue working in the trade, she entices her younger relatives or neighbors to follow suit in order to sustain the earnings. Similarly those who make money overseas often return to lure other young women to follow in their footsteps.

Transnational migration does not provide a long-lasting solution to village problems of relative poverty and lack of opportunities. Certainly some migrants succeed and return home with money. These migrants mostly work under proper contracts in countries whose governments willingly receive them. In countries where the workers are illegal, the situation is very different. In Japan, for example, unskilled male workers are all illegal and can face harsh penalties if caught. To enter Japan they must pay an exorbitant fee to agents. Few succeed in making a fortune. Japanese authorities estimate that for each year in the early 1990s more than 100 Thai workers died, mostly from suicide. Thai prostitutes in Japan, however, can earn a lot of money. But they also face the hazards of AIDS, abortion complications, and other health problems. Suicides also occur among this group. Yet the young men and women of poor villages all over Thailand continue to follow the same path and face similar tragedies.

Many villages that send out migrants develop new values which uphold migration as a new avenue for self-improvement. In one poor village in Chiang Rai, over 200 male migrants went to Japan to work as illegal workers. One paid 200,000 *baht* to an agent who smuggled him into Japan on a cargo ship. He then spent eight months unsuccessfully looking for a job during the recession and committed suicide as he could not face returning home a failure. Other migrants from this village returned with enough savings to improve their housing and buy a few consumer goods. But the productive capacity of the village remained poor. As a result, villagers continue to migrate to Japan.[26]

The Thai government may congratulate itself that by promoting transnational migration it helped to find employment for the population. But this strategy provides a rationale for not paying attention to rural development and human resource development at the village level.

The same questions can be asked about inward migration to Thailand. Many young women from Laos and Burma who come to Thailand to support their families, end up as indentured labor in brothels and become HIV-positive before they return.[20]

COMBATING INTERNATIONAL TRAFFICKING IN WOMEN

The trafficking in women for sex services has increased in this present age of globalization for three major reasons: the push factors in the sending countries, the demand in receiving countries, and the resulting profitability which creates incentives for agents.

A 1997 study by the Foundation for Women shows that the impetus for migration has been changing over time. In the 1960s straightforward poverty forced young Thai women to migrate to cities in search of cash work so that they could send remittances to their families. Ignorance and lack of information made them fall prey to agents and traffickers in the sex trade. In the 1970s, as rural households became used to the higher standard of living underwritten by the remittances sent by their daughters, parents began urging their female children to seek work in the urban sex industry.

In the 1980s and early 1990s Thailand experienced high economic growth but also increasing income inequality. This produced two effects in relation to trafficking in women. High economic growth raised the demand for sex services among those with higher income inside Thailand and abroad. Meanwhile poor rural households became more vulnerable. Agents and traffickers went into villages specifically to recruit young women for sex services in urban Thailand and abroad.

In the mid-1990s traffickers began to diversify their supply source by recruiting immigrant women from Burma, Laos, China, and other neighboring countries. The inflow of low-cost recruits prompted more Thai sex workers to go overseas in search of higher income. Thailand became a center for both importing and exporting young women.

Thai government policies support export of labor in general. This implicitly includes women for sex services. In the early 1980s recession, labor export was seen as a means to solve local unemployment problems and to attract foreign exchange. This policy did not change with the economic boom in the late 1980s and early 1990s. A politician suggested that a special fund should be designated for loans of up to 50,000 *baht* to pay for the cost of workers going overseas. At the onset of recession in 1997, businessmen and officials again looked to labor export to counter the strains of growing unemployment.

Thus, two major factors on the supply side have contributed to the rise in the global trafficking of Thai women: the domestic sex trade and sex tourism, and the national labor export policy.

On the demand side, the international labor markets for Thai women have also changed. In the 1960s and 1970s the primary demand was for domestic workers. This quickly changed to more profitable "brides" and sex services. Thai women were trafficked first to neighboring countries, such as Singapore and Malaysia, and then later to European countries, Japan, and Taiwan. In the 1990s agents operating in Thailand also export young women from hill areas and illegal immigrants from neighboring countries. Most of these young women do not possess proper legal identification and risk becoming stateless persons if caught.

Current policies of receiving countries also aggravate the vulnerable position of women who are trafficked for sex services. Women are seen as criminal offenders both for being illegal immigrants as well as being prostitutes. In fact, by being trafficked to work as sex workers, women find their human rights violated on multiple counts. They do not know their employment terms. Many are sold and resold as indentured labor with debts imposed on them. They have to work in slave-like conditions, are denied their freedom, and often robbed of their income. In many countries their children are denied the right to nationality. Most of the receiving countries enforce only their immigration laws to punish and deport women, rather than considering them victims of trafficking, a modern form of slavery. According to the Foundation for Women, "They have become targets of racial prejudice and punishment".[27]

POLICY ISSUES

Trafficking in transnational workers has become a lucrative business for two reasons: workers have poor information about the labor market in which they operate, and recipient countries deny migrants legal status and hence, create opportunities for exploitation. Economic growth in recipient countries creates a demand for in-migrant labor. As long as there is demand there will be agents willing to meet it. Yet recipient governments refuse to acknowledge this demand and are either unable or unwilling to block the in-migration. In effect, the recipient country benefits from the high rate of exploitation of the in-migrant workers.

Every country has the right to control in-migration. However, to render all migrant workers illegal, while the demand for them is high, is simply unrealistic. An alternative is for sending and receiving countries to agree on a standard set of wage and working conditions on a bilateral basis, to regularize the flow of migration through government-to-government agreements, and to suppress trafficking and its associated corruption flows.

Thailand is both a sending and receiving country. In the past Thailand benefited significantly from exporting workers because of local problems of unemployment and foreign exchange shortage. Yet these benefits did not come without a cost. The promotion of external migration drained young and capable people away from the local labor market. Following its transition to a more industrialized economy, Thailand needs to be more careful about conserving and developing its labor resources.

The influx of migrant labor from Thailand's neighboring countries, especially from Burma, is a complicated issue. To remain competitive in world markets, Thailand needs to restructure industries and move up the technological ladder. This requires more educated and skilled manpower. But the large supply of unskilled in-migrant workers suppresses local wage rates, induces entrepreneurs to remain in labor-intensive production processes, and blunts the urgency to invest in education and skill creation. The over-supply of unskilled workers is also a potential source of discontent among local workers.

The issue even goes beyond the labor market. Many Burmese migrant workers were pushed out of their country not only for economic but also for political reasons. In the long term, greater economic and political stability in Burma should reduce the flow of migration into Thailand. The Thai government should press for the restoration of democracy and the revival of the economy in Burma. But in the short-term, Thailand has little option but to manage the problems generated by the inflow.

The trafficking of women across borders for the sex trade raises its own set of issues. The Foundation for Women has found that local women are willing to take action to stem such trafficking. NGOs and community groups must educate more women about the dangers inherent in the trade in order to decrease the flow at its source.

The Thai government must launch a plan to suppress trafficking in women. Thailand must reverse its image as a center for export and import of women for sex services. At present, some corrupt government officials openly participate and benefit from the trafficking.

Trafficking in humans is by definition an international issue. Hence, international organizations should devote more resources to combating the business. There is no international campaign against human trafficking comparable to the campaign against drug trafficking, although social costs are comparable. Perhaps this is because the costs fall on some of the world's poorer countries, unlike drugs which are largely a rich country's problem.

Decriminalization of adult prostitution would reduce the vulnerability of migrant sex service workers to exploitation by agents. Adult prostitution should be regarded as an occupation which an adult can choose. Prostitutes should be protected by labor laws like any other kind of work. Migrant workers could request a permit to work as a prostitute.[28]

APPENDIX:
CASE STUDIES OF THAI PROSTITUTES IN JAPAN

The following are real life stories of Thai women who went or were trafficked into Japan to work as prostitutes.[29]

Lek who never returned. Lek came from a broken family in Phayao. Her mother had once been a prostitute in Bangkok. After completing six years of compulsory primary education, Lek continued to lower secondary but could not finish. She left school and stayed at home. In her village some young women studied, but many "went south" to work as prostitutes in Bangkok. Lek wanted to work as she was bored with staying around the house. Her mother did not know how to prevent her daughter from going. Then an agent came to look for young women to work in the city.

Lek asked for 20,000 *baht*. But her mother asked for only 8,000 *baht*, as she had the experience herself and did not want her daughter to be too much in debt. The agent took Lek to work in Songkhla in the south of Thailand. She endured it for 11 months and then fled back home. Her pimp followed her and claimed that she owed him 25,000 *baht*. The mother argued that Lek only took eight thousand, and after working for almost the whole year, the debt should be paid off. Lek could not stand the work because clients beat and tortured her. So she often ran away. When she returned the pimp would charge her more debt and cheat her on fees. She eventually ran back home. The pimp felt he had not received sufficient income from her and was determined to squeeze Lek for what he thought was his due.

The pimp threaten to kill Lek if she did not hand over "his money". Lek's parents were so scared that they decided to sell their paddy land to pay off the debt. They took Lek to stay with a relative who runs a brothel and told their daughter to earn her keep there. In October 1991, Lek decided to go to Japan to try her luck. An agent organized the travel arrangement for her. She had to work as an indentured laborer with a forced "debt" of 800,000 *baht*. She worked in Japan for about eight months. On July 1, 1992, she wrote her mother that she had worked off all the debt except for 30,000 *baht*. As she was about to be free and she had some savings from tips, she asked her mother to open a bank account where she could send her remittances. Four days later, the mother received a telegram that Lek had died of heart failure. The person who brought Lek's remains back to Phayao said she had died in an abortion attempt.

The person who told this story is a teacher in the Phayao village. Lek's mother had told her this story so that the teacher could relate the tale to other young women in the school.

Nu who came home in a wheel chair. Nu came from a poor farming village in Roi Et in the northeast. When she was 17, she went to work as a bar waitress in Bangkok. In 1989, when she was 30, she decided to go to Japan through a network for illegal foreign workers. On arrival she was made to work off a debt of 2.5 million *yen*. After clearing the debt, she went to live with a Japanese man, became pregnant, but lost the child. Six months later the man abandoned her. She was so desperate that she decided to throw herself from a second floor window. She fractured several ribs and her right leg, and suffered paralysis on the left side of her body. She tried to strangle herself with an electric cord but was restrained. A network of volunteers who take care of foreigners in Japan came to her rescue. Three hospitals in Japan were forced to pay for her medical bills totaling 4.6 million *yen*, as the central and local government refused to take the responsibility. Nu is one among many who were lucky to gain assistance from NGOs.

Noi and her Japanese husband. Noi came from the same village as Lek and went to Japan in the same way. But she was luckier. She spent three years in Japan and succeeded in earning lots of money. She sent the money back home for her parents to build a house and buy an additional piece of paddy land. Later Noi married a Japanese man and together they began working as agents to bring Thai women to Japan. Her husband would provide a recommendation letter for a fee of 100,000 *baht*. In 1993 when this story was told at a seminar, Noi was still selling the recommendation letter to young women from her own village. She has continued to travel back and forth between Thailand and Japan plying her lucrative trade.

Phonsi who may go again. Phonsi from Korat went to school until she completed ninth grade. Then she earned approximately 1,000 *baht* per month helping in her family's grocery store. She had a son in a non-registered marriage. When she was 21, she decided to try her luck in Japan. An agent organized everything for her. She arrived in Japan in the summer of 1992 and was told she had to work off a debt of 370,000 *yen* (about 700,000 *baht*). In addition, she had to pay her employer 80,000 *yen* a month for food and lodging. She claimed she serviced on average one client a day and her gross income was 200,000 *yen* per month. On this basis it would take her two years and two months to regain her freedom. Soon after she worked off her debt in 1995, she was caught by the police and detained at the immigration office in Osaka. To the question whether she would return to Japan again if she could, she replied "don't know".

NOTES

The author gratefully acknowledges the support which the Asia Foundation and the Thailand Research Fund gave to this research.

1. Estimates of the numbers and economic value of migrants in and out of Thailand are not easy. This research relies on existing information from government sources, available studies, and well-informed guess/estimates of field researchers. Thanks to: Associate Professor Somphop Manarangsan of Chulalongkorn University; Khun Pairat Lamyong of the Ministry of Interior; Khun Niyom Watthammawut of the Ministry of Foreign Affairs; Khun Niwat Suwanphatthana at Chiang Mai University; Khun Naiyana Suphapung of Friends of Women in Asia; Khun Siriporn Skrobanek of the Women's Foundation; and Shoko Sasaki of the Ministry of Justice in Japan. Criticisms and suggestions are welcome so that the study can be improved and be useful to policy makers and those who fight for the rights of migrant workers.
2. The number of deported Thai women and Thai overstayers in Japan are from the Japanese Ministry of Justice. The number of deportees has increased in the 1990s. The total of deportees from 1986 to 1990 is 4,186. The fees paid to agents were obtained from FOWIA, an NGO which interviews women returnees. A questionnaire survey of Thais being detained in the immigration office of Japan in Osaka in July-August 1995 yielded similar figures. At the time of this research, the exchange rate was roughly 25 *baht* per U.S. dollar.
3. Pasuk Phongpaichit, Sungsidh Piriyarangsan, and Nualnoi Treerat, *Guns, Girls, Gambling, Ganja: Thailand's Illegal Economy and Public Policy* (Chiang Mai: Silkworm Books, 1998).
4. Peter Stalker, *The World of Strangers: A Survey of International Labor Migration* (Geneva: International Labor Office, 1994).
5. Siriporn Skrobanek, Nattaya Boonpakdi, and Chutima Janthakeero, *The Traffic in Women: Human Realities of the International Sex Trade* (London and New York: Zed Books, 1997).
6. Voravidh Charoenlert, "Trend and Pattern of International Labor Migration: the Prospect for Thailand", Mimeo. Faculty of Economics, Chulalongkorn University (1992), p.20.
7. The national minimum wage in 1994 was 4,757 *yen* or around 1,189 *baht* a day. The national average wage for construction workers was 14,430 *yen* or around 3,607 *baht*. Illegal workers receive approximately minimum wage or maybe half of the national average for construction workers. Figures obtained from consultation with Dr. Piyasiri Wikramasekara of the ILO in Bangkok.
8. Pasuk Phongpaichit and Samart Chiasakul, "Services", in Peter Warr (ed.), *The Thai Economy in Transition* (Cambridge: Cambridge University Press, 1993).
9. Jagdish Bhagwati and Martin Partington, *Taxing the Brain-Drain: A Proposal* (Amsterdam: North Holland, 1976).
10. In 1994 migrant workers in Japan totaled around 560,000, including 300,000 illegal migrants

and 260,000 registered as "aliens". This latter group included those with student visas, but mostly working. The figures are based on records of the Ministry of Justice, Japan.

11. *Daily News,* July 12, 1997.

12. Siriporn Skrobanek, speaking at the focus group on "The Trafficking of Thai Women for Prostitution Abroad", at the Political Economy Centre, Chulalongkorn University, Feb. 9, 1996.

13. The information on client fees, food, lodging and clothing costs was obtained from questionnaires completed by Thai prostitutes who were detained at the immigration office in Osaka in July–Aug., 1995 and from interviews of those who sought help from an NGO in Osaka. I am grateful to Khun Naiyana Suphapung who shared with me the information she obtained from interviewing Thai prostitutes who came under her care.

14. *Bangkok Post,* June 3, 1995.

15. Estimates based on Ban Ying Co-ordination Centre, *The Traffic in Foreign Women in Berlin* (Berlin, 1994), p.19.

16. Carey Goldberg, "From Thai Grocery Store to New York Brothel", *Bangkok Post*, Sept. 12, 1995.

17. Phornsuk Koetsawang and Kritaya Atchawanitkul, "Kan Lamoet Sitthimanutsayachon Nai Prathet Bhama Jak Phu Liphai Su Rangngan Khamchat" (The Denial of Human Rights in Burma, from Refugees to Transnational Migrants). Paper presented at the Seminar on Policy Options for the Importation of Foreign Labor into Thailand: A Study of Interest Parties, Legal Issues and the State Management System, organized by Institute of Population and Social Research, Mahidol University, at Siam City Hotel, Bangkok (May 27–29, 1997).

18. These included 340,819 who, as of March 7, 1996, reported themselves with the Ministry of Labor, following the government's decision in mid-1995 to regularize the employment of illegal immigrants in 43 provinces in unskilled occupations. 288,511 were issued with permits. Those who failed to apply for the permits (around 50,000) may have already moved out of the locality after reporting themselves. See Kritaya Archawanitkul, Wanna Jarusomboon, and Anchalee Warangrat, "Khwam Sapson Lae Khwam Sapson Ruang Khon Khamchat Nai Prathet Thai" (The Complexity and Confusion over the Numbers of Transnational Workers in Thailand). Paper presented at the Seminar on Policy Options for the Importation of Foreign Labor into Thailand: p.68. By November 1996, 372,242 had reported for registration, of which 82 percent were Burmese, 4 percent Lao, and 8 percent Cambodian. See *Bangkok Post*, July 18, 1997, p.7.

19. Asia Watch and the Women's Rights Project, *op.cit.*, p.1.

20. Kritaya and Phornsuk, *op.cit.*; Vorasak Mahatthanobon, *Kan Kha Prawani Ying Jin Nai Thai* (The Trading of Chinese Women for Sex Services in Thailand) (Bangkok: Institute of Asian Studies, Chulalongkorn University, 1996).

21. Information in this section comes from a social worker at the Foundation for Women who works in border areas. See also Asia Watch and the Women's Rights Project, *A Modern Form of Slavery: Trafficking of Burmese Women and Girls into Brothels in Thailand* (New York, Washington, Los Angeles, London: Human Rights Watch, 1993).

22. Kritaya, Wanna, and Anchalee, *op.cit.*, p.68.

23. Kritaya and Phornsuk, *op.cit.*, p.41.

24. Charit Tingsabadh, "Maximizing Development Benefits from Labor Migration: Thailand" in Tashid Amjad (ed.), *To the Gulf and Back: Study on the Economic Impact of Asian Labor Migration* (New Delhi: ILO Asian Employment Program, 1987).

25. It has been found repeatedly that the pattern of aunts bringing in nieces, sisters bringing sisters, neighbors bringing in neighbors, has persisted. See Pasuk Phongpaichit, *From Peasant Girls to Bangkok Masseuses* (Geneva: International Labor Organization, 1982), and Siriporn, Nattaya and Chutima, *op.cit.*

26. *Bangkok Post*, Feb. 4, 1995.

27. Kopkun Rayanakhon, *Kan Suksa Kotmai Kiewkap Kan Kha Praweni Lae Kan Kha Ying* (A Study of Laws Concerning the Trade in Sex and Women) (Bangkok: Foundation for Women, 1995), p.7.

28. In some European countries which have legalized prostitution, there is a debate about giving work permits to migrant women who want to work as prostitutes. Some groups only support permits for short-term stays (e.g. three months). At present, three countries allow foreign women to apply for work permits as prostitutes: Curacao, Aruba, and Surinam.

29. Lek and Noi stories came from Niwat Suwanapatthana, *Raingan kan sammana rueng panha raeng ngan ying thai nai tang daen praden kan aw priep tang pet* (Report of a seminar on the problems of Thai women working abroad) (Chiang Rai: YMCA, 1993). Nu is from stories printed in *Asian Women's Association Newsletter*, Shibuya-ku Tokyo (Oct. 3, 1992). Phonsi is constructed from a questionnaire returned by a Thai prostitute who was detained in the Japanese immigration office in Osaka, July–Aug. 1995.

Organized Crime and Trafficking in Women from Eastern Europe in the Netherlands

GERBEN J.N. BRUINSMA
GUUS MEERSHOEK

INTRODUCTION

In 1996, in a brothel in the southern part of the country, Dutch police discovered 15 women from Poland, Ukraine, Estonia, and Latvia. Many were recruited, most of them under false pretenses. Their average age was 21; three of them were minors. The brothel was part of a series, owned by a couple. Eleven pimps or recruiters were also affiliated to the brothel. The prostitutes were not allowed to leave the building and were working 9 to 19 hours a day. After closing hour the fence around the building was hermetically closed. The women were sleeping in a dirty, damp cellar. There were also other women working independently as prostitutes in the brothel. They received the regular 50 percent of their earnings. The women from eastern Europe were promised only 25 percent of the earnings. In practice, they did not receive anything. The couple imposed all kinds of fines on them, for example for failing to smile to customers. The women also had to pay for all kinds of unwanted services like sleeping in the cellar. If a woman somehow succeeded in acquiring a surplus, she was sold by her pimp to another pimp in the same brothel and had to pay back to her new owner the money he had paid for her. Some of the women declared to the police that they had been treated badly by the pimps; one of them claimed that she had been raped.

As a business in which large amounts of money can be earned, prostitution is quite often exploited by pimps and sometimes by organized crime. In the Netherlands, both kinds of exploiters can be found. Until the 1970s prostitution was mainly a local affair, dominated by Dutch pimps and Dutch prostitutes. Since then, the number of prostitutes has increased rapidly.[1] Many of the newcomers were women from abroad (Philippines, Thailand, Colombia, Brazil, and several countries in Africa). In the 1990s the newcomers are women from central and eastern Europe. In many cases these women were brought to Holland and forced to work in prostitution in conditions similar to those in the aforementioned brothel.

This essay presents the results of an empirical study on trafficking in women from central and eastern Europe. The study was conducted by researchers at the University of Twente in close cooperation with a team of policemen and criminal analysts from a special inter-regional criminal investigation department focusing on organized crime from eastern Europe and Turkey. It is based on empirical data from police sources, information provided by local police units concerned with supervising prostitution, and interviews with persons involved in the prostitution business. Special attention is given to the *modus operandi* and to the nature of the criminal groups involved.

BACKGROUND

Nowadays prostitution in the Netherlands has a number of specific characteristics that mak it highly vulnerable to trafficking in women.[2] The business has a semi-legal status. Prostitution in itself is not an offense: neither women nor men can be prosecuted for it, and customers can not be prosecuted for soliciting. Running a brothel and giving opportunity to prostitution is still a crime. As in most western countries, however, criminal prosecution is not taking place. For more than ten years, the government has declared its intention to legalize prostitution and many government agencies, such as the tax inspectorate, treat brothels like ordinary businesses.

The labor market in prostitution is informal and unregulated.[3] There are no formal arrangements concerning education, grades, and recruitment (although advertisements in which women are requested for prostitution are openly published in the newspapers). Brothel owners, who are legally organized in the Netherlands, informally "invite" women and sometimes men to work for them. This labor market is functioning unnoticed and unhindered by society and official social control agencies. Only the local government of Amsterdam tries to regulate labor relations in prostitution by police measures, based on a complex legal construction.

In this profitable economic sector the economic relationships are non-transparent and unregulated.[4] Nobody knows exactly how much money is flowing into this economic sector. There are some estimates of the average earnings of prostitutes and brothel owners are assessed for tax based on notional sums.

The prostitution sector employs many illegal people. A significant number of illegal immigrants find their way to prostitution as a way to earn money for a living. A repeated count by the Amsterdam police in 1994 and 1995 indicated that about 75 percent of all prostitutes behind windows in the Red Light district, De Wallen, are foreigners and that 80 percent of all foreign prostitutes are in the country illegally.[5] Law enforcement agencies and local administrations in the Netherlands hardly control prostitution. The control is most intensive on the streets and other public places, and less intensive in private clubs and bars. The police are not allowed to control escort bureaus.

Criminals are involved in the business. For criminals, prostitution is a traditional field for the supply of illegal services. Sometimes organized crime groups are involved;[6] sometimes professionals or those working independently.[7] In addition, many criminals spend their money on prostitutes in brothels, bars and clubs. For them, these places are also a favorite meeting ground.[8]

In the Netherlands the estimated number of prostitutes is about 25,000.[9] Most prostitutes are women: thirty percent of them are employed in private clubs; fifteen percent are in escort bureaus; thirty percent are doing their work behind windows in the Red Light districts; ten percent are on the streets; and fifteen percent of them are active in peepshows, sex theaters, porno business, or prostitution at home. Most of the time (between seventy and eighty percent) the women are waiting for or actively looking for customers. This implies that prostitutes have "to make" a lot of hours each day.

Since the beginning of the 1990s, the number of prostitutes in the Netherlands from eastern and central Europe has increased very rapidly. They are coming from Russia, the Visegrad countries (Poland, Hungary, and the Czech republic), Ukraine, and the Baltic States. In just a few years the number of women coming from central and eastern Europe has increased to approximately 4,500, twenty percent of the estimated total of 25,000. The fall of the Iron Curtain offered the opportunity to travel to western countries. Many people, most of them women, from the former Soviet bloc travel legally or illegally to the

Netherlands. Often they intend to find work, although the legal opportunities are very limited. The immigrants face many difficulties in trying to enter Holland legally. This provides opportunities for criminal organizations in their home countries, which offer them the facility to travel, to cross the frontiers and to earn money in the Netherlands.

A second indicator for eastern European involvement in trafficking in women is the number of known suspects from these countries in police registers. In the mid-eighties, most suspects came from the Netherlands, the former Yugoslavia, and Turkey. Nowadays, the majority of police files about trafficking in women concern offenders from countries in eastern and central Europe. Important countries of origin are the Czech republic, Poland, and Russia.

Another indicator of this kind of trafficking in women is the increasing number of East European prostitutes that were reported as victims by the Dutch *Stichting tegen Vrouwenhandel* (STV: Foundation against Trafficking in Women), the most important of three government sponsored organizations that help victims of trafficking in women. The number of victims from central and eastern Europe increased from 10 in 1991 to 100 in 1994, and 117 in 1997. For several years, this category has made up two-thirds of the total number of victims who apply to the STV for support.

These three indicators make clear that a large number of women from central and eastern Europe have been the victim of trafficking during the last few years and that criminals are involved in this process.

RESEARCH QUESTIONS, METHODS, AND EMPIRICAL DATA

In a major study on organized crime in the Netherlands, Fijnaut, and his colleagues stated that although various policies to combat trafficking in women have been put into effect in the Netherlands since the early 1980s this "does not necessarily mean that we now have clear picture of the nature and the scale of this form of crime".[10] Although some empirical data on this subject does exist, more detailed and systematic criminological research is needed. The problem of trafficking in women as described above leads to two specific research questions:

- What kinds of criminal groups engage in trafficking in women from eastern and Central Europe into the Netherlands?

- What *modus operandi* is adopted by these criminal groups?

In order to answer these questions the research group collected data from various sources, mostly from the police. First, from the whole country, 23 police files of criminal cases on trafficking women from eastern and central Europe between 1994 and the middle of 1996 were extensively studied. This was done according to the framework for analysis of organized crime groups developed as part of the criminological research carried out for the Parliamentary Commission of Inquiry on Police Methods.[11] Second, information was collected from sources in the Ministry of Justice and the police organizations about all suspects trafficking women from eastern and central Europe during the specified period. Third, data on victims of trafficking in women were available on a limited scale from STV and the police forces. Additional qualitative material was gathered from 50 open interviews with victims, policemen, public prosecutors, pimps, social workers, and prostitutes. All this, sometimes confidential, information was combined with different types of demographic statistical data from official Dutch agencies.

We are aware of the possibilities and the limitations of police sources for scientific research, especially the selectivity, reliability, and validity of data concerning organized crime.[12] It also proved to be difficult to assess the validity of the data from the known victims. They can not be considered a random sample of all women. Those women had the courage to report the perpetrators to the police. Many of the women did not have this courage and did not go to the police or solicit help from the STV or government agencies. Within the limits of the data we are nevertheless able to describe the criminal groups and their *modus operandi*. But, it is only possible to describe the Dutch part of the story. We have only limited knowledge of the other side of the trafficking chain, that is those parts of the organized crime groups that are active in eastern Europe.

THE *MODUS OPERANDI*

Trafficking in women from one country to another involves a number of activities that can be roughly classified in three phases:

- the recruitment of the women in the home countries;
- the trafficking of the women from the home country to the new country;

- the employment and forms of social control in the prostitution sector.

The Recruitment in the Home Countries

Police sources and data from STV indicate clear shifts over time in the countries of origin of the victims. In 1992 and 1993, victims mainly came from Poland and Ukraine. In 1994 and 1995, they were joined by victims from the Czech Republic, Slovakia and the Newly Independent Countries. In 1995 the number of Polish victims decreased. In the next years there were also less known victims from the other Visegrad Countries. There continue to be many victims from Russia and Ukraine. These shifts seem to be related to the economic transformation which started in Poland and still has hardly begun in Ukraine. To be more precise, the changes seem to be related to the level of inflation that in most transitional countries was very high in the first two years after the start of the reforms and that continues to be high in (not reforming) Ukraine. This hypothesis is supported by declarations of the victims who indicate that they left home for economic reasons, to earn money for their family. However, more recently the number of victims from central Europe has risen slowly again. In 1997, 14 percent of the victims in the Netherlands were from the Newly Independent Countries, 7 percent from Ukraine, and 7 percent from the Baltic States – and 22 percent of the victims were from the Visegrad countries. Among the remaining 50 percent there were many women from Bulgaria, Romania, and the former Yugoslavia.

Illustration

In 1996, the police found a woman and her daughter in a brothel near Amsterdam. The daughter used to live with her mother in the countryside of Ukraine. She did not earn much; her mother had a small pension. When inflation reduced this pension to almost nothing, the women started an extra business to wash clothes during the night. At that time a friend of her daughter put her in contact with a businessman. He was quite helpful and told the women that he could help them to work legally in prostitution in Western Europe. He promised them that together they could earn 5,000 U.S. dollars in three months. For those women that amount of money was a fortune. The businessman was able to arrange the legal affairs and promised to bring them back to Ukraine after three months and to pay them the money. The women did not fully trust the man but in the end they accepted the offer for financial reasons. The man took their passports, arranged the visa, and brought them with a colleague by car to the Netherlands. He set them to work in a brothel. They had to work there for many hours a day and for a far longer period than three months. The women did not receive any money.

The victims are generally quite young. Even minors are recruited as prostitutes by the offenders. The average age is 20 years while the average age of Amsterdam prostitutes for instance is 27. In general, victims from central Europe are younger than those from eastern Europe. Their stories resemble one another. Often they live in families that are struck by unemployment or high inflation. They have little experience in earning money when they meet a man who offers them a job in a restaurant or cafe in Western Europe. Alternatively, they read an advertisement in a newspaper with the same invitation. Quite often, the women realize that it is a fake-story and that they will have to work as prostitutes. In about 50 percent of the cases, the women were already active as prostitutes. Almost always, however, they have a far too positive view of prostitution in Western Europe, identifying it with drinking expensive drinks with young, well-dressed businessmen in high-ranking hotels. They know nothing about Dutch society; they do not speak any foreign language (except a few English words); and they have no relatives or friends living in the Netherlands. After the contact has been established the recruiter asks for their passport, offering to arrange the visa for them.

In East European countries, recruiting is almost always done by natives, who are somehow affiliated to the criminal group or organization in the Netherlands. It is rarely done by Dutch, Turkish, or former Yugoslav criminals, (even though the groups from the Balkans have some linguistic affinity with parts of eastern Europe). There were a few cases in which the criminal groups bought women in the Czech Republic. In a majority of the cases that were investigated by the police, the recruiters possessed or were able to utilize travel agencies to obtain visas for their victims. At many embassies in eastern European countries, it is not necessary to apply for a visa in person.

Trafficking

The Netherlands is part of the Schengen group (Germany, France, Belgium, Luxembourg, and Italy) that has abolished border-controls between the member countries. Inhabitants of the central European countries, that are affiliated to the European Union, do not need a visa to enter the countries of the Union. The embassies of these countries give tourist visas that are valid for three months in the whole Schengen territory. Many victims enter the Netherlands on this kind of visa. But, in half of the cases, their passports are replaced by forgeries "for reasons of facilitating the entrance and working in the country of destination". In reality, this practice makes the women more dependent on the offenders.

In general, the women are brought to the Netherlands by car. It takes more than a day to travel. Usually the trip is used to assert control over the women who originally went with the men voluntarily. The women are maneuvered quickly and powerfully; they are placed in a dependent and vulnerable position by taking away their passports, preventing them from contacting their family or friends, and bringing them to places which are unknown to them. Sometimes the perpetrators threaten to inform relatives about the real reason for their departures. The kindness at the beginning of the trip is replaced by threats and violence. In addition, the women are informed about "the hostile surrounding in the strange societies where policemen and governmental employees are corrupt and keeping an eye on them". The result of this process is to create an atmosphere of menace and uncertainty for the women which facilitates their exploitation.

Working in the Prostitution Sector

Although the women of East Europe are not legally permitted to work in prostitution during their stay, in many parts of the country their presence is tolerated by the police. Prostitutes work in clubs all over the country. In eleven cities they work behind windows in so-called Red Light districts. Between January 1994 and July 1996, 326 victims from central and eastern Europe were identified in police investigations: 147 of them were working in clubs, 165 behind windows. There are some quite convincing explanations why trafficking in women appears most frequently in clubs or behind windows. Both situations offer criminal groups good opportunities to control and supervise the women. Apart from that, in prostitution behind windows, the sexual techniques used to serve the clients are less complicated and there is no great demand for conversational skills. In clubs, there is far less police supervision than on the streets. Victims working in escort bureaus might be under-represented in the police files, because local police do not have legal permission to supervise such businesses. Much seems to depend on the local police behavior. When the police start to supervise a Red Light district, criminal groups transfer their victims from behind windows to escort bureaus or to places on the street.[13]

Inhabitants from the countries that are affiliated to the European Union are allowed to start their own business in the Netherlands. Amsterdam brothel owners have utilized this rule to arrange for prostitutes from these countries who are legally required to have their own "papers". In exchange for 150 U.S. dollars women receive from the brothel owners a collection of documents that make any police action impossible. Criminal groups use legal opportunities. Women from the former Soviet Union, for example, are given false Polish identity cards and then obtain the documents from the brothel-owners under a false name. Most criminal groups are able to put their victims to work in more than one city.

A Dutch prostitute who works in a club or behind windows, earns on average approximately 300 U.S. dollars a day. In a club she is allowed to keep 150 U.S. dollars herself; behind windows she can keep 200 U.S. dollars. Being young and new in town, a victim of trafficking is generally able to earn more than would an established and known prostitute, sometimes as much as 500 U.S. dollars per day. Often, her pimp only allows her to keep some 25 U.S. dollars every day. Because the victims are working long hours and many days a week, trafficking in women is a profitable business. The Groningen police was able to prove that a criminal organization engaged in trafficking in women from Ukraine had monthly earnings of some 12,000 U.S. dollars for each victim.

Police investigations revealed that in big cities in the Netherlands and other European countries clandestine markets exist in which East European women are bought and sold by traffickers. The possibility of staying legally for a period of three months on a tourist visa has the effect that many women are sold every three months. In a steady, ongoing carousel, the women are bought and sold by brothel owners and traffickers from different regions across the borders of Germany, Belgium and the Netherlands.[14] Between January 1994 and July 1996, the Dutch police discovered 54 cases in which this had happened. In 29 cases, the average price was 2,500 U.S. dollars but prices varied between 300 and 10,000 U.S. dollars, depending on the age of the victim, her appearance, the distance of her place of origin and the time she had already been involved in prostitution. However, the interviews make clear that only a few women from eastern and central Europe succeeded in sending money back home.

THE CRIMINAL GROUPS

Who are victimizing these women? Where are the perpetrators coming from? The preceding analysis confirmed that a number of offenders are always involved and that they organize their activities from a long distance. But, are they all members of organized crime groups? If we use the definition of organized crime provided by Fijnaut and his colleages (i.e. "when groups primarily focused on illegal profits systematically commit crimes that adversely affect society and are capable of effectively shielding their activities, in particular by being willing to use physical violence or eliminate individuals by way of corruption")[15] then it is clear that not all offenders are members of such criminal groups. Our analyses of the police files, police records, and other data reveal a more differentiated picture varying from loosely organized professionals to organized crime groups linking recruiters from the homeland, the traffickers, and the recipients in the Netherlands.

TABLE 1

ABSOLUTE NUMBER OF POLICE SUSPECTS FOR WOMEN TRAFFICKING BY LAND OF ORIGIN

Country	1995	1996	1997	Total
Poland	2	4	1	7
Czech and Slovakia	8	3	3	14
Hungary	-	5	1	6
Russia	3	5	4	12
Ukraine	2	–	2	4
Baltic	–	3	–	3
Former Yugoslavia	4	7	6	17
Holland	8	28	12	48
Others	4	26	20	50
Total	31	81	49	161

Source: Dutch Police Files

Table 1 shows that most offenders arrested by the police for trafficking in women during the three years from 1995 to 1997 are Dutch. All of them are recipients, owning or exploiting brothels, clubs, and other places of prostitution. More than a third (63) of all arrested offenders have their origin in eastern and central Europe. The "others" category in Table 1 consists of offenders coming from different countries, a great number of them from Germany, Belgium, Morocco, and Turkey. This emphasis on Dutch, German, Moroccan, and Turkish offenders is the result of the police activities that are predominantly focused on the recipient side of the trade in women. Attention must also be paid to the growing number of offenders from the former Yugoslavia. According to the latest study on organized crime in the Netherlands, the number of criminals and criminal groups from the former Yugoslavia that are involved in prostitution is increasing.[16] In our data this growth had just began to emerge.

Of all arrested offenders 90 percent are male, and their average age is 34. They all have a criminal career in Holland as well as in their home countries, especially in violent crimes such as assault and robberies. Trafficking in women is not the sole criminal activity of the offenders. A majority of them is also involved in smuggling arms, drugs, or stolen cars. In some cases, the traffickers in women use the return trip for smuggling drugs in stolen cars to their home countries.

In the police files, 23 criminal groups are identified. These can be divided into two categories:

Cliques of professionals.[17] Eleven small loosely organized cliques are active each consisting of two or three professionals in the field. These professional criminals work together regularly without one man being the leader and without any clear division of labor or responsibilities. Most of them are traditional pimps having or aiming at personal relationships with the women. They are incidentally involved in trafficking women from eastern and central Europe, and the number of women is relatively small. Whenever necessary, they contact their criminal acquaintances in international networks ranging from the Netherlands, Germany, or Belgium to eastern and central Europe with requests to deliver new prostitutes.

Organized crime groups. Twelve criminal groups were identified by the Dutch police in the research period. These groups have a greater number of individuals (an average of 11 people) with a clear division of labor among the members. The groups employ more violence than the professional cliques and traffic more women from eastern and central Europe.

These 12 criminal groups can also be further divided again: *Four* of the groups have their center in their home countries where they own brothels, discotheques and bars. These criminal groups make use of travel agencies or mediation agencies (sometimes in their hands) to traffic the women and take care of the false passports, visas, or other necessary documents. They also corrupt civil servants in order to obtain such documents. Although these kinds of criminal groups handle a far greater number of women during a year, they have no regular customers in the Netherlands. They offer the women to anyone who is interested. Part of their criminal activities consists of smuggling drugs and stolen cars from the west to the east. There is not enough valid data to determine whether and to what extent these four criminal groups are part of or linked with other organized crime groups in their homelands.

The other *eight* criminal groups have the same origin and operate in a similar way as the aforementioned groups. However, their center is in the Netherlands. These organized crime groups possess brothels, clubs, and windows in different cities. The owner of the club is usually an active member of the group. In these criminal groups, Dutch offenders organize their criminal activities in close collaboration with criminals from eastern and Central Europe, Turkey, and Morocco with the Dutch sometimes – but not always – playing the leading part. The Dutch do not always dominate, because they are dependent on the "delivery" of the women for their clubs and they fear the violence of their Eastern companions. In a few cases the Russian partners extort the recipients of the women by using violence. Their extortion involves collecting money from them but also a forced delivery of women.

CONCLUSIONS

During the last few decades, the prostitution sector in the Netherlands has expanded rapidly and has become more international. There recently has been an increase in the number of prostitutes from eastern and central Europe who are active in Holland in brothels, clubs, and behind windows in Red Light districts in the cities. Although the majority of the women travel to the Netherlands voluntarily, they are victimized by cliques of loosely organized professionals as well as by organized crime groups from different nationalities. All arrested offenders are career criminals. Most of the criminal groups are also involved in smuggling drugs, arms, and stolen cars. In the field of trafficking women, there is close collaboration between eastern and central European criminals and their Dutch, Turkish, and former Yugoslav counterparts. Initial recruitment in the homelands is done by the local offenders.

Because prostitution is seen as a more or less legal economic activity the police, until recently, neglected the social problem of victimization of prostitutes.[18] Moreover, criminals active in trafficking and exploiting women from eastern and central Europe do not fear detection and prosecution – and will not be deterred by relatively low sentences. When confronted with the police, they seem more concerned about their merchandise than about themselves.[19] However, our study based on police and other empirical data shows the serious circumstances in which the women often end up after leaving their homeland.

NOTES

This essay is a revised and enlarged version of a paper presented at the 50th Meeting of the American Society of Criminology in Washington D.C. November 1998.

1. A.B. Meulenbelt, *De Verdiensten van Prostitutie* (Amsterdam: Amsterdam University Press, 1993) and L. van Mens, *Prostitutie in Bedrijf: Organisatie, Management en Arbeidsverhoudingen in Seksclubs en Privéhuizen* (Prostitution in Action: Organization, Management, and Labor Relations at Sex Clubs, and Brothels) (Delft: Eburon, 1992).
2. M. de Boer, "Vrouwenhandel: Beleid in Beeld. Eindrapport" (Trafficking in Women: a Focus on Policy. Final Report) (Utrecht: Willem Pompe Institute for Criminal Sciences, 1994).
3. Van Mens, *op.cit.*
4. *Ibid.*
5. IPIT/IRT-NON, "Mensenhandel Vanuit Centraal – en Oost-Europa" (Trading people from central – and eastern Europe), *Enschede*, IPIT/IRT-NON, 1997.
6. H. Abadinsky, *Organized Crime* (Chicago: Nelson Hall, 1990).
7. C. Fijnaut, *Prostitutie, Vrouwenhandel and (vermeende) Politiecorruptie in Antwerpen* (Prostitution, trafficking in women (supposed) police corruption in the city of Antwerp) (Leuven: Acco, 1994) and G.W. Potter, *Criminal Organizations: Vice, Racketeering, and Politics in an American City* (Prospects Heights: Waveland, 1994).
8. C. Fijnaut, F. Bovenkerk, G.J.N. Bruinsma en H.G. van de Bunt, *Organized crime in the Netherlands* (The Hague: Kluwer Law International, 1998). Hereafter cited as Fijnaut *et al.*
9. Meulenbelt, *op.cit.*
10. Fijnaut *et al.*, p.102.
11. *Ibid.*
12. *Ibid.*, pp.35–58 and G.T. Marx, "Notes on the Discovery, Collection, and Assessment of Hidden and Dirty Data", in: J.W. Schneider and J.I. Kitsuse (eds.), *Studies in the Sociology of Social Problems* (Norwood: Ablex, 1984) pp.78–113.
13. (IPIT/IRT-NON, 1997, *op.cit.*

14. H.G. van de Bunt and E.R. Kleemans, *Criminaliteitsbeeld Georganiseerde Misdaad* (Den Haag: Ministry of Justice, forthcoming).
15. Fijnaut, *et.al.*, pp.226–27).
16. Van de Bunt and Kleemans, *op.cit.*
17. H. Abadinsky, *The Criminal Elite: Professional and Organized Crime* (Westport: Greenwood Press, 1983).
18. De Boer, *op cit.*
19. Van de Bunt and Kleemans, *op.cit.*

Prostitution and the Mafia:
The Involvement of Organized Crime
in the Global Sex Trade

SARAH SHANNON

Common interpretations of the nature of organized criminal activity invariably include money laundering, drugs and arms smuggling, and racketeering schemes. Indeed, criminal gangs are heavily involved in each of these pursuits. Crime syndicates, however, are also involved in forced prostitution, a form of illicit activity that is not only increasingly prevalent but also has a significant transnational dimension. Commercial sexual exploitation of women and children is a global phenomenon of tremendous proportion from which organized crime realizes huge profits. Yet the role of transnational organized crime in the global sex trade has rarely been seriously explored. This analysis is a preliminary attempt to address this situation. It begins with an overview of the global sex trade, highlights its distinctive features, and explores its regional manifestations. It then examines the involvement of international criminal syndicates and assesses their importance in the industry.

THE GLOBAL SEX INDUSTRY

The global sex trade involves the trafficking of persons for the purposes of commercial sexual exploitation. It may be described simply as the transfer or sale of human beings for sexual purposes. According to the World Congress Against the Sexual Exploitation of Children, three main forms of sexual exploitation exist:[1]

1. Prostitution: to engage or offer the services of a person to perform sex acts for money or other recompense.

2. Trafficking and sale of persons for sexual purposes: to transfer persons from one party to another for commercial sexual purposes in exchange for money or other recompense.

3. Pornography: to create, distribute, use or otherwise participate in material which portrays persons in a sexual context. Such depiction may include explicit sexual actions or the exhibition of genitals in an attempt to provide sexual gratification to the user.

In many cases, these three forms of sexual exploitation are interconnected. For example, trafficking in women is normally associated with subsequent involvement in imposed prostitution, while children exploited by pornography are often forced into prostitution. The most unique aspect of this form of transnational criminal activity is its vast contribution to human suffering. Although other forms of illicit criminal ventures are certainly unfortunate activities, which may well undermine political and economic systems, the global sex trade has been described as, "the most denigrating, dehumanizing of all crimes that can possibly be imagined".[2] In denying its victims the freedom and dignity normally associated with even the most primitive existence, the sex industry becomes fundamentally different from all other international criminal businesses. Only in this realm are women and children viewed exclusively as commodities of economic value rather than human beings.

Scale

The size of this industry is difficult to assess. It is clear, however, that the global sex trade is a multi-billion dollar venture, which infects every geographical area of the world, including the richest first world nations.[3] Estimates suggest that each year more than one million children and teenagers are forced into commercial sexual exploitation.[4] The figures for women are comparable. If wholly reliable estimates are elusive, it is still possible to make broad assessments, which facilitate a general interpretation of the issue.

Children

Estimates suggest that 1,380,000 children are involved in the commercial sexual industry in Southeast Asia and the Pacific Islands[5] and more than 702,000 are involved in Latin America.[6] In the United States, between 100,000 and 300,000 youngsters are presently working as prostitutes.[7] Global profits from trafficking in children for sexual exploitation reach approximately five billion dollars per year.[8]

Women

Over 525,000 women are victims of forced prostitution in Southeast Asia.[9] The European Union's illicit sex market supports between 200,000 and 500,000 female prostitutes.[10] In Italy, 19,000–25,000 women working in the sex industry are foreign prostitutes;[11] in Belgium, at least 2,000 females have come from abroad.[12] Additionally, 75 percent of the prostitutes working in Germany are foreign.[13] It is important to understand that women who are not indigenous to a country yet work in that nation's sex business are often victims of trafficking schemes.

The profit from female sexual exploitation is higher than the five billion dollar estimate associated with the child sex business. While global assessments are inherently uncertain, regional assessments reveal the scale of the phenomenon. For example, in Russia alone trafficking in women has been estimated to yield seven billion dollars annually.[14] In addition, Dr. Sangsit Phiriyarangsan, director of Thailand's Chulalongkon University Political Economy Center, calculated that country's sex trade to be worth 20 billion dollars a year.[15] He emphasizes the seriousness of the problem by noting that illicit businesses are "bigger than the national budget".[16]

TECHNIQUES

Essential to an understanding of the global sex industry is the comprehension of its most basic facts. How does it happen? How are victims procured, transferred, and then used? The three primary modes of operation are kidnapping, sale by family, and the false promise of work.

Kidnapping

Victims of kidnapping come from every geographic region, social class, and age group. Organized criminal gangs may take girls off the streets of Paris, London, or Frankfurt and sell them to intermediaries in Africa or Arab world.[17] Similarly, such syndicates realize large profits from kidnapping teenagers and young women from countries like Burma, Laos, Vietnam, and China and then forcing them into the sex industry in Thailand.[18] Kidnapped women face even more significant barriers to escape than victims procured by other means simply because no one knows what has happened to them. Furthermore, women who are kidnapped are purposely transported to a foreign country to live out their sexual servitude. Factors such as language barriers, solitude, and the insensitivity of nationals to a non-native's plight all contribute to an increasingly hopeless situation for these women.[19]

Sale by Family

Although a depressing acknowledgment of the disintegration of familial authority and a disturbing comment on the nature of society, the reality is that many victims are sold into prostitution by their families.[20] Most often the guilty party is a father or uncle, who decides that his daughter or niece could provide much needed cash. The girl may be sold to a criminal group or pimp and never acknowledged or thought about again.[21] Conversely, she may continue to live with the family while she is pressed into sexual service. This seems to happen more often with younger girls, who are frequently sold for sex only as long as they are still too young to become pregnant.[22]

False Promise of Work

Job scams abound and are especially tempting to women who feel they have no real economic opportunities in their own environment.[23] Young women are promised work as dancers, waitresses, maids, models, or entertainers in another city or country.[24] Naive and desperate, the women readily believe the sales pitch often made by a member of a crime group. They are subsequently given forged passports or other needed documents, transportation, and contacts upon arrival. Sometimes fake contracts are presented to increase the illusion of legitimacy.[25] Upon arrival in the new city, women quickly realize their fate. Greeted by unsympathetic con-men who are frequently members of cooperating crime gangs, they are sometimes informed that their contract was bought and that they are now owned by another, who expects a different service.[26] In some instances, they are told that they must repay their transportation expense immediately and are offered only one way of earning the money. In other cases, there is no explanation whatsoever; the women are simply stripped of documents, money, and belongings.[27] Through a combination of such tactics, the women are quickly forced into prostitution. Those who resist are beaten, starved, raped, and tortured until they are broken and submit without further opposition.[28]

Each of these tactics leads to similar involvement in the international sex market. However snared, every female shares the common problem of how to extricate herself from this fate. Yet, escape is difficult if not impossible. Victims of forced prostitution are rarely allowed to keep the money they earn. If they do receive a portion of their pay, they are frequently prisoners of debt bondage, wherein they owe their captors more money than they can possibly accumulate.[29] Besides the financial impossibility of escape, there are more immediate, concrete constraints. For example, women are frequently locked in the brothel or even chained to a bed.[30] Children may be similarly confined. Child victims in Bombay, for example, are sometimes kept in cages.[31] Furthermore, the ramifications of repeated physical abuse and continual exposure to numerous sexually transmitted diseases can be deadly. These factors, compounded by inadequate food and medical care, often cause serious illnesses, from which many victims do not recover. Those healthy enough to attempt escape have no money for rail or bus fare. Some who do attempt to flee are simply killed by the criminals who control them. For all of these reasons, escape is a difficult and rare accomplishment.

CONTRIBUTING FACTORS

Several other factors contribute to the success of the commercial sex industry.

First, this market is demand driven. As long as there are men who prefer to buy sex rather than engage in reciprocal intimacy, pedophiles who seek to satisfy their perverted tendencies, and unscrupulous individuals ready to operate as intermediaries there will be numerous unwilling victims. Unfortunately, much of the supply must be involuntary because the demand for women and children for the use of sexual purposes is so great.

Second, poverty is a great supporter of sexual exploitation. Desperate circumstances breed desperate measures. In many poor regions of the world, the sale of a woman or child provides food and clothing to individuals who might otherwise not have a meal or a shirt. The vast socioeconomic inequities that encourage the involuntary supply of this market greatly benefit the agents, middlemen, and organized criminals who derive most of the profits from this business.

Finally, cultural attitudes also play an important part in the prosperity of the sex business. In many societies, women and children are still viewed as second class citizens or even inferior beings who do not deserve the same rights and liberties as others. Discriminatory attitudes and patriarchal perspectives extend to the belief that one of the main purposes of a female is to please the male, especially sexually. Sexism and gender roles are taught from childhood and in some countries are intensified by traditional religious doctrine.[32] For example, in historically Roman Catholic countries where the influence of the church pervades most aspects of everyday life, women suffer under traditional canons and codes of conduct. A case in point is Bolivia, which maintains strict laws against pre- or extramarital sex that apply even to widows and divorcees. A woman believed to have been less than chaste, even if unwillingly, acquires a permanently tarnished reputation and may then be acceptably abused by other male members of society. These women additionally suffer because the concept of rape does not apply to "tainted" women and there are no laws to protect them from further sexual exploitation.[33]

Another example of distorted religious beliefs is the Hindu Devadasi tradition in India. This doctrine requires that young girls be given to a temple for their training as deified sexual slaves. As one report noted, Devadasi followers, "have been dedicating their daughters to a religiously sanctioned life of prostitution for well over a millennium".[34] It is extremely difficult to combat the problems of child prostitution and sexual abuse in nations where "sexual involvement with children is still given a religious respectability".[35] Ancient religious beliefs are a facet of more general cultural attitudes that fortify the existence of widespread sexual exploitation.

Players

The circumstances of commercial sexual exploitation differ greatly and fluctuate constantly. They can range from one teenage girl grabbed from a bus stop to a group of women promised similar jobs in the same city and transported there under false pretenses. Those responsible for the exploitation may be professional criminals or first time pedophile offenders. The range of possible engagements in sexual commerce is expansive. So too is the range of those who facilitate and control the business. However a number of distinct players contribute to the viability of the sex market enterprise. For example, the business would not run efficiently without the involvement of numerous intermediaries and aides such as pimps and brothel owners. Similarly, family members who sell relatives into the world of forced sex endow the industry with many new and unsuspecting recruits every month.

Any business would collapse without customers; the sex industry in particular is driven by the demands of its consumers. These include numerous businessmen who spend their vacation time participating in what are most commonly deemed "sex tours". A report prepared by the United Nations Commission on Human Rights describes this sub-industry as, "Tourism organized to facilitate, directly or indirectly, a commercial sexual relationship".[36] For example, vacation tours are sold with the understanding that the provision of children for sex is included in the package. Thailand, Brazil, the Dominican Republic, Sri Lanka, and India are known destinations for such tours and offer resorts and beaches that cater specifically to the sex tourist.[37] Other common target countries are Cambodia, China, Laos, Burma, and Vietnam.[38] Current customers include men from many areas, especially Europe, Japan, Australia, North America, and the Middle East.[39]

Additionally, governments and police forces play an important part in the sex trade, either through explicit cooperation or deliberate inaction. Often law enforcement agencies are purposely negligent in their protection of victims, especially if the women are non-natives. Furthermore, authorities frequently act in collusion with pimps or organized crime figures, as is the case when they return girls who have escaped to their former captors. In some cases when girls escape, corrupt police actually go to the victim's home and threaten the family, demanding that the pimp be repaid for the girl's value.[40] Yet authorities cooperate in other ways as well. For example, in January 1997 Turkmen President Saparmurad Niyazov spoke about the problem of forced prostitution in Turkmenistan and accused Turkmen police of, "direct complicity in the widespread cases of prostitution in the republic".[41] He indicated that the police participated in the illegal activity and regularly accepted bribes.

Similarly, indifferent governments are directly responsible for the proliferation of the sex business. Many authorities are hostile to victims of forced prostitution, seeing them as somehow criminal rather than innocent. For example, the Japanese government will not provide medical care to prostitutes.[42] Likewise hospitals in India will not treat prostitutes who show signs of HIV. In Bombay's J.J. Hospital, the largest medical center in Asia, the staff refused to help a prostitute in labor who was HIV positive. Although her condition was extremely serious, she was sent away to deliver the baby in the brothel.[43] An even more horrendous example is that of the government of Burma, which routinely executes prostitutes infected with AIDS. In April 1993, the *Chicago Tribune* reported on the fate of 25 Burmese females who were kidnapped and sold into prostitution in Thailand. Thai police eventually rescued the women who, by then HIV positive, were promptly sent back to Burma. Upon arrival, Burmese health officials injected the women with cyanide in order to help stem the spread of AIDS.[44] Such governmental antagonism encourages the efforts of sex traffickers and is one of the multiple components of the total global sex business.

Commercial sexual exploitation involves many actors, both directly and indirectly, yet those who run this business are often transnational criminal organizations.

THE ROLE OF ORGANIZED CRIME

One of the most important actors in the world of illicit sex is organized crime. Mafia groups are an essential part of the structure that controls this market and their involvement takes many forms. For example, organized crime syndicates might act independently or in cooperation with other individuals, such as authorities, pimps, and even other mafia groups. Joint ventures between organized crime groups and persons not formally involved with a mafia organization are common for at least two reasons. First, established criminal groups are more easily able to operate transnationally in part due to the links between the syndicates. Second, mafia groups are experienced and skilled at operating outside legal boundaries, and evading prosecution by authorities. For example, sometimes the criminal group provides protection services to enterprising brothel owners.[45] Other times the group may run the prostitution ring itself. For instance, Japanese Yakuza or Chinese Triad members regularly obtain victims from large cities, often employing the job scam tactic. They may then provide the girls with fake passports and smuggle them out of the country, where they are promptly sold to brothel owners. In the 1991 article "Imprisoned Prostitutes", Paul Kaihla described how a member of a Hong Kong gang had transported approximately 20 girls into Canada in this fashion.[46] Similarly, in a 1993 piece, Susan Moran explained how Chinese criminal groups used the false promise of a job to obtain new victims. She related:

> Fukinese women ranging in age from 17-20 are promised a job in a factory by the smugglers and charged 25,000 to 35,000 dollars for the trip ... The hardships start on the trip over, when the women risk rape by the gang members. "These women are placed at great risk on the high seas in a lawless situation, sometimes for months", says Wayne McKenna of the INS, coordinator of the interagency Chinese Boat Smuggling Task Force.[47]

Moran also illustrated the subsequent fate of the migrants:

> Gang rape and narcotics often are used to condition the young women to prostitution. The smugglers then introduce them to managers of established massage parlors, clubs or barbershops, usually in New York, San Francisco, Houston, and other American cities with large Asian populations.[48]

Unfortunately, simply being aware of what goes on does nothing to stop it. In fact, convicting traffickers is a difficult task. As Moran noted, "Proving that Asian gangs smuggle women for prostitution is difficult. Often the smugglers will say they didn't know the women were prostitutes, intended to be prostitutes, or would be forced into prostitution".[49]

A 1997 report discussed the attempts of the UN-led police force in Slavonia to confront the problem of forced prostitution run by the mafia in the Serb controlled territory. UN Spokesman Douglas Coffman explained in August 1997 that the victims were, "mainly women from Eastern European countries who had been brought to the region under false pretenses, had their passports taken away and were forced to work as prostitutes".[50] Coffman went on to emphasize that mafia related activities regularly disrupted the smooth running of the region and indicated that prostitution was only one of such activities that also included operations like car, fuel, and cigarette smuggling.[51]

Organized crime groups employ other tactics besides the false pretense of work to procure women. For example, they buy girls from families desperate for money or simply take them from the streets of major cities as well as from rural areas. Moran offered an instance of Triad involvement in this activity: "Members of Chinese crime syndicates will pay ... parents for their unwanted daughters. If the girls are very young, the gangs often will sell them into slavery as child prostitutes to pedophiles, primarily in Bangkok".[52] Moran further explained that the girls are generally then trafficked into the United States, Australia, and Japan.[53] Usually it is only the older females who are trafficked into America because child molestation laws make it too dangerous to smuggle especially young victims for use in American pedophile rings.[54]

One burgeoning characteristic of gang activity is that some mafia groups now move around the country, exploiting situations where they find them. They stay in one place only as long as their operation is profitable and easy. A few years ago, a Houston Police Department detective uncovered a network of Vietnamese pimps who used Korean women in their operations. The discovery supported the beliefs of some law enforcement officials who feel that, " ... these pimps are members of Vietnamese gangs that move around the country like nomads, use more violent methods of extortion than the other Asian gangs, and are the most difficult to identify and track".[55]

Interestingly, criminal organizations frequently conduct trafficking activities in conjunction with other illicit ventures. Some operations are run jointly. For example, Japanese Yakuza groups may manage their gambling activities or sell crystal methamphetamine from the massage parlors that house their prostitution rings.[56] The Ravna Gora, a mafia group active in the former Yugoslavia, is primarily known for arms smuggling but is simultaneously involved in trafficking women and children.[57] Even the International Organization for Migration has recently asserted that, "Criminal organizations, operating across continents, have found that trafficking in migrants is even more lucrative than drug trafficking and they often succeed in combining the two".[58]

In another instance, an investigator for the Global Survival Network who was researching the mafia's role in wildlife smuggling discovered that, "a group trading tiger bones and skins to Chinese and Japanese buyers had developed a sideline in supplying sex clubs abroad with Russian women".[59] Finally, an April 1997 article in *U.S. News and World Report* reported that, "in Russia, women have become a favorite commodity of the criminal class along with such illicit trade as smuggling enriched uranium and cocaine".[60]

Increasing cooperation is a significant development in the operations of transnational criminal organizations. For example, the Yakuza gangs that direct much of the Asian sex business sometimes act in collusion with American operatives in California. Teamwork on false employment schemes is particularly popular. Frequently American contacts advertise entertainment jobs in Japan, where Yakuza members wait for susceptible recruits.[61] The Bureau of International Labor Affairs reports connections between child pornography rings in the United States and Western Europe and trafficking groups in the United States and Thailand.[62] Charles Ferrigno, supervisory anti-smuggling agent for the INS in New York, maintains that organized criminal syndicates in Hong Kong and New York regularly cooperate. He states, "A gang boss in Chinatown will have a relationship with the Hong Kong-based gangs, like the Sparrows and 14K".[63] Even Tho Siju, a former minister of public security in China, reiterated this idea. In an April 1993 news conference, he admitted that members of the Chinese police force, "have dealings with Mafia-style gangs based in Hong Kong ... ".[64]

Furthermore, with increasing globalization, national criminal gangs are now operating outside their traditional jurisdictions. Not only do mafia groups work in association with other criminal organizations, but they also set up their own operations in other countries. For example, the Russian mafia traffics women from Germany, a known destination for Czech, Polish, and Slovak girls who travel there in search of work.[65] Russian gangs also frequently operate out of Turkey, where their influence is similarly strong.[66] Another case of nationals working in foreign lands is the recent Triad activity in Canada. The Dai Huen Jai and the Big Circle Boys are two examples of Chinese gangs that help direct a network of prostitution that runs through Toronto, Calgary, and Vancouver.[67]

The instances of organized crime's operations and collusive activities are numerous and varied. Reliable information on the nature and extent of gang businesses is not readily available. Much remains to be discovered. However, it is possible to present some known facts about the role of organized crime in the global sex trade and its regional variations.

Asia

Asia remains the most notorious of regions in which commercial sexual exploitation is rampant. This area of the globe has a long history of such activity. In their book *Yakuza*, David E. Kaplan and Alec Dubro comment on Japanese criminal gangs' control of prositution rings. They acknowledge that, before World War II, most prositution in Japan was legal and even fairly respectable. However, the devastating effects of the war inspired Yakuza control of what would become a multi-billion dollar industry. The authors explain that, "Out of the economic desperation many women were sold by their families to Yakuza, who used them as prostitutes in the cities. . . nearly all organized crime fell into the hands of the Yakuza and their associates".[68] Furthermore, Kaplan and Dubro illustrate how sex tourism was linked to the huge growth of the sex business in the late 1960s. Although the Japanese tourist industry had expanded tremendously, the motivation to travel was not a wholesome one. Rather, "men from around the country lined up for prostitution junkets across much of East Asia ... . The "sex tour" was born".[69] And the Yakuza became involved early:

> The Japanese sex tours encouraged the Yakuza to follow the excesses of their countrymen across East Asia ... the tours introduced the gangs to the international trade in sexual slavery, a merciless enterprise that they would soon help expand around the Pacific.[70]

Today, Japan remains a haven for customers of the sex industry. A Methodist missionary who directs a rescue center in Tokyo explained that, "feminine sexual slavery remains a pillar of Japanese male society".[71] Most sexual commerce that transpires is governed by the Yakuza. In his book *Enslaved*, Gordon Thomas describes how women are trafficked by the Yamaguchi-gumi and sold in Tokyo's Yoshiwa district.[72] Additionally, he reports on the number of children and foreign women that the Yamaguchi-gumi provides to brothels, massage parlors, bars, and teahouses. The latest trend is "pantyless clubs" where the floors are completely mirrored.[73] These bars are the most recent agency to demand girls from the Yakuza.

Bangkok's Center for the Protection of Children's Rights estimates that 6,000 Thai children were snatched from the streets in just a few months in 1988, some of whom were eventually trailed to the Middle East.[74] If Yakuza and Triad gangs are not directly responsible for a number of the kidnappings, they are undoubtedly involved in the trafficking process. Some of the children taken in 1988 were thought to be destined for sale into the North American and European sex markets. Given the links that exist between Yakuza members and their American counterparts and the recent Triad activity in Canada, such a transfer seems entirely probable. A 1996 article in the *Bangkok Post* noted the movement of prostitutes in Thailand:

> Prostitutes ... from Laos, Burma, and Southern China enter Thailand along border points in the Northeast and Northern provinces. Major destinations include Bangkok and other major cities such as Chiang Mai, Khon Kaen, and Hat Yai. Many eventually head overseas to Japan and Singapore through Don Muang Airport.[75]

Additionally, a December 1997 article related the breakup of Taiwan's "Lily" international sex ring, an operation that was not only involved in peddling sex but also smuggling humans for the same purpose. The report stated:

> Police investigations show that the Lily ring had recruited foreign women to work as prostitutes through an underworld syndicate which ran an efficient human smuggling operation from Southeast Asia. The human smuggling ring forced those women to serve as prostitutes by confiscating their passports upon their arrival in Taiwan. Police estimated that more then 120 women from Thailand, Malaysia, Singapore, mainland China, Macau, and Hong Kong had been forced into the sex trade by the syndicate.[76]

In 1997, Italian police cracked a major international sex racket linked to pedophile activity in many regions of the globe. The discovery of forged documents by Milan customs officials led authorities to participants of a global child sex ring that was one of the largest in Europe.[77] A rescued twelve-year-old Chinese girl explained to police that she had been sold into prostitution by her parents, forced to work in a brothel in Thailand, and was shortly destined for further sexual exploitation in Miami, Florida. In connection with the case, a Japanese man and Chinese woman were arrested in Milan on charges of kidnapping, extortion, and associating with the mafia. According to the *BBC News*, Italy is a common departure point for children victimized by Asian organized crime syndicates who are headed for pedophile exploitation in Europe and the United States.[78] The BBC's report stated, "Italian police believe the discovery marks only the tip of the iceberg of pedophile crime run by Chinese triads or mafia gangs and the Japanese gangsters".[79]

India has become a favorite destination for pedophiles and tourists seeking the sexual company of children. Furthermore, women and children are increasingly trafficked from India to Pakistan, Oman, Cyprus, United Arab Emirates, the Middle East, and Sri Lanka.[80] India's mafia is a powerful and pervasive force that is heavily involved in the booming sex market. In an article in *The Nation*, Robert Friedman described the nature and extent of the mafia's control of the sex trade. He cited an instance in which a Dutch doctor working for the World Health Organization was kidnapped by the mob in Bombay and warned to stop investigating the links between prostitution, the mafia, and local politicians.[81] In particular, Indian criminal organizations resent inquiries about the prevalence of AIDS among their prostitutes. This is not surprising. As Friedman noted, "Publicity about AIDS has already cut into its profits and the mob is keen to avoid further scrutiny".[82] Health and social workers must obtain the mafia's permission before they are allowed to work in the area and even then organized crime dictates the extent of their activities. For example, they are often instructed to ignore child prostitution.[83] Dr. Jairaj Thanekar, director of Bombay's Municipal Health Clinic, attributed the growth of the city's red light district to the spread of organized crime and the desires of Arab customers who came to Bombay for sex with children.[84] Thanekar observed, "The mafia paid the police and politicians a lot of money to close their eyes".[85] Yet their involvement did not stop there. Friedman explained the intricacies of Bombay's sex market in his article:

> Bombay's flesh trade has evolved into a highly efficient business. It is controlled by four separate though harmonious crime groups: one is in charge of payoffs to the police, another controls money lending, a third maintains internal law and order, and one procures women from a vast network stretching from South India to the Himalayas. Of the four mafia kingpins, the most powerful is Mehboob Thasildar, the procurer of women, according to well-placed Indian government sources.[86]

Not surprisingly, these criminals have close links to politicians. In return for protection and support, the politicians receive the votes of pimps and prostitutes.[87]

The Middle East

An interesting trend in the global sex trade is the increasing sexual exploitation of women from the Newly Independent States, who end up far from their homelands. Since the demise of the Soviet Union, women from the former Communist empire have probably become the most frequent victims of trafficking schemes. A March 1998 *Prime Time Special* focused on Russian women who had been trapped into forced prostitution and explained how hundreds of these women were bought from an organized crime network that traffics women from the former Soviet Union to Israel. Cynthia McFadden interviewed the owner of one of the busiest brothels in Tel Aviv, Jacob Golan. He admitted to purchasing the girls from the mob and justified the trade by saying, "We need a lot of girls and, in Israel, we cannot find so many girls to give this service. So we have to bring girls from other countries like Russia".[88] Investigations led by the Global Survival Network and reported elsewhere in this volume highlight the scope and dynamics of trafficking.[89] The following is an excerpt from a conversation between Golan and McFadden:

McFadden: Do you actually have a hand in importing the girls from Russia?

Golan: No, this business belongs to other guys from Russia.

McFadden: The Russian mafia?

Golan: Yes, they bring [the] girls from the airport and they sell the girls.

McFadden: For how much money?

Golan: It depends how the girls look. It's between 5,000 to 15,000 dollars.[90]

Furthermore, Golan spoke about his ties to Israeli criminal organizations. He told McFadden that he initially paid the Israeli mafia five to six percent of his monthly profits. However, because the mafia continually increased their fees, he eventually negotiated a partnership deal with the mob.[91] Such cooperation facilitates the smooth running of the brothel.

Yet it is not just the local mob's involvement that helps Golan stay in business. He also bragged about his connections to corrupt officials inside the Israeli Interior Ministry. As McFadden related, "Golan told us he pays his contact in the Interior Department 1,000 dollars for fake Israel identification papers for each girl".[92] When asked about such allegations of corruption, an employee of the interior department immediately denied them. Yet, upon further questioning, the official acknowledged that the ministry was aware of the trafficking. He justified the government's lack of action by explaining how difficult it was to stop the illicit trade and by noting that, "those girls who come to Israel have to take the responsibility to find out exactly what they are supposed to be doing in Israel".[93] After being asked how a woman could know in advance that she was going to be sold into sexual slavery, the official replied, "Before I visit a foreign country, I plan it in advance".[94] This is a telling example of how indifferent and corrupt government officials support the global sexual exploitation of women and children.

In a special report appearing in *The New York Times* in January 1998, Michael Specter discussed the involvement of Russian organized crime in trafficking women from the former Soviet Union to many regions of the globe. He described the forced prostitution these females encounter upon their arrival in cities like Tel Aviv and Ramle, Israel and contended that, selling naive and desperate women into sexual bondage has become one of the fastest growing criminal enterprises in the robust global economy.'[95] In particular, Russian organized crime is a key player and Specter highlighted a particularly Russian alternative to the popular job scam tactic. He noted that these groups sometimes procure victims through fake mail order bride businesses. And even if these businesses are not run by the mafia, Specter acknowledged that, "few such organizations can operate without paying off one gang or another".[96] What makes this particular illicit market so attractive to Russian organized crime? Michael Platzer, of the United Nations' Center for International Crime Prevention, noted that many factors encourage the mob's participation:

> The mafia is not stupid. There is less law enforcement since the Soviet Union fell apart and more freedom of movement. The earnings are incredible. The overhead is low – you don't have to buy cars and guns. Drugs you can sell once and they are gone. Women can earn money for a long time. Also ... the laws help the gangsters. Prostitution is semi-legal in many places and that makes enforcement tricky. In most cases punishment is very light.[97]

Specter similarly observed that the fragile socioeconomic conditions of a state in transition or a developing state can give rise to organized crime. He described how areas like Russia, Belarus, and particularly Ukraine have become the busiest centers for procuring women to serve the needs of the global sex industry. Specter explained that, "the Ukrainian problem has been worsened by a ravaged economy, an atrophied system of law enforcement, and criminal gangs that grow more brazen each year"[98] Mikhail Lebed, head of criminal investigations for the Ukrainian Interior Ministry, reiterated this logic in speaking about the great monetary advantage criminal gangs have over law enforcement officials. He said, "It is a human tragedy but also, frankly, a national crisis. Gangsters make more from these women in a week than we have in our law enforcement budget for the whole year".[99] Indeed, the problem in Ukraine is immense. The networks controlled by gangs based in Kiev, the Ukrainian capital, operate as far east as Japan and Thailand.[100]

Latin America

Traditionally, organized criminal groups in Latin America have specialized in drug trafficking and money laundering, due to their control of the cocaine industry and the huge profits that naturally flow from such a lucrative business. The Medellin and Cali cartels were infamous for their dominance in the international cocaine trade. While it is still difficult to assess the involvement of Latin American criminal organizations in different illicit ventures, certain trends in the region indicate that organized criminal groups are involved in the sexual exploitation of women and children. In recent years, the scale of the sex industry in South America has increased tremendously. It would be remarkably unrealistic to imagine that such a vast enterprise could be conducted so efficiently without criminal enterprises that are practiced at circumventing national law enforcement agencies. In "Child Prostitution in Latin America", Dorianne Beyer suggests why precise information on the nature and extent of organized crime's participation in the sex trade in this area is hard to obtain. She explains:

> An additional Latin American aspect that makes data difficult to come by is the pervasiveness of the Roman Catholic Church and its teaching about morality, sex within marriage, etc. In addition to the usual secrecy that surrounds illegal child prostitution all

over the world, in Latin America there is an overlay on the family level, the community level, and the governmental level, of shame, denial and covertness due to the permeation of the Roman Catholic culture.[101]

Many Central and South American nations face significant child prostitution problems domestically. Countries such as Argentina, Bolivia, Brazil, Chile, Colombia, Costa Rica, Ecuador, Mexico, and Peru are among those that have not yet begun adequately to address the sexual exploitation suffered by millions of the children that live in the streets of their capital cities and the hills of their rural communities.[102] Unlike Asia, there are few governmental programs that deal with child prostitution in Latin America. Additionally, while there may be laws against pimping, no laws exist specifically prohibiting child prostitution.[103]

How many of these children are victims of mafia groups? Again, although precise details remain elusive, certain specific reports do exist. Beyer discusses organized crime's involvement in the sexual exploitation of young females in Brazil for instance. In her report, she describes how teenage girls are transported to remote areas by traffickers who have promised them restaurant jobs: "Young girls, around 15 or 16 years old, are imported like chattel after being lured to these isolated areas by traffickers promising them employment in the canteens and restaurants of the Amazonian mining towns".[104] Furthermore, Beyer demonstrates the prevalence of this particular activity.

> ... (there are) large groups of male laborers working in isolated outposts and criminal rings anxious to serve them with mass importations of young girl prostitutes ... it is not a phenomenon found only in the remote mining communities ... but it is also common as a criminal exploitative adjunct to continuing civil engineering projects. It is therefore no surprise that Brazil has the largest and most sophisticated criminal rings and syndicates to provide these girls for workers.[105]

Another example of children who are victimized by mafia groups in this region comes from the west coast of South America. Some years ago Ecuador's then Under-Secretary for Child Welfare, Elsa Maria Castro, halted all adoption of Ecuadorian children by foreigners after it was discovered that babies were being kidnapped and sold to customers in Norway and Great Britain. The operation was controlled by an efficient gang that had already succeeded in dozens of such transactions.[106] Furthermore, a member of the Dutch parliament, Piet Stofflen, alleged that like minded gangs were involved in the same trade in Guatemala. This time however, the children were being sold to middlemen in the United States for approximately 15,000 dollars each.[107]

Africa

The January 1998 issue of "Trafficking in Migrants", a quarterly bulletin issued by the International Organization for Migration, reported on the trafficking and sexual exploitation of African children. According to the article, children between the ages of 8 and 15 are kidnapped from rural areas in poorer countries like Togo and Benin and then sold to brothels in countries such as Gabon, Nigeria, Ghana, Burkina Faso, Cameroon, Cote d'Ivoire, and Equatorial Guinea.[108] In autumn 1997, local police blocked two trafficking attempts in the Benin cities of Porto Novo and Cotonou, where well dressed men were loading numerous children into trucks and buses. The IOM states that this trafficking is conducted by "professional" organizations, which operate efficiently and systematically.[109]

The same bulletin discussed the activities of a Nigerian criminal group that trafficked women from Nigeria to Belgium, Italy, and Germany. In September 1997, a Brussels court convicted nine members of this network for trafficking women for forced prostitution. The victims were given false documents and promised asylum in the new country. Upon arrival, the women were sold to agents who supplied the local sex markets with fresh flesh. The women were offered the opportunity to buy their freedom for 25,000 dollars.[110]

Europe

In September 1997, a court in Liège, Belgium sentenced eight persons for their participation in a criminal ring that trafficked pre-pubescent girls from Hungary and Romania to Belgium for purposes of forced prostitution.[111] The guilty included five Hungarian and Romanian nationals and three Belgian associates.

Women from Eastern Europe and the newly independent nations of the former Communist empire have nearly replaced women from the developing world as the "main prey of the sex trade and its complex web of organized crime".[112] In Milan in late December 1997, police discovered a prostitution ring, "that was holding auctions in which women abducted from the countries of the former Soviet Union were put on blocks, partially naked, and sold at an average price of just under 1,000 dollars".[113] Similarly, it has been claimed that 50 to 55 percent of prostitutes in Athens are from the former Soviet bloc.[114] Furthermore, reports from UNICEF and UNESCO indicate that international criminal organizations in Eastern Europe and Russia are becoming increasingly involved in trafficking children from these areas into Western Europe for use in many of the richer nations' child prostitution and pornography markets.[115] Human rights groups relate incidents of international gangs trafficking Filipina women to the Netherlands and Scandinavia.[116] Additionally, the Italian mafia presently participates in trafficking women from Albania and other Eastern European countries.[117] One of the most surprising developments, however, has been the growing involvement of Albanian criminal organizations in prostitution in Italy. One commentary observed that Albanians are not only able to import tens of thousands of sometimes very young girls to Italy, but that they also control much of the prostitution in the country.

> In the large Italian cities anyone who is a prostitute – woman, man, or transvestite and no matter what country they come from – has to pay their dues. The volume of work is such that the Albanians must often use North African collectors, the same ones hired to sell light drugs at the retail level. The prostitution sector, which the judges increasingly refer to as being reduced to slavery, has provided the primary source of capital. But it has also been a brutal arena ... The methods of persuasion are terrifying".[118]

Ironically, Italian organized crime groups seem content with such an arrangement. Although Milan, for example, is, in part, the preserve of the Calabrian 'Ndrangheta, Albanian clans seem to run the business without interference.[119] It is possible although not certain that a small percentage of the profits goes to the Italian group in return for the freedom to operate on their territory.

In another case, in October 1997, Spanish police dissolved an international smuggling operation that transferred Chinese from the province of Fujian to destinations in Canada, the United states, and Great Britian.[120] In short, there are multiple suppliers and multiple destinations for women and children who have become part of the global sex trade.

United States

The United States provides no exception to this overall pattern. In his Keynote Address to a Symposium on Forced Labor and Prostitution of Children, Representative Joseph Kennedy II acknowledged that, "...child prostitution is a growing problem in both developing and developed countries ... . I am ashamed to say that in the United States the problem is of unimaginable proportions".[121] Indeed, criminal groups that control child prostitution rings in the United States sometimes tattoo the victims they exploit.[122]

According to Susan Moran, the increase in prostitution operations in the United States is due partly to the increase in Asian organized crime. The Immigration and Naturalization Service reportedly estimated that more than 100,000 women were smuggled into the United States the late 1980s and early 1990s years to provide services for these sex rackets.[123] Many have come from Asia.

> The increase is a direct result of the expanding power of Asian gangs in the United States. The gangs supply the houses with new girls, provide them with clients and protect them from extortion by other gangs and busts by the police. Highly organized, these gangs often work for larger, more powerful and more established organizations known as tongs and for Chinese secret societies called triads.[124]

Four main tongs operate from New York City. Each appears to coexist with smaller criminal gangs that perform critical functions for the larger syndicate. For example, the On Leong runs a number of operations on Mott Street, where the Ghost Shadows gang supervises daily business. Other subsidiaries of more established criminal organizations are groups such as the Fuk Ching and the Flying Dragons. Bruce Nichol, coordinator for the INS on the interagency Violent Crime Task Force maintains, "The triads are definitely involved in smuggling young Fukinese females into the United States for the purpose of prostitution".[125] Yet it is not only girls from the Fukin province who are victimized. Before 1980, most were Korean.[126] Increasingly however, women are being taken from all over Asia, including countries like Malaysia, Vietnam, Laos, and the Philippines. Such clandestine operations are nothing new. In the early 1900s, the U.S. government recruited Chinese men to help build the railway system in California and Chinese Triads smuggled native women into America to service the desires of the workers. During the Korean War, the Triads used a sneakier tactic. Organized crime groups paid American GIs between 5–10,000 dollars to marry Korean prostitutes so that the women could enter the U.S. legally and then be used in the sex market of America.[127] Unlike their Chinese counterparts, the Japanese Yakuza elect to import foreign prostitutes rather than export native flesh. Caucasian women are a highly prized commodity. A typical procurement scenario would follow a pattern similar to the following description:

> The Yakuza often advertises in trade magazines around Los Angeles and San Francisco for singers and models to try out in Japan, offering to pay the airfare. When the women arrive, however, they quickly learn that more is expected of them. If they resist or try to escape, they are beaten, gang raped, or threatened with imprisonment or death.[128]

It is clear that each region of the world yields its own peculiarities, depending on which gangs control the sex trade. Cultural differences notwithstanding however, many similarities exist. For example, each group involves itself in the sex industry because it yields large profits. Furthermore, each gang exhibits similarly callous and brutal attitudes in its treatment of victims. And no criminal organization presently involved in the sex market exhibits a propensity towards exiting the industry. Moreover, the fact that criminal gangs now operate increasingly transnationally and cooperatively suggests that their interests and operations are more similar than disparate. This may serve as a further catalyst for the promotion of this industry.

Two broad conclusions emerge from the geographical survey. First, the size and extent of the global sex business is phenomenal. No region of the globe remains unaffected by this illicit activity. Furthermore, the facets and dimensions of the industry are numerous and dynamic, making effective countermeasures difficult to design and implement. Second, the role of organized crime in the global sex trade is multifaceted; in many cases the exact functions performed by organized criminal associations remain unclear. In other cases, even when the nature of involvement is evident, the scale of such participation is vague. The lack of dependable data continues to be a major impediment for law enforcement officials, governments, and human rights groups. As Ko-Lin Chin has noted, "there is a lack of information on the link between Asian gangs and prostitution ... this is a growing problem".[129] Certainly this sentiment could be expressed about any criminal organization, particularly those operating across borders. It is clear that criminal organizations frequently traffic women and children for forced prostitution, and that these organizations provide security, support, or liaison services to pimps, brothel owners, and other mafia groups. Obviously their involvement is essential to the efficiency and success of the sex industry. Yet much more needs to be known. If effectual countermeasures are to be developed and implemented, a firmer knowledge of the role organized crime plays in this illicit market is essential.

NOTES

1. Background Document for the World Congress Against the Commercial Sexual Exploitation of Children. UNICEF and ECPAT, NGO group for the Convention on the Rights of the Child, pp.2–3. (http://www.acapa.org.za/back.html).
2. Forced Labor: The Prostitution of Children, U.S. Department of Labor, Bureau of International Labor Affairs (1996), p.1.
3. Ibid.
4. Background Document for the World Congress Against Sexual Exploitation of Children, op.cit., p.1.
5. "Forced Labor", op.cit., p.2, Carol Aloysius, "Is Our Paradise Islands Becoming a Haven for Pedophiles?", Aug. 25, 1996, p.1. (http://www.lanka.net/lakehouse/anclweb/observr/weekl/features/25fea06.html), Phil Williams, "Major Trends in Transnational Organized Crime", Paper prepared for UN Crime Prevention and Criminal Justice Division, p.7; and Rahul Bedi, "India: Bid to Protect Children as Sex Tourism Spreads", March 19, 1996, p.1. (http://www.alternatives.com/crime/INDCHILD.HTML).
6. "Forced Labor", op.cit., p.32, 39.
7. Ibid, p.2.
8. Brian Freemantle, Europe in the Grip of Organized Crime. (London: Orion, 1995), p.125.
9. Matsui Yayori, "Eliminating Trafficking in Asian Women", p.1 (http://www.alternatives.com/crime/ASIAWOM.HTML); Youngik Yoon, "International Sexual Slavery", p.2 (http://law.touro.edu/AboutTLC/journals/ internationallawrev/vol16/part7.html); "Trafficking in Women from the Dominican Republic for Sexual Exploitation" (Geneva: International Organization for Migration, June 1996), Migration Information Programme (http://www.iom.ch); and Phil Williams, op.cit., p.3, 5.
10. Ibid, p.5.
11. "Trafficking in Women to Italy for Sexual Exploitation", International Organization of Migration, Migration Information Programme (June 1996) (http://www.iom.ch).
12. Phil Williams, op.cit., p.6.
13. Ibid, pp.5–6.
14. Victoria Pope, "Trafficking in Women: Procuring Russians for Sex Abroad – even in America", U.S. News and World Report (April 7, 1997), p.42.
15. Chirachari Chaimusik, Chirathat Niwatphumin and Butsaba Siwasombun, "Cleaning up the Dirty Money Game", Bangkok Post (May 13, 1996), p.28.
16. Ibid.
17. Youngik Yoon, op.cit., p.2.
18. Ibid.

19. *Ibid*, pp.2–3.
20. *Ibid*, pp.2–4 and Aaron Sachs, "The Last Commodity: Child Prostitution in the Developing World", *World Watch* (July–Aug. 1994), Vol.7, No.4.
21. Yoon, *Ibid*.
22. "The International Sex Market in Children", *WIN News*, Vol.19, No.2 (Spring 1993), p.51.
23. Phil Williams, *op.cit.*, p.5.
24. Yoon, *op.cit.*, pp.3–4 and Freemantle, *op.cit.*, Chapter 12.
25. Yoon and Freemantle, *Ibid*.
26. *Ibid*.
27. *Ibid*.
28. *Ibid*.
29. "Plight of Burmese Women Detailed", *Burma News Network* (Nov. 12, 1996), p.1. (http://www-uvi.eunet.fr/asia/euro-burma/fbc/nov1/a18nov96-4.html).
30. Yoon, *op.cit.*, p.3.
31. Ellen Lukas, "Saving the Children", *National Review*, Vol.48, No.24 (Dec. 23, 1996)p.2.
32. "Forced Labor", *op.cit.*, pp.34–35.
33. *Ibid*, p.35.
34. Sachs, *op.cit.*, p.5.
35. Gordon Thomas, *Enslaved* (New York: Pharos Books, 1991), p.210.
36. United Nation's Commission on Human Rights, Rights of the Child, Report of the working group in its second session, p.19. (http://www.unhcr.ch/refworld/un/chr/chr96/thematic/1996–101.html).
37. Dick Ward, "Child Victimization is a Global Problem", *Criminal Justice International* (Nov.–Dec. 1996), p.4, Carol Aloysius, *op.cit.*, p.1, and Rahul Bedi, *op.cit.*, p.1.
38. "Forced Labor", *op.cit.*, p.22.
39. *Ibid*.
40. Youngik Yoon, *op.cit.*, p.3.
41. "Turkmenistan: Niyazov States Police Involved in Widespread Prostitution", *Tashkent Radio Mashal in Uzbek*, 11:30 GMT (Jan. 23, 1997).
42. "Plight of Burmese Women Detailed", *op.cit.*, p.1.
43. Robert I. Friedman, "India's Shame: Sexual Slavery and Political Corruption are Leading to an AIDS Catastrophe", *The Nation*, Vol.262, No.14, April 8, 1996, p.10.
44. Youngik Yoon, *op.cit.*, p.2 and "Forced Labor", *op.cit.*, p.22.
45. Vincenzo Ruggiero, *Organized and Corporate Crime in Europe* (Aldershot: Dartmouth Publishing Company, 1996), p.140.
46. Paul Kahila, "Imprisoned Prostitutes: the Gangs Run Lucrative Brothels", *Maclean's* (March 25, 1991), Vol.104, No.12, p.24.
47. Susan Moran, "New World Havens of Oldest Profession", *Insight on the News*, Vol.9 No.25, June 21,1993, p.2.
48. *Ibid*.
49. *Ibid*, p.3.
50. "Croatia: UN-Led Police To Halt East Slavonia Forced Prostitution", *Paris AFP*, 18:07 GMT (Aug. 30, 1997).
51. *Ibid*.
52. Moran, *op.cit.*, p.1.
53. *Ibid*, p.2.
54. *Ibid*.
55. *Ibid*.
56. Christopher Seymour, "Yakuza Diary: Doing Time in the Japanese Underworld", *Atlantic Monthly Press*, New York (1996).
57. Brian Freemantle, *op.cit.*, p.137.
58. "Trafficking in Migrants", *Quarterly Bulletin of the International Organization for Migration* (Dec. 1997/Jan. 1998), No.17, p.1.
59. Victoria Pope, *op.cit.*, p.42.

60. *Ibid.*
61. Yoon, *op.cit.*, p.4.
62. Forced Labor, *op.cit.*, p.26.
63. Susan Moran, *op.cit.*, p.5.
64. *Ibid.*
65. Freemantle, *op.cit.*, p.137.
66. Michael Specter, "'Traffickers' New Cargo: Naive Slavic Women", *The New York Times*, Jan. 11, 1998, p.6.
67. Paul Kahila, *op.cit.*, p.24.
68. David E. Kaplan and Alec Dubro, *Yakuza: The Explosive Account of Japan's Criminal Underworld* (Reading: Addison Wesley Publishing Company, Inc., 1986), p 77.
69. *Ibid.*
70. *Ibid*, p.201.
71. Thomas, *op.cit.*, p.31.
72. *Ibid*, p.32.
73. *Ibid.*
74. *Ibid*, p.149.
75. Chaimusik, *et al*, *op.cit.*
76. "Taiwan: "'Lily' International Sex Ring Disbands", *Taiwan Central News Agency*, 10:46 GMT, Dec. 22, 1997.
77. "Chinese Girl blows lid on Global Child Sex Trade", *BBC News* (November 7, 1997), p.1.
78. *Ibid.*
79. *Ibid.*
80. "The International Sex Market in Children", *WIN News* (Spring 1993), Vol.19, No.2, p.51.
81. Friedman, *op.cit.*, p.3.
82. *Ibid*, p.4.
83. *Ibid.*
84. *Ibid*, p.5.
85. *Ibid.*
86. *Ibid*, p.9.
87. *Ibid*, p.8.
88. "Girls for Sale, Young Russian Women Lured into Prostitution", *Prime Time ABC* (March 18, 1998), p.2. (http://www.abcnews.com/onair/ptl/html_files/transcripts/pt10318a.htm).
89. *Ibid.*
90. *Ibid*, p.5.
91. *Ibid*, p.11.
92. *Ibid*, p.9.
93. *Ibid.*
94. *Ibid*, p.10.
95. Michael Specter, *op.cit.*, p.1.
96. *Ibid*, p.6.
97. *Ibid.*
98. "Trafficking in Migrants", *op.cit.*, p.2, 3.
99. *Ibid*, p.2.
100. *Ibid.*
101. Forced Labor, , *op.cit.*, p.34.
102. *Ibid.*, p.32–40.
103. *Ibid.*
104. *Ibid*, 37.
105. *Ibid*, pp.37–38,
106. Gordon Thomas, *op.cit.*, p.149.
107. *Ibid.*
108. "Trafficking in Migrants", *op.cit.*, pp.2, 3.

109. *Ibid.*
110. *Ibid.*
111. *Ibid,* pg. 3.
112. "Europe Urged to Curb Sexual Exploitation of Women", *AIDS Weekly Plus* (June 24, 1996), p.16.
113. Michael Specter, *op.cit.*, p.6.
114. Dh. Nikolakopoulos, "Greece: Russian Mafia's Laundry" Athens To Vima Tis Kiriakis in Greek, Feb. 15, 1998, pp A28-A31.
115. Laura J. Lederer, "Poor Children Targets of Sex Exploitation", *National Catholic Reporter* (Nov. 22, 1996), Vol.33, No.5, p.1.
116. *Ibid,* p.2.
117. *Ibid*
118. Gianfrancesco Turano, "Report of Albanian 'Mafia' in Italy", Il Mondo in Italian, Jan 3, 1998, pp.55–58.
119. Roberto Ruscica, "Albanian Mafia, This Is How It Helps The Kosovo Guerrilla Fighters", Milan Corriere della Sera in Italian, Oct. 15, 1998, pp.79, 80.
120. "Trafficking in Migrants", *op.cit.*, p.2.
121. Forced Labor, *op.cit.*, p.2-3.
122. Forced Labor, *op.cit.*, p.26.
123. Moran, *op.cit.*, p.1.
124. *Ibid.*
125. *Ibid,* p.2.
126. *Ibid,* p.1, 4.
127. *Ibid,* p.4.
128. *Ibid,* p.5.
129. *Ibid, op.cit.*, p.3.

Trafficking in Women and Children: A Market Perspective

PHIL WILLIAMS

I. INTRODUCTION

Control of prostitution is perhaps the world's second oldest profession. It is also a profession that, during the last 150 years, has expanded considerably and taken on new dimensions with the development of a wide range of trafficking networks that bring women and children from a variety of sources to destination countries, sometimes voluntarily, sometimes under false pretenses, and sometimes through the use of coercion. In the 1990s these networks are ubiquitous. They take women and children from one country to another in the developing world as well as from east to west and south to north.

The more recent growth in the trafficking of women and children can be explained in terms of the new opportunities provided by globalization, the ease and speed of travel, the breakdown of barriers between east and west, the emergence of a market that has become much more cosmopolitan, and the desires of customers who are enticed by the exotic elements provided by foreign prostitutes or the depravities of child sex. Foreign women and children are also more vulnerable than their domestic counterparts and easier to control for the pimps and criminal organizations which profit from their activities. Moreover, the inhibitions on and obstacles to the development of these markets have been minimal. At both the domestic and international levels, there are real gaps in prevention and enforcement activities. At the international level, there are conventions and norms in place, but these are not vigorously implemented. At the national level, legislation is often lacking or inadequate while law enforcement is poorly equipped, both legally and operationally to counter trafficking operations, especially those that are transnational in scope. As in many other areas of criminal activity, law enforcement still operates in a bordered world whereas transnational criminal organizations operate in what for them is virtually a borderless world. Where market opportunities are lucrative, criminal organizations, large and small, ignore borders and typically violate or transcend national sovereignty; when they need safe havens they hide behind borders and exploit sovereignty. Against this background, trafficking in women and children for commercial sex can be understood as an activity where two distinct but overlapping phenomena come together – organized crime and illegal immigration – and result in a phenomenon that is distinct from both.

- Organized crime traditionally has been seen largely as the supply of illicit goods and services. It has long been involved in the commercial sex trade, either directly or indirectly. Prominent among criminal organizations active in the sex industry are the Yakuza which has traditionally controlled a significant portion of the prostitution in the Philippines and other parts of southeast Asia, Chinese criminal organizations operating in a wide variety of locations from Canada to Australia, and the Bombay Mafia which controls a large red light district.

- Illegal immigration shares many of the same dynamics as legal migration except that it involves illegal entry to the destination country either through avoiding border controls or passing through immigration and customs checks with false documentation. Trafficking in women and children overlaps with alien trafficking more generally but has certain distinct characteristics. Whereas aliens who are smuggled into the United States or Western Europe often endure enormous and unexpected hardships, the decision to migrate is usually a voluntary one. In effect, the demand comes from the would-be migrants, and those who arrange the transportation and false documents are simply responding to demand from willing if often unwitting customers. With trafficking in women and children, however, the demand tends to come from the other end of the chain, from legitimate entrepreneurs requiring cheap or forced labor and unscrupulous businessmen, semi-legitimate enterprises or criminal entrepreneurs seeking a regular supply of participants for the commercial sex trade.

The analysis here is a preliminary attempt to understand the phenomenon of trafficking in women and children through the application of a market analysis. The underlying assumptions are:

- The market for commercial sex has long had a transnational dimension so that, in one sense, there is little new about the contemporary manifestations of the phenomenon. In 1885, for example, the *Pall Mall Gazette* in London began a series on the white slave trade and the abduction of English girls which caused a sensation not only in Britain, but also in Europe, especially France and Belgium, and the United States.[1] Similarly, in the late nineteenth century Argentina and Brazil emerged as lucrative markets for traffickers in women. Those who controlled the trafficking business were predominantly French, Jews from Poland and Russia, and Italians.[2] Among the women who were trafficked were significant numbers of Slavic women taken to work as prostitutes in a wide variety of places including the Ottoman Empire and Argentina as well as New York and other major cities in the United States.[3] As one of the predecessors of today's NGOs lamented in 1903: "the white-slave traffickers are in close contact in all parts of the world, in great cities as in small villages ... in order to benefit fully from the techniques of the traffic and the advantages of combination".[4] Moreover, "the advantages of the traffickers were indeed substantial. They had the steamship and the railway to move women quickly and the telegraph to help dispatch them efficiently. With the exception of Britain and Germany, the police were corrupt or compliant to varying degrees everywhere".[5] It is clear from all this that the difference in today's world is not the trade as such, but the speed, ease and variety of the flows of women – and that even this is a difference in degree rather than kind.

- The markets in women and children for commercial sex are similar in their essentials to any other illicit market whether drugs, nuclear materials, illicit arms, fauna and flora, or art and antiquities. This is not intended to be cold or inhumane; it is simply to suggest that we have to engage in detached analyses of an emotion-driven subject if we want to enhance both our understanding and our capacity to do something about it. The major players in the market do not take an emotional approach: in effect, they trade in human misery and treat women and children as simply more commodities that can be trafficked and sold for substantial profits. From the point of view of domestic and transnational criminal organizations or shady entrepreneurs, women and children are a product, like any other.

- There are, nevertheless, certain distinct features of the markets in women and children, which serve to differentiate them from other illicit products. In effect, both women and children are treated as consumer durables to be used and abused repeatedly by clients, and to be passed on from one trafficker or brothel owner to another in what is little more than a modern form of slavery. This makes them an attractive product. The markets in women and children obviously overlap with one another but also have some distinct features.

- By understanding the market dynamics it should be possible to develop more effective counter-measures that, in effect, create disruption and dislocation, impose risks, and establish barriers in the markets.

Accordingly, the paper initially sets out a market framework and then within this framework looks first at trafficking in women and then explores trafficking in children as part of the broader issue of child prostitution. In both cases, it looks at the responses that governments and law enforcement agencies can take in order to create market barriers. It recognizes, however, that both preventive and remedial measures will take time to implement, and that the markets will continue to flourish so long as there is a demand for commercial sex, so long as there are limited opportunities for women in licit sectors of the economy, and so long as there are individuals who see this as a lucrative area of activity.

II. A MARKET FRAMEWORK

In looking at illicit markets, there are several dimensions that need to be identified and elaborated:

- the size and scale of the market and in particular the extent to which national, regional, and global markets can be understood as an integrated whole or as separate and overlapping.

- emerging trends in the market and in the location and direction of the flows of women and children.

- the profitability of the market.

- the dynamics of supply and demand.

- the main participants in the market and, in particular, the extent to which the market is transaction based or dominated by well-established and large criminal organizations.

• facilitators and inhibitors.

• the vulnerability or resilience of the markets. Most functioning markets are based on the predominance of facilitating factors over market barriers. If something is to be done about the markets in women and children for commercial sex, the facilitators have to be weakened or removed and the inhibitors have to be strengthened.

III. TRAFFICKING IN WOMEN

The standard definition of trafficking in women emphasizes its transnational character as a *sine qua non*.

> Trafficking in women occurs when a woman in a country other than her own is exploited by another person against her will and for financial gain. The trafficking element may – cumulatively or separately – consist of: arranging legal or illegal migration from the country of origin to the country of destination; deceiving victims into prostitution once in the country of destination; or enforcing victims' exploitation through violence, threat of violence, or other forms of coercion. One trend in trafficking in women ... is migrant women forced into, or forced to remain in, prostitution.[6]

Although this definition is useful and important there is another dimension to the problem – which occurs simply at the national level. This does not involve trafficking across national borders, but it involves women being taken from their home environment to another location where they are basically compelled directly (that is, through intimidation) or indirectly (through lack of feasible economic alternatives) to become involved in the sex trade. Whether the trafficking is within one nation or across borders, however, it is clear that in the vast majority of cases, most of the financial benefits accrue to others rather than the women themselves.

DIMENSIONS OF THE MARKET

Taking this extended definition, it appears that trafficking in women (and children) takes place at three distinct levels – global, regional, and national. Examples of global trafficking include the trafficking of women from Russia or Ukraine to the United States or Israel, the trafficking of women from Southeast Asia to the United States and Western Europe, and the trafficking of young Nigerian women from their home country to Italy and other states in Western Europe. Regional trafficking generally involves crossing one or two contiguous borders such as from Nepal to India or from Cambodia or Burma to Thailand. It can also involve travel between countries that, while not contiguous, are in relatively close proximity. The movement of women from Thailand to Japan very clearly falls into this category. At the national level, trafficking can involve moving women from their home town to the capital or other big cities where prostitution is more prevalent. Furthermore, once women are more or less indentured into sexual servitude they are often sold from one brothel to another, and have little or no opportunity to escape. This is frequently the case in Israel where Slavic women are passed on from "owner" to owner, a phenomenon which underlines the fact that the trafficking process can continue after the transnational component has been completed.[7]

An important question, however, concerns the extent to which these markets are integrated or remain distinct from one another. The answer is mixed: while many markets are predominantly national or regional, there are also global trafficking flows that are smaller and less systematic but that can nevertheless develop rapidly when they prove lucrative. The flow of Slavic women to the United States and to Israel is an example of regional success – trafficking from the states of the former Soviet Union to Western Europe – being extended into a global pattern. This is not surprising. Once the trafficking process goes beyond movement within national boundaries then the traffickers build or acquire expertise in immigration laws and regulations and how they are best negated. The acquisition of false documentation, for example, can be as useful for global travel as for regional. Moreover, as ethnic networks develop in a variety of countries then trafficking connections can become better established. It is not inconceivable, for example, that Slavic women who are initially trafficked to Western Europe for prostitution will subsequently be taken to the United States.

Among the countries which supply women at the global level, Thailand, Brazil, the Dominican Republic, and the Philippines are prominent. All have significant numbers of women working overseas in the sex trade. It has been estimated, for example, that (based on the number of Thai workers who overstay their visas) there are well over 23,000 Thai women staying illegally in Japan where they work as prostitutes.[8] A study has also been done of women from the Dominican Republic, about 50,000 of whom work abroad in the sex trade – mainly in Austria, Curacao, Germany, Greece, Haiti, Italy, Netherlands, Panama, Puerto Rico, Spain, Switzerland, Venezuela, and the West Indies.[9] In the case of the Dominican women, the proceeds from prostitution are used to support parents or children. For those women really concerned about providing such support, opportunities in the licit economy are very limited in a society where 80 dollars a month is the minimum salary for domestic work. Those who came to Europe traveled first to Denmark or Italy where visas were not required. The majority knew what they were involved in and were not deceived by being contracted as dancers. Significantly, however, many of those who returned to the Dominican Republic did so with mental disorders.[10]

There has also been a substantial growth in trafficking of women from Eastern Europe to Western Europe. Estimates suggest that between 200,000 and half a million women are working illegally as sex workers in the European Union.[11] In Germany 75 percent of prostitutes are believed to be foreigners, while the figure in Milan is 80 percent.[12] In Italy one study suggests that there are between 19,000 and 25,000 foreign prostitutes, approximately 2,000 of whom have been trafficked, with 70 to 80 percent of these being used for street prostitution.[13] Particularly alarming is the fact that some of the victims were as young as 14 when first brought to Italy. They were recruited by "deception, physical threats, or payments made by the women's families".[14] Nigerian women in particular are easily controlled because their families are forced to repay a huge debt, and many of them have never even attended school. Witchcraft and threats to harm their family are also used to keep them in line. Women from the former Yugoslavia and from Albania also loomed large. In Italy the number of people charged with trafficking women for sexual exploitation increased from 285 in 1990 to 737 (258 of whom were foreigners with 158 from Central and Eastern Europe and 57 from Africa including 18 from Nigeria) in 1994.[15]

The pattern in Austria is of women being trafficked mainly from Central and Eastern Europe. In Vienna, in 1990, there were 800 registered prostitutes and 2,800 illegal prostitutes; by 1995 only 670 were registered while the number of unregistered prostitutes had increased to 4,300. The number of cases of trafficking increased by six times from 1990 to 1994 (with a dip in 1993) but the number of convictions has lagged far behind. Of the 751 victims of trafficking identified in an 18 month period from January 1994 to the end of June 1995, 48 percent were from the Czech and Slovak Republics and another 16 percent were from the Dominican Republic. Most women are under 25 and many are in the 15 to 18 age range. Sentences against traffickers are light, and there have been few successful convictions.[16]

A similar picture exists elsewhere in Western Europe. Following earlier waves of trafficking involving women from Asia (Thai and Filipinas), women from the Caribbean and South America (Dominicans and Colombians) and women from Africa (Ghanaians and Nigerians), the mid-1990s witnessed a wave of trafficking from Central and Eastern Europe.[17] In the Netherlands in 1994, for example, nearly 70 percent of trafficked women were from Central and Eastern Europe.[18] In Belgium, at least 10 to 15 percent (that is 200–300) of the 2,000 foreign prostitutes are victims of trafficking.[19] Women in the former Soviet bloc are particularly vulnerable. In the Russian Federation in 1992, for example, women made up 52 percent of the labor force but 71 percent of the unemployed.[20] The vagaries of the Russian economy since then and the major economic collapse in Russia in 1998 can only exacerbate this situation and heighten the vulnerabilities of women who are looking to escape from dire economic circumstances. The lure of overseas employment makes them an easy target for agents, pimps, or organized criminals looking to diversify their activities. Moreover, from the perspective of those who control the sex trade in the destination countries it is easier and cheaper to have women brought to Western Europe from Russia and other Newly Independent States than it is to have them brought from developing countries.

Some of the markets are regional with women from Belarus, for example, involved in prostitution in the Baltic states and in Poland. Others are global. Women from Russia, Ukraine, and other parts of the former Soviet Union have been trafficked to the United States, Israel, Macao, Dubai, and Australia.[21] As far as the trafficking from Russia and Ukraine to the United States is concerned, this seems to be the second wave of women trafficking – following the earlier wave of the mid-1990s, which seemed to focus largely on the West European market. It is something that has only appeared on the policy agenda of the United States during the latter half of the 1990s – largely through the activities of the Global Survival Network – even though there were earlier, if sporadic and scattered, indicators that the phenomenon was developing and that the United States was becoming an important destination.

In short, trafficking in women is an area of activity that knows no geographic boundaries. It is also an area where accurate figures remain highly elusive. Nevertheless, enough is known to reveal that it is a significant phenomenon and one with a very substantial human cost. From the perspective of those who control and benefit from the trade, of course, these costs are irrelevant, especially when compared to the profits that can be made.

THE PROFITABILITY OF THE MARKET

Trafficking in women for prostitution is clearly something in which organized crime is involved, but prostitution itself is an activity which covers the spectrum from individual women acting independently to highly organized arrangements in which women are controlled by pimps or members of criminal enterprises. Prostitution and its control, especially at the more organized level, is also a highly lucrative business, albeit one that is very difficult to estimate with any degree of accuracy. Although there are few good assessments of either turnover or profits that are derived from the sex trade, it is clear that this market is a profitable one – for several reasons. In the first place, prostitution involves continuing enterprises with enduring if replaceable "commodities" that are consumed repeatedly rather than just once. Second, the overheads are generally low and the women themselves are usually paid a pittance, with the result that profit margins can be extremely high. Buying the women who are trafficked is a limited once off investment; the sale of their services continues to generate profits long after the initial outlays have been covered. Third, in some cases, the women can be sold to other brothel owners, providing yet another accretion of profit. Indeed, there are perhaps few other criminal activities in which the profit to cost ratio is so high.

THE DYNAMICS OF SUPPLY AND DEMAND

The supply side of the market is generated partly by poverty but also by social and economic dislocation. Where the economic and social condition of women has deteriorated, the incentives for migration are increased. This can take the form of migration from the licit to the illicit economy or migration to another country, or indeed, a combination of the two. Where opportunities in the licit economy are circumscribed and rewards are limited, the temptations for women to become involved in commercial sex increase. In some cases, this is voluntary, the result of what is in effect an economic or cost benefit calculation – albeit one based on limited, erroneous, or misleading information. In other cases, the women migrate in the hope of greater opportunity within the legal economy and once they are vulnerable, alone, and in a foreign country, are forced into prostitution. The supply side covers the spectrum from willing recruits to women who are coerced or tricked into prostitution.

The dynamics of the demand side go beyond the scope of this paper, but are certainly sufficient to generate the large profits that attract criminal organizations into the business and to encourage the emergence of a variety of intermediaries whose role is to bring the supply to where there is clear demand. Cultural and psychological factors that encourage the treatment of women as little more than objects for sexual gratification provide the underpinnings for the demand side of the global sex trade in many societies. An additional set of non-paying customers come from corrupt policemen and officials who facilitate the trafficking in return for free sexual services. From the traffickers' perspective, this is a very small price to pay for the ability to operate with a very limited level of risk.

In specific instances, of course, the demand has been related – at least in its early stages – to military bases overseas or to large scale military involvement in regional conflict. The importance of Thailand in the global sex industry, for example, is generally traced back to the late 1960s and the use of Thailand as a place for "rest and recreation" for American G.I.s in Vietnam. The recommendation by the World Bank in 1971 that Thailand develop " mass tourism" as a means to pay off its debts, encouraged what became, in effect, the peacetime institutionalization of the sex industry in Thailand.[22]

THE MARKET ACTORS[23]

Although it is tempting to see trafficking in women for commercial sex as something that is dominated and controlled by organized crime, the picture is actually rather more complex than this. There is, in fact, a wide range of participants in the trade including:

- women who through force of economic or personal circumstances decide that travel abroad to work as dances, maids, or in some cases, prostitutes is better than living in current conditions. Some of these are trafficked voluntarily but are then coerced into prostitution. In other cases the whole process is voluntary.

- women who are tricked into going abroad for work or romance and who then find themselves in a position of servitude and used for commercial sex.

- women who are coerced or forced into traveling abroad for prostitution. Such cases are involuntary at every stage. In some cases the women go and stay because of threats to their families.

- brokers and agencies who recruit the women, often using false promises of employment.

- criminal organizations which either engage in the trafficking directly or facilitate the trafficking for the agencies and entrepreneurs involved.

- corrupt officials who assist in provision of passports, visas, work permits, and any other documentation that is required.

- brothel owners and criminal groups who pay the suppliers and initially put the women to work.

- "guards" who help to ensure that the women do not escape and inflict punishment in the event they try. These can range from the men who provide muscle for organized crime to Nigerian "mamas" who are often associated with forms of witchcraft and exercise psychological rather than physical control.

- additional brothel owners to whom women are sold as part of a constant process of turnover.

- corrupt policemen and officials who take payoffs – in money or in kind – for turning a blind eye to the sex trade in their jurisdiction.

- politicians who provide protection for the criminal organizations and brothel owners who control the sex trade in their constituencies.

- governments which place a premium on development through tourism and tacitly condone prostitution and trafficking in women as essential to the continued dynamism of the tourist industry.

This brief overview of the market actors suggests that the process is best understood not in terms of a few dominant syndicates, but in terms of a mixed market with a variety of actors who form networks of convenience for trafficking and networks of corruption to protect both the trafficking and the prostitution. Trafficking not only goes through a variety of stages but is made possible by the connivance, corruption, and collusion of authorities in source, transshipment, and destination countries.

FACILITATORS AND INHIBITORS

For the criminal organizations and the various intermediaries involved in the market this is generally a low risk activity. Penalties for participation in the trafficking of women are often minimal and sometimes nonexistent. In many cases there is no legal framework within which efforts to counter trafficking can be based, while there is often a lack of law enforcement concern, partly because of the continued myth that prostitution and other forms of commercial sex are victimless crimes. Even when there are efforts to do something about the problem, the women are often afraid to testify against those who have been exploiting and abusing them – a reluctance that is even greater in those societies where the women are treated as the perpetrators rather than as the victims of crime. Moreover, this is not an area of law enforcement activity that is driven by need for spectacular successes in terms of interdiction or buy and bust. For transit and destination countries, those who are being trafficked are foreigners and the problems are not seen as having any impact on one's own citizens. As suggested above, few traffickers ever go to court and fewer still are convicted. When set against the financial incentives from participation in women trafficking and control of prostitution the limited risk or cost typically imposed by law enforcement means that this is an area of criminal activity where there are many facilitators and few inhibitors.

ATTACKING THE MARKET AND CREATING MARKET BARRIERS

There are signs, however, that governments are moving towards a more concerted and vigorous campaign to combat trafficking in women. President Clinton – partly in response to a *New York Times* article on trafficking in women from Ukraine – on March 11, 1998, issued a

Presidential Directive on Steps to Combat Violence against Women and Trafficking in Women and Girls. Among the measures envisaged were greater efforts to protect victims, partnership with non-governmental groups, more effective use of criminal law, enhanced cooperation with source, transit, and destination countries, and public awareness campaigns.

The European Union has also been looking at this issue for several years and, in 1997, the Council of the European Union announced a Joint Action to combat trafficking in women and the commercial exploitation of children. Complementing these national efforts, the United States and the European Union have also started to develop a joint approach at various levels including education. Working closely with the International Organization for Migration, the United States and the European Union initiated an educational campaign in Ukraine that was carefully targeted at those women determined to be most at risk.[24]

While such measures are welcome, cooperation needs to be more extensive. The issue is now firmly on the policy agenda of discussion between the United States and Russia and there have been helpful exchanges of information and ideas for policy development and innovation. Nevertheless, it is difficult to escape the conclusion that this issue needs a much more innovative and comprehensive approach with sustained and systematic multilateral cooperation among sender, transit and recipient countries. It also requires increased resource allocations to underpin and consolidate such cooperation. Indeed, containing, let alone reducing trafficking in women is not something that will be accomplished quickly or easily unless governments start to pursue much more focused and effective policies that fundamentally alter the existing balance between facilitators and inhibitors by introducing greater costs, risks and difficulties into the market. The inhibitors have to be increased significantly. With this in mind, the major components of a market based response include:

- The creation of market barriers at all stages – supply, trafficking, and demand. At the supply level, this can be done through large scale education programs that alert women to the dangers. In terms of trafficking, greater efforts can be made at interdiction through better intelligence, greater awareness among officials, and sting operations. It is essential to attack both the major players and the support structures. In addition, at the demand stage, the customers should also be subject to legal action. Such activities, some of which are in place, need to be used more extensively and with greater vigor. This will help to disrupt existing markets by increasing risks and costs for the trafficking organizations, the intermediaries, the facilitators and the customers, while also retarding the development of new markets.

- Seize the commodities – which, in this case, means rescuing the victims and changing their incentive structure. It is critical to recognize that the women are being treated as commodities and as such need to be removed from the market. This should be done not by treating them as perpetrators of crimes but through the provision of expanded witness protection and special care programs that change their incentives and encourage cooperation with law enforcement. The Clinton initiatives go some way in this direction, but similar measures need to be initiated by a variety of other countries.

- Create public-private partnerships for the care and protection of trafficked women. NGOs, especially women's organizations in a wide variety of countries have considerable skill and experience in this area and could provide important advice and support for governments as they seek to develop more effective measures. Important steps have been taken in this direction, but much more needs to be done.

- Make the trafficking process more difficult through more careful scrutiny of immigration or tourist applications and by tightening visa requirements. Destination countries, especially those in the European Union, need stricter visa requirements on certain categories of workers such as "dancers' and artists.[25] At the same time, greater emphasis needs to be placed on identifying false documents and on suppressing the corrupt activities of officials who are willing to issue real documents for appropriate payment. Attacking the support apparatus is an indispensable component of an attack on the market.

- Introduce risk into the market through legal changes, more effective law enforcement and the imposition of tougher penalties. In many criminal codes, trafficking in women is not given the seriousness it warrants.[26] Some countries have no specific laws against trafficking in women while such trafficking is merely a misdemeanor in other states. Even in several West European countries, which supposedly take the problem seriously, the maximum penalties for trafficking in women involve no more than a few years in jail. Specific legal definitions of trafficking for commercial sexual exploitation need to be developed in substantive laws at the domestic level, while there is also a strong case for strengthening and modernizing international legal instruments. Without changes in the legal framework the entrepreneurs, criminals, corrupt officials, and other beneficiaries of trafficking in women will continue to make considerable profit while incurring little or no risk. If the risk component is to be significantly increased, however, legal measures have to be accompanied by more effective and focused policing and the imposition of tougher penalties. As well as meaningful jail sentences for trafficking, control of prostitution should be made a predicate offence for money laundering and also be subject to asset forfeiture. The money thereby obtained could appropriately be used to assist victims of trafficking. In short, human commodity trafficking has to be treated with at least the same seriousness as drug trafficking and given penalties that reflect the fact that this crime involves fundamental and flagrant violations of human rights.

TRAFFICKING IN CHILDREN AND CHILD PROSTITUTION

An even more emotive and difficult issue than the trafficking and sexual exploitation of women is the commercial sexual exploitation of children. Defined as "... the sexual exploitation of a child for remuneration in cash or in kind, usually but not always organized by an intermediary (parent, family member, procurer, teacher, etc.)", child prostitution is an old phenomenon, but one that has become more salient as a result of globalization, tourism, and technological developments.[27] While there is obvious overlap with women trafficking, there are several distinctive features of this phenomenon, including the degree of exploitation, that make it worth treating as a separate problem.

SCALE OF THE MARKET

Transnational trafficking in children for commercial sex has become a global problem that merges with the issue of child prostitution as a local or domestic, rather than a cross-border activity. There is no part of the world that is truly free of these inter-connected phenomena. In the United States, for example, estimates for the number of child prostitutes range from 100,000 to 300,000.[28] In Asia, the problem is extensive, and UNICEF estimates that the number of children exploited for commercial sex is 200,000 in Thailand, over 650,000 in the Philippines and 400,000 in India.[29] The phenomenon is less extensive in Africa, although it is reportedly a growing problem in Senegal, Zimbabwe, Sudan, Kenya, Ghana, in Cote d'Ivoire, and Burkina Faso.[30] The problem is greater in Central and South America where it is inextricably connected to the problem of street children, many of whom become involved in prostitution as a matter of sheer survival. Argentina, Bolivia, Brazil, Chile, Colombia, Ecuador, Mexico, and Peru all have significant numbers of children involved in prostitution, although precise numbers in which it is possible to have a high level of confidence are difficult to obtain. In Brazil, estimates for the number of child prostitutes range from 200,000 to 500,000 revealing both the difficulty of data collection, and the extent of the problem.[31] There are also cases of children who are effectively trafficked within the country and taken from the major cities to the mining towns. Once there they are virtually held as slaves and subject to violence, torture, and killing. "And in Peru, it is estimated that about half of the one million adult prostitutes are in fact minors working with false identification cards".[32] The average age of the children is between 13 and 17, although cases of much younger children have been documented in Brazil.[33] In Chile, there is a close link between drug addiction and child prostitution: "traffickers and pimps will addict the children to inhalants such as benzene gum and glue. The children taking these inhalants are as young as nine, ten, or eleven years old. They are kept addicted".[34] The prevalence of child prostitution in Latin America is explicable partly in cultural terms with the pervasiveness of machismo and a dichotomous approach to women and girls which divides them into those who are pure and those who are soiled and thus are not worthy of being treated with respect.

While accurate global figures are not readily available, a rough accumulation of national estimates suggests that the number of child prostitutes world-wide could easily exceed five million. The number trafficked across national borders is far less, but certainly not insignificant. As one analyst has observed, "Children are increasingly sold and trafficked across frontiers – between developing and developed countries, among developing countries, and among developed countries.

The spread of child prostitution worldwide is part and parcel of the less positive aspects of globalization".[35] The main child trafficking pipelines include those from Nepal to India and from Burma to Thailand. In addition, girls and young women from India and Pakistan are frequently sold to wealthy Middle Eastern men. "Abduction, false documentation and sham marriages" are all used to facilitate this movement.[36] In many cases, organized crime controls much of the prostitution in the destination countries. Organized crime groups also participate in global trafficking, as was revealed by an episode in which a 12 year old Chinese girl was being taken to Miami via Milan – a case in which Chinese and Italian criminal organizations seemed to be heavily involved.[37]

THE MARKET DYNAMICS

The underlying dynamics that contribute to trafficking in children for commercial sex operate at the level of supply and demand. At the supply level, it is possible to identify both push and facilitating factors. Perhaps the biggest push factor is the poverty in rural areas that can lead villagers to sell their daughters and the desperation that in urban areas can draw young girls into prostitution as a means of survival. In this connection, it is worth emphasizing that the number of street children is likely to increase rather than decrease. Indeed, one consequence of the AIDS epidemic in Africa and Asia is an increase in the number of children of either gender who are orphaned, have to fend for themselves at a very early age and have few alternatives to becoming involved in prostitution. Cultural barriers to such developments are weak or nonexistent in many traditional societies where there are exploitative and demeaning attitudes towards girls and women and tolerant attitudes towards homosexual sex with young males. In other words, the supply side of the child sex trade is rooted in structural factors that are difficult to alter, at least in the short term. In addition, the ready availability of "street children", girls and boys with few skills (apart from survival skills) and little future in the licit economy, provides an enormous opportunity for those looking to position themselves as intermediaries between supply and demand by recruiting children for prostitution. The economic crisis in Asia can only fuel these opportunities as will the crisis in Russia, where there are now an estimated three million street children.[38]

At the demand level, there are five factors in particular which have contributed to the exploitation of children for commercial sex:

- the growth of global tourism including sex tourism to countries such as Thailand or Sri Lanka where child prostitutes are readily available and where, until the last few years, customers could act with a high level of impunity. As one Interpol report noted: "The incredible escalation of child prostitution over the last ten years is directly caused by the tourism trade. Child prostitution is the newest tourist attraction offered by developing countries. The parallel to this phenomenon in the Western countries is the explosion of a huge underground trade in child pornography in videos and magazines. Since laws against child prostitution are stringently enforced in most affluent countries, pornographic films and photographs often have their origin in countries where child prostitution has become a temporary escape from poverty for struggling rural people".[39]

- the prevalence in certain cultures of myths regarding the rejuvenating power of sex with virgins and young girls. Among some Chinese men this is even believed to add to their longevity. Similarly, in parts of the Middle East, the desire for young brides leads them to purchase Indian or Pakistani girls who are then forced into a life of sexual servitude.

- the spread of AIDS, which has led many men to seek younger partners for commercial sex in the belief that they are less likely to be infected. This belief, in fact, is erroneous since children are more susceptible to sexually transmitted diseases, less knowledgeable about the requirements of safe sex practices, and unable to determine the terms on which their customers have sex.

- the exploitation of computer networks by pedophiles who share photographs and experiences, and provide a ready and lucrative market for child pornography which is distinct from but closely related to trafficking and child prostitution.

- the increase in juvenile drug use. As one commentator has noted: "As more girls and boys become addicted to drugs ... more are turning to or remaining in prostitution to support habits. Others are sexually enslaved into prostituting themselves in order to feed addictions and maintain loyalty to pimps, gangs, and flesh traders".[40]

THE PROFITABILITY OF THE MARKET

Estimates for the value of the child sex industry are even more elusive than those for commercial sex in general. Nevertheless, there are once again grounds for seeing this as substantial. One reason is the inextricable connection to the tourism industry in countries such as Thailand and Sri Lanka. It has been estimated, for example, that each year as many as 50,000 Australian men participate in sex tourism, not only in Thailand and the Philippines but also in Indonesia and West Timor.[41] Another is the fact that young girls – even more obviously than trafficked women – are not in a position to make demands on those who control them, a situation that makes for minimum overheads and maximum profits. The third is that where the child sex trade is controlled and institutionalized in ways that go beyond street children acting alone, then it is possible for the procurers and brothel owners either to charge a premium or to make the children provide sex for even more customers. In practice, of course, there is also a seamless web between the various aspects of the commercial sex business, so that child prostitution is simply one branch of the broader industry.

MARKET ACTORS

The demand and supply components of the child sex market are brought together by a wide variety of intermediaries. The intermediary can be an agent who buys children in rural villages and transports them to the towns or cities where they are turned over to brothel owners who can be either individual entrepreneurs or members of criminal groups. Reportedly, "brothel owners in Chiang Rai, Chiang Mai, and the south of Thailand ... have well-established networks of agents. These people systematically target families who are undergoing economic hardship and other difficulties in order to convince them to sell their daughters for much needed cash".[42] The intermediary can also be a transnational criminal network that arranges for the children to be trafficked into countries where they then work as prostitutes for other members of the network. Although in some cases children enter prostitution as a means of survival, this is also an area in which "there are criminals at work – intermediaries, pimps, and procurers – all benefitting and profiteering from children".[43] Indeed, a 1996 United Nations report noted that sexual exploitation of children "is a highly profitable business. It involves both *ad hoc* or individual "entrepreneurs" and international profiteers using systematic methods of recruitment within a highly organized syndicated network, which is often also involved in other criminal activities such as drug dealing".[44] Moreover, as with trafficking in women, there is considerable connivance, corruption, and collusion on the part of officials, and police. Ladda Saikaew of the Development and Education Program for Daughters and Communities (DEP), a non-governmental organization working in Thailand, has neatly encapsulated the extensive distribution of benefits from the exploitation of children for commercial sex, in what she terms "the exploitation spiral".[45] The direct beneficiaries are able to act with support and with a minimum of risk because of the indirect beneficiaries.

FACILITATORS AND INHIBITORS

In many cultures, child sex abuse and the commercial sex trade in children are wholly abhorrent. In some countries, however, there is a far greater level of tolerance. The resulting asymmetries in what is or is not permissible behavior, the desire of developing countries to attract tourists, and the desire of potential consumers of child sex to move beyond the moral restrictions and legal prohibitions of their own communities, have all contributed to the growth in trafficking children, in child prostitution and in child sex tourism. Even where government and business have not encouraged sex tourism there has been astonishing indifference to the plight of children and a failure to develop serious inhibitors on the child sex trade. In fact, this is an area where it has been the work of NGOs such as End Child Prostitution in Asian Tourism (ECPAT) that has been critical in placing the issue on the international agenda. The United Nations has also tried to come at the problem from a variety of angles including international conventions on labor and an emphasis on the rights of the child. It is only in recent years, however, that there has been a serious international effort to change the balance between facilitators and inhibitors and an attempt to create effective and enduring market barriers to child prostitution and trafficking in children for commercial sex. The steps that have been taken in this connection are the theme of the next section.

ATTACKING THE MARKET

The response of the international community to the issue of child prostitution *per se* is relatively recent. As mentioned above, international efforts to deal with prostitution more generally date back to the beginning of the twentieth century and the concerns over the white slave trade. More specifically, an international convention in 1922 was designed to suppress trafficking in both women and children. For its part, the International Labor Organization (ILO) has exerted pressure for international legislation against forced labor, something that also covers child prostitution. The Forced Labor Convention (No. 29) of 1930, and the Abolition of Forced Labor Convention (No. 105) deal with child prostitution as part of the broader issue of forced labor. Another important international instrument targeting sexual exploitation was the 1949 Convention on the Suppression of Traffic in Persons and of the Exploitation of the Prostitution of Others. This document targeted those who procured and exploited prostitutes rather than the prostitutes themselves. The 1979 Convention on the Elimination of All Forms of Discrimination Against Women provides in Article 6 that signatories "shall take all appropriate measures, including legislation, to suppress all forms of traffic in women and exploitation of prostitution of women". The 1959 United Nations Declaration on the Rights of the Child and the 1989 Convention on the Rights of the Child focused specifically on children and how they should and should not be treated. Article 34 of the convention required the adherents to "undertake to protect the child from all forms of sexual exploitation and sexual abuse. For these purposes, States shall in particular take all appropriate national, bilateral, and multilateral measures to prevent: a) the inducement or coercion of a child to engage in any unlawful sexual activity; b) the exploitative use of children in prostitution or other unlawful sexual practices ... ". Taken together, these measures established an international legal and normative framework against the exploitation of children including sexual exploitation.

As with most international conventions, however, there has been a major gap between aspiration and achievement. The international norms and standards enshrined in these declarations and conventions have been far less effective than desired. Even when states have acceded to them there has been insufficient or ineffective monitoring of the problem while national implementation has been sporadic, uneven, and incomplete. This is not to deny that there has been some progress. Positive developments to combat trafficking in children include:

- the work of the Non-Governmental Organization, End Child Prostitution in Asian Tourism (ECPAT) which was established in

1991 by welfare groups in Thailand, Taiwan, Sri Lanka, and the Philippines. ECPAT has done a great deal both to focus attention on the problem and to pressure states to pass legislation dealing with extra-territorial child sex abuse.

- the Tourist Code adopted in 1985 by the World Tourism Organization. The code exhorted both tourist professionals and tourists themselves to refrain from exploiting others for prostitution purposes, although once again the degree of responsiveness and peer pressure has been offset by the direct or indirect benefits to the tourist trade from sexual exploitation of children and sex tourism more generally.

- the creation by Interpol in 1992 of a Standing Working Party on Offenses Committed against Minors. In 1993, Interpol established sub-groups to look into the issues of law enforcement, legislation on child prostitution, international cooperation, liaison networks, sex tourism, victim assistance, police structures, missing children, free telephone help-lines, prevention models, training, research, and statistics. The Working Party has met regularly since then and in March 1998 published a Handbook on Good Practice for Specialist Officers Dealing with Crimes against Children, providing advice on all aspects of investigating sexual crimes against children. Interpol has also developed a close working relationship with ECPAT.

- regional and bilateral initiatives. These include the 1987 African Charter on the Rights of the Child, which called for protection of children from various forms of exploitation. Similarly, the Council of Europe in 1991 adopted the Recommendation on Sexual Exploitation, Pornography and Prostitution of and Trafficking of Children and Young Adults, emphasizing the need for information and educational campaigns, data collection, interaction with travel agencies, accession to international instruments, expansion of national jurisdiction to cover the misdeeds of nationals abroad, exchange of information, and more research on the link between the sex industry and organized crime.

- the fact that more and more countries are criminalizing sexual abuse of children by their citizens while overseas. In addition, some of the countries in which sex tourism is most rampant have began to adopt a more punitive approach, if on a somewhat selective basis. Thailand in 1996 sentenced a German citizen to 43 years while the Philippines sentenced an Australian to 17 years imprisonment for child sex abuse. More recently, Thailand jailed a British citizen for sexual involvement with a child. It is far from clear, however, that these cases go beyond demonstrative show trials designed to deflect international criticism rather than a sustained commitment to breaking the child sex tourism nexus. Consequently, although these cases suggest that some risk for customers is being introduced into the market much more has to be done in this area. Laws need to be developed or tightened up and more severe penalties imposed. In addition, both more punitive laws and successful prosecutions should also be given maximum publicity, especially where they send a message that traditionally permissive societies are no longer willing to tolerate the exploitation of children for commercial sex.

- the growing emphasis by the United Nations on practical actions to implement the international legal framework that is already in place. A Program of Action for the Prevention of the Sale of Children, Child Prostitution, and Child Pornography was adopted by the United Nations Commission on Human Rights in 1992. The Program called for better law enforcement and more cooperation between key organizations such as Interpol and United Nations and its various agencies. It also included an international information campaign and educational measures to raise awareness of the issue; alternative educational programs for street children; and various forms of development assistance. More recently, an Interim UN Report in 1996 emphasized not further commitment by states but the ways in which existing commitment could be translated into effective actions designed both to "stop the supply and eliminate the demand".[46] This required both substantive laws making child prostitution and child pornography criminal offenses and the introduction of procedural provisions to protect children during criminal proceedings.[47] The media, education, and criminal justice systems were identified as the three catalysts for responding to commercial sexual exploitation of children.[48] In terms of criminal justice and law enforcement, considerable emphasis was placed on the need for enhancing national capabilities to deal with the problem. Priority was also to be given to international cooperation, ranging from information sharing, and synchronization of national laws to "arrangements by which abusers in a foreign country may be subject to prosecution either where the offense took place or in the country of the offender. This could be done either through extradition or expansion of jurisdiction through extraterritoriality".[49]

- the convocation in Stockholm in 1996 of the First World Congress Against the Commercial Sexual Exploitation of Children. Attended by over 1,300 participants from 125 countries the Congress (which resulted from an initiative by ECPAT) brought together governments, inter-governmental organizations, and NGOs. It also formulated a Declaration and Agenda for Action that provided guidelines for specific initiatives at the local, national, regional, and international levels. The agenda included the development and implementation not only of "comprehensive, cross-sectoral and integrated strategies and measures" but also of monitoring mechanisms.[50] Among the principles to guide the development of these strategies the Congress emphasized: the participation of the children themselves; the need for prevention through education and the creation of early-warning systems; the protection of children through more effective laws against child trafficking, child pornography as well as the provision of hotlines, mobile services and shelters; the recovery and reintegration of children; the collection and diffusion of information regarding all aspects of the problem and appropriate responses; and international cooperation at all levels.[51]

All these developments are very positive. Yet much remains to be done if serious and effective market barriers are to be created. In this connection, emphasis should be placed on enhancing national capabilities through more effective and punitive laws and more effective policing of laws already in place. Measures should include increased undercover and sting operations that would introduce far greater risk into the market whether the market operates through the internet or more traditional means. Furthermore, asset forfeiture should be applied to traffickers in children even more vigorously than to drug traffickers. The money thereby obtained could be used to make provision for the treatment and re-integration of children. Similarly, stricter codes of conduct in the tourism industry are essential. Although UNICEF has been working with the World Tourism Organization, The United Federation of Travel Agents, and the Hotel and Tourism Branch of the International Labor Organization, and some progress has been made, the overall impact has been modest. Self-regulation has clearly not worked. Consequently, governments and law enforcement agencies should become more active and interventionist in this area rather than allowing the industry to police itself. More extensive use by more countries of the extra-territorial application of laws against child sexual exploitation is also essential.

In sum, the scale of the problem requires a concerted and comprehensive program in which the emphasis is placed firmly on implementation and in which more explicit efforts are made to attack the market in all its dimensions. The vigor with which these measures will be pursued, however, remains uncertain. Trafficking in women and children has created considerable vested interests not only on the part of criminal organizations but also corrupt politicians, officials, and law enforcement personnel who benefit either directly or indirectly from what can only be described as human commodity trafficking. If what is rightly described as a modern form of slavery is to be abolished then not only do more effective market barriers have to be created and maintained but the support structure also has to be dismantled.

NOTES

1. Mary Ann Irwin, "'White Slavery' As Metaphor: Anatomy of a Moral Panic", on http://www.sfsu.edu/~hsa/ex-post-facto/wslavery.html.
2. Edward J. Bristow, *Prostitution and Prejudice: The Jewish Fight Against White Slavery 1870–1939* (New York: Schocken Books, 1983) p.118.
3. See the analysis in *Ibid.* for a fuller discussion of these destinations.
4. The Hamburg-Jewish Committee Against White Slavery quoted in *Ibid*, p.124.
5. *Ibid.* p.124.
6. *Trafficking and Prostitution: the Growing Exploitation of Migrant Women from Central and Eastern Europe* (Geneva: International Organization for Migration, May 1995), p.7.
7. This emerged very clearly in "Girls for Sale" *ABC Prime Time Live*, March 18, 1998.
8. See the analysis of Thailand by Pasuk Phongpaichit elsewhere in this volume.
9. *Trafficking in Women from the Dominican Republic for Sexual Exploitation* (Geneva: International Organization for Migration, June 1996).
10. *Ibid.*
11. Mugur Gabriel Stet, "Europe-women: Social Measures Urged to End Women Trafficking", *Inter Press Service English News Wire*, June 17, 1996.
12. *Ibid.*
13. *Trafficking in Women to Italy For Sexual Exploitation* (Geneva: International Organization for Migration, June 1996).
14. *Ibid.*
15. *Ibid.*
16. *Trafficking in Women to Austria for Sexual Exploitation* (Geneva: International Organization for Migration, June 1996).
17. *Trafficking and Prostitution: The Growing Exploitation of Migrant Women From Central and Eastern Europe*, p.8.

18. *Ibid.* p.4.
19. *Ibid.* p.12.
20. *Ibid.* p.12.
21. Victoria Pope, "Trafficking in Women", *U.S. News and World Report*, April 7 1997, pp.38–44.
22. For a brief but useful discussion of Thailand see R. Barri Flowers, *The Prostitution of Women and Girls* (Jefferson, North Carolina: McFarland, 1998), p.166. The discussion is part of a broader survey of countries that are particularly important in the sex trade. See pp.165–175.
23. This section draws heavily on the author's editorial overview in *Trends in Organized Crime* Vol.3 No.4 (Summer 1998), pp.3–9.
24. *Information Campaign against Trafficking in Women from Ukraine: Project Report* (Geneva: IOM, 1998).
25. *Trafficking and Prostitution: The Growing Exploitation of Migrant Women From Central and Eastern Europe*, p.35.
26. This point is made repeatedly in the IOM studies.
27. Quoted in Vitit Muntarbhorn, "International Perspectives and Child Prostitution in Asia" in *Forced Labor: The Prostitution of Children* (Washington D.C.: U.S. Department of Labor, 1996), p.9.
28. Joseph Kennedy II in "Keynote Address" in *Ibid.* places the figure at 100,000. The higher figure is estimated by UNICEF and quoted in "Fighting the Child Sex Trade" *World Press Review* (November 1996), p.6.
29. Quoted in "Fighting the Child Sex Trade" *Ibid.* pp.6–7.
30. Muntarbhorn, *op.cit.*, p.24.
31. Jack Epstein, "Maybe the Worst in the World", *World Press Review* (Nov. 1996), p.10 reproduced from *Globe and Mail*, August 26, 1996.
32. Dorianne Beyer, "Child Prostitution in Latin America" in *Forced Labor: The Prostitution of Children* (Washington D.C.: U.S. Department of Labor, 1996), p.32.
33. *Ibid.*
34. *Ibid.* p.35.
35. Muntarbhorn, p.9.
36. *Ibid.* p.12.
37. "Chinese Girl Blows Lid on Global Child Sex Ring", *BBC News*, November 7, 1997.
38. Street kid numbers soar in Russia" Moscow, *AFP*, Dec. 16, 1998.
39. "The International Law Enforcement Response against Child Sexual Exploitation" Appendix A in *Forced Labor: The Prostitution of Children*, p.87.
40. Flowers, p.184.
41. See "Sexual Exploitation in Australia", Coalition against Trafficking in Women (Summer 1993). A copy of the report can be found at www.uri.edu/artsci/wms/hughes/catw/catw.htm.
42. Ladda Saikaew, "A Non-Governmental Organization Perspective" in *Forced Labor*, p.65.
43. Muntarbhorn, p.11.
44. *Sale of Children Child Prostitution, and Child Pornography. Note by the Secretary-General*, General Assembly Document, Fifty-first session, Agenda item 106, A/51/456/ (Oct, 7,1996), p.5 hereafter cited as *Sale of Children*.
45. Saikaew, p.71.
46. *Sale of Children*, p.11.
47. *Ibid.* p.13.
48. *Ibid.* p.16.
49. *Ibid.* p.24.
50. World Congress Against the Commercial Sexual Exploitation of Children, pp.27–31, August 1996, Stockholm Sweden: The Report of the Rapporteur-General, Prof Vitit Muntarbhorn, p.4.
51. *Ibid.* pp.14–21.

Child Pornography in the Digital Age

ANNA GRANT
FIONA DAVID
PETER GRABOSKY

INTRODUCTION

The rapid development of sophisticated and affordable computers and the increased accessibility of global telecommunications networks have revolutionized the manner in which information is transferred around the world. While the benefits of the global information exchange are enormous, attention has been drawn to the dangers of the free flow of certain material that has traditionally been the subject of control by law enforcement and customs authorities.

As the twentieth century draws to a close, few public issues rival child pornography in their capacity to arouse public indignation. Although child pornography has been around for some time, only recently has it risen to prominence on the policy agenda in western industrial societies. Explanations for the recent emergence of child pornography as a subject of public and official concern are diverse. Followers of Durkheim might suggest that the end of the Cold War, and the personal insecurities which accompany life in an era of rapid globalization, have necessitated a search for new demons. The specification of negative referents, of which child pornography constitutes an archetype, helps bolster social solidarity amongst those members of society who would like to regard themselves as relatively virtuous. Opponents of sexual explicitness in general may select child pornography as the most objectionable form of sexually explicit content, and thus the softest target in a campaign to increase censorship of public expressions of sexuality. Others may see the success of feminism in making the personal political, finally giving a voice to child victims of sexual abuse.

More concretely, the growing recognition that certain forms of premature sexual activity can have lasting harmful effects on a child has made depictions of such activity increasingly objectionable, since these depictions may themselves constitute *prima facie* evidence of abusive behavior, or may indicate risk of such behavior at some time in the future. This increasing attribution of harm is reflected in the position advanced by a number of policy entrepreneurs, both at the grass roots and in government, who have tenaciously carried the issue forward. Horrific instances of child sexual abuse, such as the notorious Dutroux case in Belgium, have provided further momentum. The convening of the World Congress Against the Commercial Sexual Exploitation of Children in 1996 focused world attention on child pornography among other forms of child sexual abuse, elevating the issue even higher on the policy agenda of many jurisdictions.

Among the most significant developments impacting on the issue of child pornography are those in telecommunications and computing technology. These have markedly facilitated the production and reproduction of child pornography, and greatly assist in concealing this activity from the attention of law enforcement or other adversary interests. Even more dramatic is the manner in which these technologies permit the dissemination of the content in question almost instantaneously to many recipients, over vast distances.

This article explores the issue of child pornography as it has been transformed by new technologies. Following a discussion of definitional issues, we turn to an overview of contemporary manifestations of child pornography, particularly its transnational dimension. We then review some of the counter-measures that are being mobilized against child pornography in the digital age, and indicate what the most appropriate configuration of these countermeasures might entail, in both domestic and transnational contexts.

DEFINITIONAL ISSUES

Public discourse on child pornography is afflicted by extreme definitional ambiguity. Precisely what child pornography is, and what it is not, might not be explicitly defined in a given jurisdiction. Moreover, definitional boundaries may expand or contract over time, depending upon evolving social and political values. And they can vary significantly across jurisdictions. Without embarking upon an exhaustive inventory of legislation relating to child pornography, it might be useful to explore some of its definitional properties. Among the parameters of a definition of child pornography are the following:

- What type of behavior is being depicted? The narrowest definition would embrace only depictions of children engaged in explicit sexual activity. One could, however, imagine suggestive depictions of children entailing other than sexually explicit behavior. To some observers, there is a significant difference between pornography and erotica; to others, not.

- Who is a child? In some cultures, the attainment of adulthood is marked by a ritual, such as marriage, or death of the head of the family, rather than the attainment of a certain chronological age. In other cultures, adulthood is a legal concept, defined by the legislature of the particular jurisdiction. The legal age of consent for consensual sexual activity varies significantly around the world, as does the age of consent for participation in depictions of sexual conduct, whether implicit or explicit. Children's physical characteristics also differ significantly. Definitions of prohibited material may be based on the actual age of the person in the depiction, or on the person's apparent age.

- Do the depictions record actual, or imaginary behavior? In addition to considerations of apparent age, child pornography might be produced without the involvement of children, or indeed, of any other person. Photographic images can be enhanced or altered in a manner which gives the appearance of child subjects. In reality, the image might be created *ex nihilo* (as is the case with cartoons) or transformed by technical means (the colloquial term for this is "morphing"). Verbal depictions can be based on fact, or on fantasy; as is the case with pictorial images, it is not always possible to determine whether the product is fictional or real.

- What is the intended effect of the material on its consumer(s)? In some jurisdictions, the definition of child pornography might be based in part on the intended use of the material. Erotic (but not sexually explicit) depictions of children often appear in art or in commercial advertising. Indeed, what is regarded as erotic will vary over time and space, and from one individual to another.

In some jurisdictions mere advocacy of sex with children may be defined as child pornography. The point at which public advocacy of, for example, the lowering of the age of consent, moves from political speech to criminal conduct might not always be clear.[1]

Some jurisdictions seek to get around these difficulties by defining child pornography rather broadly, including a subjective element, and trusting in the discretionary processes of the criminal justice system to do the right thing. For example, the Australian National Classification Code refers to publications, films and computer games that:

(a) describe, depict, express, or otherwise deal with matters of sex, drug misuse or addiction, crime, cruelty, violence, or revolting or abhorrent phenomena in such a way that they offend against the standards of morality, decency and propriety generally accepted by reasonable adults to the extent that they should not be classified; or

(b) describe or depict in a way that is likely to cause offence to a reasonable adult, a minor who is, or who appears to be, under 16 (whether the minor is engaged in sexual activity or not); or promote, incite or instruct in matters of crime or violence.

According to the law of the Australian State of Victoria, child pornography:

> means a film, photograph, publication, or computer game that describes or depicts a person who is, or who looks like, a minor under 16 engaging in sexual activity or depicted in an indecent manner or context (Crimes Act, 67A).

The Criminal Code of Canada (163.1 (1)) specifies:

(a) photographic, film, video, or other visual representation, whether or not it was made by electronic or mechanical means,

    (i) that shows a person who is or is depicted as being under the age of eighteen years and is engaged in or is depicted as engaged in explicit sexual activity, or

    (ii) the dominant characteristic of which is the depiction, for a sexual purpose, of a sexual organ or the anal region of a person under the age of eighteen years; or

(b) any written material or visual representation that advocates or counsels sexual activity with a person under the age of eighteen years that would be an offence under this Act.

By contrast, U.S. federal law (18 U.S.C. Sec. 2252 (a) (1)) is more narrowly drawn, to include visual depictions if:

1. the producing of such visual depiction involves the use of a minor engaging in sexually explicit conduct; and

2. such visual depiction is of such conduct

Child pornography was defined by World Congress Against Commercial Sexual Exploitation of Children (1996) as:

> ... any visual or audio material which uses children in a sexual context. It consists of the visual depiction of a child engaged in explicit sexual conduct, real or simulated, or the lewd exhibition of the genitals intended for the sexual gratification of the user, and involves the production, distribution, and/or use of such material.[2]

Despite the efforts to arrive at a modicum of international agreement about the definition of child pornography and how best to respond to the issue, it is clear that child pornography raises difficult questions which will not be resolved quickly. Policy makers will continue to address the issue but should do so with consideration for its many complexities. These include cross-national variations in matters relating to consent, complications of perception and reality, the relevance of context, and the importance of differing moral, religious, social, economic, and cultural factors.

The absence of a bright line which differentiates child pornography from other material is generally less of a problem within a jurisdiction, than is the case when interjurisdictional cooperation is required to interdict trans-border offending. Before we discuss the transnational dimensions of child pornography, however, it is important to explore its modern manifestations.

CHILD PORNOGRAPHY IN DIGITAL FORM

Technologies

In years past, child pornography, however defined, took the form of still photographs, films, and printed matter. The production and distribution of these materials often involved many hands. Although producers of pornography with the requisite knowledge and equipment to do their own developing and printing were less reliant on the cooperation of third parties, marketing of the material usually involved use of postal services in the case of mail-order transactions, or over-the-counter sales through "adult" bookstores. The visibility of production and sale of child pornography, whether to law enforcement directly or to third parties with the potential to cooperate with law enforcement, always remained a risk. The importation of child pornography across international frontiers risked attracting the attention of vigilant postal inspectors and customs authorities.

The advent of personal videocameras and digital photography reduced the visibility of production, and the risk that illegal material might be called to the attention of law enforcement by commercial photo developers. Moreover, new digital technologies allow child pornography to be copied, stored, and transmitted quickly and unobtrusively, and with perfect accuracy. When posted in cyberspace, it is potentially available to anyone, anywhere in the world, who has access to a personal computer and a modem. These developments, and the abundance of child pornography available in cyberspace, mean that in the fullness of time, traditional printing and photography are likely to be eclipsed by digital technology as the dominant media for the production and distribution of this material.

The introduction of digital technology has dramatically enhanced the amount of material available to those who would access child pornography, as well as the speed and privacy with which it may be accessed.

Online child pornography takes two basic and very different forms. The first is the more overt, unabashed activity occurring in Internet Relay Chat (IRC) and newsgroup facilities; the second, the covert, sophisticated activity which takes place in relative privacy.

Internet chat rooms are provided by Internet Service Providers (ISPs). These are accessible to anyone with an internet connection and the requisite software, which is freely available, if not a standard part of the service. IRC facilities exist for almost every conceivable interest, from Australian Rules Football, to Star Trek, to pre-teen sex.

These IRC facilities permit group discussion, as well as the exchange of files between participants. These files may contain text, still photographs, sound, moving pictures, or multimedia content, all in digital form. A visitor to a typical IRC room devoted to sex with children will see offers to barter or exchange explicit images, such as '3 for 1' or '2 for 1'. When an agreement is made, digital content can be sent and received almost instantaneously.

In addition to the group discussion facilities of IRC, a further degree of organization can be achieved with software called ICQ.[3] ICQ can inform a user of other specific individuals currently connected to the Internet, and can facilitate communications between them. Each user can create his or her own contact list, and as soon as one of the other specified contacts logs on to the Internet, ICQ detects the log-on and automatically announces the presence of the specified contact to others who have named him or her on their contact list. Such a facility can be used to create networks of like-minded individuals.

In addition to the above facilities, the World Wide Web contains many websites devoted to child sex. Content may include political advocacy, vocabularies of extenuation, images of varying degrees of explicitness, and links to sites providing information relating to technologies of anonymity and encryption.

In contrast to the overt and unabashed use of IRC facilities for the exchange of materials, further exchange occurs on a more discreet basis using the more private Internet technologies. Private bulletin boards involving access control and requiring authentication limit participation to those in possession of a valid password, thereby excluding uninvited visitors. Technologies of pseudonymity and anonymity permit one to create a false identity, or otherwise to conceal one's identity altogether.

Technologies of encryption permit one to conceal the content of communications, including digital images, by converting it to unintelligible form using a mathematical algorithm or "key". Only persons in possession of the key are able to decrypt the content to an intelligible form. Anonymous remailers are services which take incoming messages and remove the source address, assign an anonymous identification code number with the remailer's address, and forward the message to the final destination. Responses can be similarly modified and the respondent likewise remains anonymous. These methods provide perpetrators with a substantial degree of security. The use of sophisticated technology is by no means limited to traffickers in child pornography, and may be applied to communications in furtherance of criminal conspiracies generally, both domestic and transnational.[4]

Commercial Aspects

In the past, commercially produced child pornography filled a niche market. A small industry that exported products around the world existed in Northern Europe during the 1960s. As governments around the world began to introduce restrictions on child pornography, the democratization of technology described above facilitated widespread amateur production and dissemination of the material. A considerable proportion of the material that is presently circulating is either home-made or recycled. Needless to say, producers of illegal material would be disinclined to assert copyright. The majority of material currently available appears to be distributed in the main through an exchange system which is considerably decentralized, and without any commercial motive. Although contemporary trade in child pornography appears to be driven largely by personal rather than profit motives, the development of electronic payments systems via the Internet may one day see an increase in the proportion of these exchanges which involve some form of cash transaction.

Volume

As we have observed, traditional forms of child pornography were obtainable by mail order, or from "adult" bookstores, by trusted clients. Even then, transactions were of such low visibility that they tended to defy quantification. Statistics on sales volume and turnover were scarce or nonexistent, and statistics on seizures tended to reflect official vigilance and law enforcement priorities rather than the actual extent of targeted behavior. Today, given that a significant amount of material is exchanged or bartered, rather than distributed in the course of a formal cash transaction, the volume of child pornography circulating around the world is difficult, if not impossible, to quantify. One could seek to analyze the volume and activity of IRC or WWW sites ostensibly dedicated to child pornography, but such analyses would ignore the presumably significant volume of traffic which occurs through private channels.

The challenge of quantification is also compounded by definitional problems noted earlier. Of that content which is publicly accessible on the Internet or World Wide Web, what is deemed to be criminal in one jurisdiction might be quite legal in another.

The "market" for Internet child pornography today appears considerably decentralized. While most content appears to originate in the United States and Western Europe, production appears to be amateur and small scale. The "home made" nature of much content was noted above. Given the availability of abundant material for free or for barter, there does not appear to be much in the way of conventional commerce. The more overt manifestations of internet child pornography entail a modicum of organization, as required by the infrastructure of IRC and WWW, but the activity appears largely confined to individuals.

By contrast, some of the less publicly visible traffic in child pornography activity appears to entail a greater degree of organization. Although knowledge is confined to that conduct which has been the target of successful police investigation, there appear to have been a number of networks that extend cross-nationally, use sophisticated technologies of concealment, and entail a significant degree of coordination.

Illustrative of such activity was the Wonderland Club, an international network with members in at least 14 nations ranging from Europe, to North America, to Australia. Access to the group was password protected, and content was encrypted. Police investigation of the activity, codenamed "Operation Cathedral" resulted in approximately 100 arrests, and the seizure of over 100,000 images in September 1998.

Two years prior, an investigation revealed The Orchid Club, a network with members in the United States, Australia, Canada, and Finland. Participants were alleged to have engaged in real time photography of children in sexually explicit poses, and transmission online in an interactive session with other network members. Access to this network was also private, subject to authentication by special password.[5]

RESPONSES TO CHILD PORNOGRAPHY

As we have noted, the suppression of child pornography has become more difficult due to technological changes. The production, storage, transmission, and retrieval of objectionable material can now occur with unprecedented speed and low visibility. The challenge these new developments pose for law enforcement agencies around the world is formidable. These developments in technology mean that the identification and investigation of child pornography offenses is becoming increasingly difficult and appears to exceed the capacity of law enforcement alone to control. With content originating in and accessible to locations anywhere around the world, the challenge is also a global one.

The following section looks at various means of controlling internet child pornography. Depending on the context, the location, and the level of visibility of the conduct in question, control strategies will involve a combination of effort by law enforcement, concerned citizens, and the online services industry.

Law Enforcement

The overt use of the Internet for the dissemination of child pornography is perhaps most amenable to control.[6] The most nonchalant and unabashed participants appear to make little effort to conceal their identity. By contrast, law enforcement agents are easily able to acquire a covert internet alias, and impersonate members of the general public. They may also use ICQ software to monitor the behavior of suspects. A suspect who joins a chat room can often be identified through an electronic (Internet Protocol or IP) address, accessible with readily available tools such as "Sam Spade" or other "digger engine" software that can be downloaded by anyone free of charge.[7] Other software can be purpose-built by law enforcement agencies. Based on these data, the suspect's name and physical address can usually be obtained from a cooperating service provider, either voluntarily, or pursuant to a judicial order, depending upon the law of the jurisdiction in question. A search warrant can then be obtained and executed on the suspect's physical premises.

The global nature of cyberspace means that law enforcement authorities in a given jurisdiction who are looking for illegal activity in publicly accessible internet sites will encounter suspects whose actual physical location might be anywhere in the world. The proportion of suspects residing in Tasmania, for example, will be extremely small. Tasmanian authorities, moreover, have no jurisdiction over the vast majority of internet illegality originating elsewhere.

On-line investigation of illegal content, of whatever form, is an extremely resource intensive and costly undertaking. Rather than invest massively in "surfing" cyberspace in search of child pornography which might originate within one's own jurisdiction, law enforcement agencies around the world are more likely to commit a modest amount of resources to this end, while coordinating their efforts with those of agencies in other jurisdictions. International cooperation in law enforcement can facilitate the identification of addresses within one's own jurisdiction which have been the originators or the recipients of illegal content. Law enforcement agents who identify a suspect in a foreign state involved in crime can disclose this to those foreign authorities with jurisdiction over the matter. The strengthening of mechanisms for information sharing and coordination is likely to become a priority for law enforcement agencies around the world.

Third Parties: Citizens and Interest Groups

Citizens' groups have been extremely successful in raising public awareness of issues relating to the sexual exploitation of children, and in striving for a degree of international consensus. They vary in size and scope from those operating on a transnational basis to those whose activities are local.

ECPAT (End Child Prostitution in Asian Tourism) is a global network of organizations and individuals campaigning against the sexual exploitation of children. It played a prominent role at the 1996 World Congress Against the Commercial Sexual Exploitation of Children. The Declaration and Agenda for Action produced by the Congress was signed by over 120 nations.[8]

In individual jurisdictions, the effectiveness of law enforcement can be enhanced by enlisting the assistance of private third parties. "Electronic Neighborhood Watch" initiatives have also begun to emerge in many locations around the world. Hotlines are under development in a number of nations that permit citizens who discover online illegality to report the conduct in question to relevant authorities. These include the Cyber Tip Line, established in 1998 in the United States at the National Center for Missing and Exploited Children. A similar hotline established in the Netherlands exemplifies collaborative public-private alliances in furtherance of law enforcement. The Netherlands Hotline for Child Pornography on the Internet is a joint initiative of the ISP industry, law enforcement, and citizens' groups.[9] Similarly, the ECPAT Norway tip-off line, (children@risk.sn.no) also seeks to identify content related to the sexual exploitation of children. Other hotlines, such as that established in the United Kingdom under the auspices of the Internet Watch Foundation, are vehicles for the reporting of online illegality more generally.[10]

There are users who avail themselves of the information technology services of their workplace or educational institution for the transmission or receipt of illegal material. This activity is often visible to the institution's systems administrator, who is usually in a position to refer suspected criminal activity to law enforcement for possible further action.

Organizations such as Pedowatch provide an online information service for members of the public, the news media, and some law enforcement agencies.[11] Content includes information on misuse of the internet, and instructions for journalists and law enforcement officers wishing to investigate IRC activity. Included in the information are links to "digger engines" and other technologies that can assist in identifying the originator and/or the recipient of illegal content.

In addition to the above, some concerned citizens engage in what might be termed electronic vigilantism. Groups such as Ethical Hackers Against Pedophilia might threaten the use of techniques, often illegal, to disable the computers of those suspected of traffic in child pornography. They can use programs that cause system instability in or freeze the target computer, forcing the user to reboot.[12] Because of its questionable legality such activity is not officially encouraged.

Third Parties: The Internet industry

Internet service providers can also contribute to such a framework by facilitating the referral of relevant information to law enforcement authorities. Depending on the laws prevailing in their respective jurisdictions, ISPs themselves may be required to disclose to law enforcement agencies any criminal activity coming to their attention.[13] In some cases, ISPs might actively assist in the conduct of an investigation. Alternatively, the ISP industry might develop its own self-regulatory mechanisms. ISPs will usually incorporate basic standards of compliance as integral to their service agreement or contract.

The Internet Industry Association of Australia has been developing a Code of Practice consistent with the regulatory regime for Internet service providers established by the Telecommunications Act 1997. The draft Code seeks to balance interests of privacy versus transparency, to foster use of the Internet for legitimate purposes, and to discourage the use of the Internet for illegal activities.

The Code contains explicit provisions aimed at preventing the communication of illegal content. It notes, for example, that "Content Providers will not knowingly place illegal content on the Internet or allow illegal content to remain on the Internet." In addition, code subscriber Internet Service Providers (ISPs) are to encourage those of their users who are Content Providers to use appropriate labelling systems.

The draft Code provides for the handling of complaints from users, as well as inappropriate conduct by users and by content providers. The draft Code would further require a subscriber ISP to cancel the account of any user who repeats offending conduct after being informed that the user's conduct is a breach of the user's service conditions, including a criminal offence. In addition to the draft Code of Practice, all ISPs are bound by legal requirements to offer reasonable assistance to law enforcement agencies in the enforcement of the criminal law.

Creation of a hostile climate for persons who would engage in blatant illegal behavior is at best a partial solution. The above efforts on the part of law enforcement, concerned citizens, and the ISP industry, might suffice to discourage the casual opportunist. But service providers cannot read all subscribers' electronic mail. Private bulletin boards lie beyond the reach of the internet industry altogether. The committed trafficker of child pornography who has not already exploited technologies of anonymity and privacy can seek refuge in more covert corners of cyberspace.

Complex Criminal Investigations

The more sophisticated and organized activities involving child pornography will be less amenable to what might be described as "beat patrols" on the information superhighway. Covert and clandestine activity can be interdicted, but usually only by more aggressive investigative methods.

While there are some individuals who traffic in child pornography but who otherwise lead law abiding lives, there are many who engage in diverse forms of criminal activity, against children, against information systems, or otherwise. To the extent that a search directed at apparently unrelated criminal activity yields evidence of an offence related to child pornography, the capacity of law enforcement to operate in the darker stretches of the information superhighway will be enhanced. As internet technology becomes increasingly pervasive in modern society, computers will be found, coincidentally or otherwise, at more and more crime scenes. Whether the scope of a search warrant will enable police to seize evidence of an unrelated crime can be an important consideration in identifying incidental evidence of online child pornography.

All else being equal, the larger a criminal organization, the greater the risk that its activities will come to the attention of law enforcement. The possibility that any one participant in a criminal enterprise will make a mistake will increase with the size of the enterprise. The existence of one weak link can be exploited by law enforcement to reveal the suspect's connections with other members of the network, and thereby unravel the entire fabric.

Child pornography networks are particularly suited to this strategy of interdiction, because they rarely exist as closed systems. The demand of members for new material will lead them to seek to recruit new members and/or to acquire new materials from non-members. Either way, the risk of disclosure from mistake or detection will persist.

One investigative strategy which might be less appropriate in the direct investigation of child pornography, but which has been useful in identifying criminal pedophile activity, is that of covert facilitation or "sting" operations. The laws of some jurisdictions may preclude the use of such methods altogether. In those jurisdictions where such methods are permissible, the activity required on the part of an undercover officer in order to gain the confidence of a suspect can have serious downside consequences. There might be ethical or legal barriers to exchanging child pornography with a suspect, much less participating in "real time" abuse of children. On the other hand, law enforcement officers posing as children seeking liaisons with adults have succeeded in identifying a range of offenses, including those relating to child pornography.[14]

The emergence of the internet as the dominant medium of child pornography raises a variety of additional legal issues that are relevant to online criminality in general rather than unique to sexually explicit material. Laws drafted for photographic and print media may not be adequate in the digital age. Incriminating material in the form of electromagnetic impulses on a floppy disk might not satisfy evidentiary requirements in those jurisdictions that require evidence to be in tangible form. It might be difficult to prove possession of data stored remotely, on a server physically located in another jurisdiction, and accessed only occasionally.

Despite the formidable technological impediments to the investigation of sophisticated internet crime, there have been some noteworthy examples of successful operations against transnational child pornography networks. One of the most recent was Operation Cathedral, which targeted the aforementioned Wonderland network. Cathedral was an international operation coordinated by the British Police and their counterparts in at least thirteen other nations.

The global nature of cyberspace requires concerted international efforts to combat transnational traffic in child pornography, as well as other forms of online illegality. Especially in circumstances where child pornography entails or is accompanied by real-time abuse of children (as was the case with the Orchid Club), this would include the development of new mechanisms for international cooperation. Such initiatives might include the establishment of a network of 24 hour points of contact to facilitate rapid response to criminal activity, as proposed by the Group of Eight industrialized nations in May 1998. If, for example, law enforcement agents in country "A" become aware of real-time abuse of a child taking place in country "B" mechanisms for the immediate notification of authorities in country "B" are highly desirable.

The international child pornography network setting differs in one important respect from some other scenarios of transnational crime. In the former, the international transactions are usually consensual. That is, participants in country "X" and country "Y" are both engaged in illegal conduct against the laws of their respective countries. Each can be prosecuted "at home," without the involvement of the other nation's authorities. In the case of some other offenses which can occur across international borders, such as intrusion, theft, and fraud, the party in country "X" offends against the victim in country "Y." Here, the cooperation of authorities in both nations will usually be required in order to make a case.

Thus, where the transnational criminal activity is consensual, cooperation between respective authorities will generally be required at the investigative stage. Police who seize a suspect's address book and determine that a number of the suspect's contacts reside in foreign locations may alert the authorities in the various foreign jurisdictions of their citizens' identities and possible involvement in illegal activity. On the other hand, when the offender in one country acts against a victim in another, additional cooperation might be required downstream in the criminal process.

In any event, current arrangements for mutual legal assistance in criminal matters are slow, and sometimes cumbersome. Moreover, not all nations have entered into reciprocal arrangements with other states that would provide the basis for mutual legal assistance.

The development of fast and effective procedures for international cooperation in criminal investigations, including arrangements for expedited mutual legal assistance, is one of the challenges facing nations of the world today. This imperative is by no means unique to child pornography, but is equally applicable to matters such as terrorism, extortion, and financial crime.

CONCLUSION

Because of its emotive nature, discussions of child pornography will continue to generate as much heat as light. The convergence of a "hot-button" issue such as child sexual exploitation, high technology, and transnational reach, means that the matter of internet child pornography is destined to remain high on the public agenda in many nations around the world. It is therefore important for those who might be in a position to contribute a degree of analytical rigor to this policy issue to do just that.

While it may be impossible to come to a universally accepted definition of what child pornography is, the effort should continue, for only when a common foundation is established can there be a dual criminality basis for mutual assistance in criminal matters.

If there is any good news about child pornography, it is that it is very difficult to become an unwilling consumer. Child pornography may not be terribly difficult to find in cyberspace, but for the most part, one must know where to go looking for it. The likelihood of stumbling across it unwittingly is slim; of having it thrust upon one against one's will even more so. For those who would take special precautions, blocking and filtering software exist to prevent access to certain internet sites. The exercise of basic parental responsibility can help children stay out of harm's way in cyberspace, especially with regard to the disclosure of personal details to strangers. Until the first generation of children born in the digital age themselves enter adulthood, a degree of education for parents seems appropriate. Fortunately, the World Wide Web abounds with materials to assist parents to help their children navigate cyberspace safely.

In these efforts to control child pornography, care should be taken not to dismiss legitimate concerns about the protection of privacy and freedom of expression. The tension between these interests and those of law enforcement are likely to endure and become one of the most hotly contested issues of public policy, at least in western democracies, over the next decade. This is not to suggest that those who would subject children to torture and record the practice for posterity should be free to do so in privacy.

But those who would condemn certain forms of legitimate political expression because they object to the message, those who would intrude on private communications and censor works of art because they find them distasteful, might encounter some resistance in a world without borders. It is important to distinguish between child pornography, communications between pedophiles for the purposes of mutual support or reinforcement of beliefs and preferences, and live communication with children in an attempt to seduce them. Vague and imprecise use of the term child pornography can be seized upon to discredit legitimate efforts in furtherance of child protection.

Regardless of the conceptualization and trajectory of these policy debates, what does the future hold for internet child pornography? It seems most unlikely that the issue will fade from public view. Its continued salience will be assured by the compelling nature of children's vulnerability to sexual exploitation.

The more publicly visible areas of cyberspace will become increasingly inhospitable to those who would traffic in child pornography. Increasing knowledge and capacity on the part of law enforcement, combined with vigilance on the part of concerned citizens, and the assistance of some ISPs, will deter most casual opportunists, and drive the residual participants underground. The future of online child pornography would thus appear to lie in more private networks whose members will depend on sophisticated technology to avoid public attention. One may thus expect a continuing game of "leap-frog" in which improvements in law and technology will facilitate detection and investigation of illegality, until the adaptive sophisticated offenders discover new ways to cover their tracks. Production and distribution will remain decentralized, with markets remaining essentially non-commercial.

The global nature of cyberspace, where transactions can occur as easily between users on opposite sides of the world as between users located in the same city, will require an unprecedented degree of coordination and cooperation between law enforcement agencies. In this regard, large scale, coordinated investigations such as Operation Cathedral are likely to play a prominent role in the control of internet child pornography in the 21st century.

NOTES

Opinions expressed in this article are those of the authors and not necessarily those of the Australian Government.

1. Patrick Forde and Andrew Patterson "Pedophile Internet Activity", *Trends and Issues in Crime and Criminal Justice*, No. 97. (Canberra: Australian Institute of Criminology, 1998).
2. World Congress Against the Commercial Sexual Exploitation of Children (1996), http://www. childhub.ch/webpub/csechome/default.htm.
3. Peter Yeomans, and Vince Hole, *Child Pornography and the Internet* (Sydney: New South Wales Police Service, Child Protection Enforcement Agency, 1998).
4. Dorothy Denning, and William Baugh, *Encryption and Evolving Technologies as Tools of Organized Crime and Terrorism* (Washington D.C.: National Strategy Information Center, 1997) and Peter N. Grabosky and Russell G. Smith, *Crime in the Digital Age* (Somerset, N.J.: Transaction, 1998) chapter 10.
5. "13 to Face Charges of Child Pornography" *The Washington Post* (July 18, 1996), p.A02.
6. Paul Duke, "New Zealand Censorship Compliance Unit" Paper presented at the Australian Institute of Criminology Conference on Internet Crime, Melbourne (Feb. 16–17, 1998). < http://taz/conferences/internet/index.html#16 >.
7. http://pedowatch.org/pedo_txt.html#Investigate.
8. http://www.ecpat.org/.
9. Grabosky and Smith, *op.cit.*, p.132.
10. http://www.internetwatch.org.uk/.
11. http://pedowatch.org.
12. http://pedowatch.org/pedo txt.html.
13. Yaman Akdeniz, "Regulation of Child Pornography on the Internet: Cases and Materials related to Child Pornography on the Internet" (1998). This analysis is available online at http://www.leeds.ac.uk/law/pgs/yaman/child.htm.
14. Louis Freeh, "Child Pornography on the Internet and the Sexual Exploitation of Children", Statement Before the Senate Appropriations Subcommittee for the Departments of Commerce, Justice, and State, the Judiciary, and related Agencies (Washington, D.C.: March 10, 1998).

The Fusion of Immigration and Crime in the European Union: Problems of Cooperation and the Fight against the Trafficking in Women

PENELOPE TURNBULL

INTRODUCTION

Since the early 1990s the member states of the European Union have attempted to create a unique institutional architecture to address internal security challenges. The fusing of immigration[1] and crime issues into an "internal security continuum" has become a defining element in both institution building and substantive policy responses. This paper is concerned with the process of fusion and, in particular, its implications for future European cooperation. Fusion, it is argued, creates significant institutional and political barriers to greater cooperation and obscures the human rights and civil liberties dimensions of many migration issues. In spite of these difficulties there has been a concerted effort to advance cooperation in the case of the trafficking in women. The paper analyzes the position of this issue on the EU's internal security agenda and its links to the question of the EU's future enlargement. The nature of the EU's response to the trafficking issue will be examined, establishing whether political rhetoric has been matched by policy practice.

JUSTICE AND HOME AFFAIRS COOPERATION IN THE EUROPEAN UNION

The Fusion of Immigration and Crime Issues

The fusion of immigration and crime issues into a single justice and home Affairs policy sector has played a significant role in the development of cooperation among West European states. In particular, the consequences of the fusion for the development of institutions and the subsequent formulation of policy responses have been marked. From a historical perspective the institutionalization of justice and home affairs cooperation in Europe has clearly produced obstacles to progress. The implications of the fusion for individual residents in the EU's territory is less concrete, but of equal consequence. In the words of Bigo, "by sliding from police and immigration questions to 'internal security' issues, there is a change of paradigm which directly concerns citizen's rights, state-citizen relations, and group relations of Europeans among themselves and towards third countries".[2]

This section of the analysis identifies the origins of the fusion concept and establishes its parameters.

The contemporary linkage between policing and immigration issues and policies in the EU originates from the Community's Single Market Program. This objective was codified in the 1986 Single European Act (SEA), which included a commitment to achieve "an area without internal frontiers in which the free movement of goods, persons, services, and capital is ensured".[3] The realization of such an area of free movement was dependent upon the achievement of progress in a number of related fields. In particular, all checks on persons usually carried out at the internal frontiers would have to be relocated to the common external frontier. Accordingly a common policy on frontier controls and the crossing of the external border, governing *inter alia* immigration, asylum and visas, was required. This in itself proved a controversial undertaking for the Community's member states.[4] Despite a common trend in the immigration and asylum policies of West European states towards more restrictive practices,[5] key elements of national policies remained distinctly idiosyncratic, defined entirely by national experiences and interests. Differing interpretations of the 1951 Geneva Convention and subsequent protocols and diverse rules regulating the family unification of immigrants are but two examples of such divergence.

The free movement principle was complicated further by the introduction of a policing dimension into the emerging debate on external and internal frontier controls. In particular, it was largely unclear what the implications of the relocation of frontier controls would be for internal security in the Community. Politicians across the EC have appeared particularly adept at emphasizing the (potential) increase in transnational criminal activity resulting from implementing free movement. Indeed, the inclusion of the General Declaration on

Articles 13–19 of the SEA is taken to be indicative of a national government perception that the removal of border controls will lead to an increase in crime.[6] Law enforcement practitioners are more cautious about emphasizing an explicit link between the removal of border controls and an increase in criminal activity. They recognize that determined criminals have already evaded the restrictions imposed by frontier controls and that they will continue to do so. Despite this caution, the potential for such a scenario has been acknowledged. The Crime Committee of the British Association of Chief Police Officers reported that "the increased mobility of people had given criminals more chance to exploit gaps in the effectiveness of law enforcement".[7] A report by the Bertelsmann Foundation, co-authored by a senior Interior Ministry official and the Head of the Federal Border Guard in Germany, took the link further: it does not seem necessary to make the establishment of a criminal investigation union, an intensification of police cooperation in all areas, the speeding up and simplifying of judicial cooperation and extradition procedures, or indeed the establishment of common supranational institutions, dependent on the complete abolition of controls at common borders. These measures constitute the precondition for the abolition of border controls and not vice versa.[8]

The Bertelsmann report was in fact describing the "doctrine of compensatory measures" which has come to dominate the internal security discourse in the Community. Although the doctrine has been described as a temporary political necessity to gain political acceptance for the Single European Market,[9] it has become a permanent characteristic of the Community's developing internal security agenda. By 1997, the Justice and Home Affairs Council referred to crime as "becoming increasingly organized, making use of the free movement of goods, capital, service, and persons".[10]

In essence the doctrine covers the policies and institutions considered necessary to compensate for any potential loss of internal security resulting from the removal of internal frontier controls. The development of the doctrine of compensatory measures has had a marked impact upon the discourses of internal security within and among EU member states. Bigo has characterized this development in terms of the emergence of an "internal security continuum", which spans asylum and immigration issues to policing and terrorism issues. The tendency to fuse immigration and crime onto one continuum of internal security issues has also been facilitated by related developments. In particular, the growth in illegal immigration and unfounded claims for asylum (discussed in greater detail below) reinforces the tendency to see migration as an issue of policing and control.[11] This, in turn, coincides with an increase in particular crimes associated with ethnic minorities in western Europe. The role of transnationally organized criminal networks in the illegal trade in drugs is a clear (and widely accepted) case in point. Additionally in the case of trafficking, the International Organization for Migration acknowledges that:

another factor, which has contributed to the growth in trafficking of women from East to West, is that some of the traffickers bringing women to Western Europe before 1989 were themselves migrants from Central and Eastern Europe. It was therefore very easy for such individuals to start recruiting women from countries where they spoke the language and had local connections.[12]

FUSION IN PRACTICE:
THE PRE-HISTORY OF THE MAASTRICHT PROVISIONS

The 1991 Treaty on European Union (Maastricht Treaty) and its provisions on justice and home affairs signified a major advance in cooperation among nation states. Although the decision of the Treaty's negotiators during the 1991 Intergovernmental Conference (IGC) to institutionalize a mechanism for the development of cooperation in these areas came as a great surprise to many,[13] it was, in fact, based on a substantial history of cooperation. The importance of this history for the analysis arises from its illustration of both the gradual development of the immigration-crime fusion and the problems encountered in attempting more advanced (that is, regulated) forms of cooperation during the early years of collaboration.

The establishment of the Trevi fora[14] under the authority of European Political cooperation in December 1975 by the member states of the European Community (EC),[15] followed initiatives by the British and German governments. Trevi's creation provided a clear signal that greater progress was desired in the field of internal security. Trevi's mandate was initially limited to the fight against terrorism (a terrorist attack at the Munich Olympics in 1972 and the constitutional provisions preventing Interpol from investigating terrorist activities provided key motivations for Trevi's creation). However, its realm of competence was gradually widened[16] to include other serious crimes (drug trafficking, environmental crime, transnational organized crime, etc.) and facets of the migration issue. In view of the Community's Single Market objective, a working group on the free movement project was established and the intergovernmental Ad Hoc Group on Immigration (see below) additionally became an informal working group of the Trevi forum. Both developments indicate a tendency towards the fusion of immigration and crime issues. The importance of this trend is that, unlike the limited operational mandate of Interpol and the very broad agenda of the Council of Europe, Trevi was designed specifically to encourage comprehensive cooperation across the field of European internal security. Thus, although Trevi's working groups were primarily consultative in nature, they did lead to informal policy coordination.[17] Similarly Trevi's membership and structure, involving national ministers, senior officials with a coordinating role, and working groups made up of civil servants and practitioners, promoted a focused and effective approach to European internal security issues.

The expansion of consultative forums for police cooperation to include elements of migration was paralleled by similar developments in bodies established to consider immigration issues. In October 1986, following an initiative from the British Presidency of the EC, the Ad Hoc Group on Immigration was established. Much of the focus of the Group's work was on the control dimension of the migration issue – securing frontiers, preventing illegal immigration, and restricting choices available to asylum seekers. During its lifetime the Group was responsible for drawing up the Convention Determining the State Responsible for Examining Applications for Asylum Lodged in One of the Member States of the European Community signed in June 1990 (the Dublin Convention) and for preparing the groundwork for the Community's External Borders Convention.[19] The Group was highly active in a number of areas, presenting a report on the harmonization of national policies on immigration to the Maastricht Summit in December 1991, drawing up plans for the European Automated Fingerprint Recognition System (Eurodac), and creating the Center for Information, Discussion and Exchange on Asylum (CIREA) and the Center for Information, Discussion and Exchange on the Crossing of Borders and Immigration (CIREFI). Though in step with the overall process of "Europeanization", a central component of the integration process in Europe, progress towards harmonization and integration in the migration field has also been identified as indicative of a move towards fortification and exclusion.[20]

Perhaps the clearest manifestation of the fusion trend is to be found in the Schengen Agreement of 1985 and the Implementing Convention of 1990. The Schengen project resulted from agreement among a "hard-core" of five member states to implement an area of free movement ahead of the Single Market's 1992 schedule.[21] Although commencing with an original membership of five, Schengen expanded to include all member states, except the United Kingdom and Ireland.[22] In attempting to implement the original agreement of 1985, it became clear that an array of policing, judicial, and customs measures would be required to enable compensatory cooperation among the signatory states. Agreement on these measures proved elusive and it took five years of negotiations before the second Schengen Convention was ready for signature. The Convention of 1990, a much more lengthy document than the original Agreement, established the institutional and decision making structures for cooperation, and included numerous articles covering policing issues. The Convention not only provided a framework for the exchange of information and a forum for policy discussion and coordination, it also explicitly enabled operational forms of cooperation. Indeed, one of Schengen's key advances was its attempt to codify a number of important innovations in international public law. The most fundamental of these was its identification of situations in which national police authorities could operate in the territory of another state (cross-border observation and cross-border pursuit). Prior to this development legitimate international police cooperation had been inherently limited.[23]

Thus, although Schengen began as a mechanism to enable free movement, it developed into a fledgling system of European internal security cooperation. Schengen can be characterized, therefore, as the first "absolute" manifestation of fusion. Its impact on future developments is clear. In the words of King, "an important effect of contemporary harmonization in the institution of restrictive policies by inner-Europe (Schengen) is that it is causing a ripple of corresponding controls to the borders of outer-Europe".[24]

The move towards a fusion of immigration and crime issues made in the Schengen Agreement was later consolidated in the Maastricht Treaty, which sought to bring greater coordination to cooperation. In addition to the forums detailed above, a plethora of other groups and bodies had developed in response to the common internal security challenges facing the member states, and efforts and energies were increasingly duplicated. The desire for a more streamlined approach to cooperation, combined with the enthusiasm of certain member states to match the moves to Economic and Monetary Union with progress towards political union, formed the basis of the decision to codify cooperation in the Maastricht Treaty. In fact, the Maastricht Treaty failed to encompass the demands of those member states who wished to see this area of policy absorbed in its entirety into the treaty structure of the European Community (EC). During the Intergovernmental Conference other member states remained equally opposed to the notion of such nationally sensitive and significant policy areas being subject to the supranational policy-making arena of the EC. This was particularly true in respect to the power of the Commission, which had undergone somewhat of a renaissance under the leadership of Jacques Delors, and with regard to the consolidation of the European Court of Justice's (ECJ) power of judicial review following a number of landmark cases.[25]

By way of the compromise, the Maastricht Treaty established three separate "pillars" of cooperation: the EC constituted the First Pillar (with a slightly expanded area of competence and a number of institutional reforms); a Common Foreign and Security Policy constituted the Second; and Justice and Home Affairs Cooperation[26] made up the third. In the case of the "third pillar", greater coordination and cooperation on free movement and policing issues were theoretically facilitated but the impact of the supranational institutions was kept in check. Thus, the Commission's right of policy initiative was shared with member states in certain sectors and abolished entirely in others; there was little provision for legally binding decisions apart from the unwieldy international convention; the European Parliament was afforded almost no role; and the jurisdiction of the ECJ was left for the member states to agree to unanimously and only in certain cases.

Fusion as a Disadvantage: Problems for Elites and Publics

The implication thus far has been that the fusion of immigration and crime issues was largely inevitable and yet, at the same time, wholly unsuitable. This paradox is, in fact, central to the whole question of the codification of international cooperation in the justice and home affairs sector. The problems relating to this paradox are twofold, matching the willingness of nation states to cooperate on one level against the rights and freedoms of individuals on another. Given the focus of this paper, the analysis concentrates primarily on the former, though concludes by raising some of the central issues regarding the micro level impact of the fusion.

It would be inaccurate to start with the hypothesis that the migration-crime fusion was solely responsible for the problems encountered during the consolidation of the Maastricht Treaty's provisions on justice and home affairs cooperation. A number of other factors clearly contributed to the Third Pillar's difficulties and this section of the paper will conclude with a brief discussion of these factors. However, it is possible to assert that the fusion played a major role in the confusion which appeared to surround the early years of cooperation under the aegis of the Third Pillar. One need only remember that one of the most significant advances agreed by the member states during the 1996 Intergovernmental Conference (convened to assess the functioning of the Maastricht Treaty and suggest reforms) was to "defuse" the immigration-crime fusion. The new Amsterdam Treaty moved all aspects of the free movement issue into the First Pillar (the European Community) and consolidated and extended the policing elements in the Third Pillar.

There is insufficient scope to describe and examine in detail the flaws and problems of the Third Pillar[27] but a number of key themes can be identified. In the early years of the Third Pillar's existence little progress was made in any of the policy sectors included in Title VI, Article 1.[28] The work program for 1994 agreed at the Justice and Home Affairs Council in November 1993 remained applicable throughout 1995 and into 1996, as few of the proposed initiatives were agreed or implemented in 1994. Indeed, no subsequent annual work program was submitted until June 1996. Furthermore, the advances that were made were largely the result of the intergovernmental cooperation which had preceded the Maastricht Treaty. In addition, acrimonious and often very public disputes arose between member states on the substantive content of policy issues as well as on the exact nature and desired influence of the Third Pillar's supranational elements. This dispute in fact spilled over into the European Commission and created a significant division between those Commission members who favored a proactive approach and those who wished to work at the pace and following the style of the member states. Finally, in cases where decisions were possible, there was a marked reluctance among member states to make use of the new policy instruments in the Treaty, and recourse was largely made to non-binding recommendations, resolutions, and the binding, but unwieldy, international convention.

The question now remains: How are these diverse problems and difficulties linked to the fusion of immigration and crime? In fact, at the heart of all the problems detailed above is the reality that, although Title VI of the Maastricht Treaty appeared to embrace the immigration-crime fusion, its provisions were unable to provide the environment in which cooperation could flourish. The Third Pillar recognized the importance of the free movement objective and clearly linked it to the integration project of the First Pillar. However, it failed to conceptualize how these elements could remain distinct from, and yet closely related to, the policing and criminal justice facets of the Third Pillar, which remained too sensitive to be considered in supranational terms. In this way the Third Pillar appeared to embrace the fusion but failed to explain how it was to be managed.

The sensitivity of the policing/criminal justice elements of the Third Pillar for national policymakers is central to an understanding of the immigration-crime fusion and the problems it creates. The significant degree of intergovernmental cooperation preceding the Maastricht Treaty suggests that nation states are not entirely averse to responding to the consequences of interdependence in this sector. However, the sensitivity of all facets of law enforcement (in particular the defining nature of the monopoly of coercive power for state sovereignty) renders this an area in which the development of international cooperation appears inherently limited. Although certain member states appear more radical in this respect than others, one need only remember the problems and constraints which accompanied the right to hot pursuit agreed between the signatory states of Schengen. Thus, although intensified cooperation was deemed necessary by all member states, there was little consensus on the actual aims of the Third Pillar. The ambiguous and contradictory provisions of Title VI of the TEU clearly indicate this fact. The conceptual disarray which characterized the Third Pillar's institutional genesis unsurprisingly spilled over into the domain of substantive policy. As a result, although rapid progress was needed for issues directly connected to the commitment to achieve free movement, the sensitivity of the required compensatory measures prevented progress. In this way the fusion issue played a role both in the institutionalization of cooperation and the subsequent attempts at policymaking.

There were, of course, other issues at play in the Third Pillar's difficulties, and these also affected attempts to consolidate cooperation. Perhaps the most significant of these concerns the negotiation of the Third Pillar's provisions. Given the centrality of the personal representatives of the Heads of State and Government in the EU's IGCs, the development of the Third Pillar was placed in the hands of non-specialists. The degree to which Interior and Justice Ministries were kept abreast of the negotiations fell to the core executives of individual member states, a task which was in certain cases entirely neglected.[29] The exclusion of those national officials who were later responsible for the implementation of the Maastricht Treaty's provision ensured their hostility. Of equal importance was their general lack of experience in the workings of the Brussels process and a reluctance to operate within the very regulated framework it offered. The increasing success of intergovernmental cooperation prior to Maastricht simply added to the frustrations of those who saw the Treaty's provisions as unnecessary and unsuitable.

Finally, with respect to the implications of fusion at the micro level, a number of issues deserve mention. It is widely accepted that certain elements of the progress made in justice and home affairs cooperation act to undermine facets of the catalogue of individual civil liberties and human rights, which is endorsed in one form or another throughout Europe.[30] In fact, both the discourse on fusion and the practical measures it has led to, have potentially significant repercussions in this respect, affecting both citizens of EU member states and residents from third countries. Among the most obvious are: increased activity affecting individuals' civil rights in a field with little or no parliamentary scrutiny or judicial review; problems of data protection given the construction of a number of European-wide databases;[31] the negative impact on refugees resulting from the introduction of control and policing issues into the discourse on asylum; and the hostility and suspicion created by a discourse which links immigration (and thus immigrants) to criminal activity and in particular to transnational organized crime. Bigo's consideration of the "internal security continuum" stresses that this "is not a sinister plot of ministerial power-seekers to attack civil liberties".[32] He does, however, concede that "the policy agenda concerning immigration control and political asylum is more security led than economic or social in approach".[33] This change of emphasis is in fact at the heart of the difficulties presented by the fusion of immigration and crime and provides the central challenge to policymakers in their attempt to consolidate cooperation among member states. This is particularly true in the case of trafficking in women where both components of the fusion are clearly evident.

TRAFFICKING WOMEN FROM EAST TO WEST: ORIGINS OF THE PROBLEM

The trafficking of humans is not a phenomenon unique to modern times, though aspects of its development are particular to contemporary political and socio-economic developments. In a speech to an international conference on trafficking in July 1998, the Deputy Director General of the IOM revealed that "while trafficking in migrants continues to grow, its more heinous form in the trafficking of women and children is a phenomenon which has increased at an even more alarming rate throughout the world".[34] Exact figures and statistics are difficult to establish as not only do collection techniques differ among countries, but more importantly women who have been trafficked are understandably reluctant to identify themselves.[35] This reluctance has its origins in a number of related factors, which include the well-founded fear of being deported as an illegal alien (the traditional response of authorities in destination countries), the fear of suffering abuse and retaliation (especially given past difficulties compiling criminal cases against traffickers), and the embarrassment caused to family members in the country of origin.

The lack of empirical data has also been a consequence of difficulties encountered in defining the term "trafficking in women". As the following analysis reveals, trafficking encompasses a wide range of scenarios in which the women may or may not have been exploited or victimized, may or may not have entered the destination country illegally, and may or may not have been trafficked against their will. The IOM's provisional definition stated:

> Trafficking in women occurs when a woman in a country other than her own is exploited by another person against her will and for financial gain. The trafficking element may – cumulatively or separately – consist of: arranging legal or illegal migration from the

country of origin to the country of destination; deceiving victims into prostitution once in the country of destination; or enforcing victims" exploitation through violence, threat of violence or other forms of coercion.[36]

Despite the lack of empirical data a number of trends with relevance to this paper are discernible. In the case of Western Europe, the source countries of those trafficked has undergone a marked change, with women from developing countries being increasingly replaced by those from Central and Eastern Europe.[37] The rapid democratic transitions in Central and Eastern European states have created an environment where trafficking has prospered. Poverty, high levels of unemployment among women and, concomitantly, the declining social status of women constitute the major "push factors" for many trafficked women.[38] Although in the past it was largely men who migrated to escape poverty and find work in other countries, this trend is changing with an "increased feminization of general migratory movements".[39] The pull factors presented by Western Europe are largely obvious, with employment opportunities, higher standards of living, and general economic wealth being most significant.

Trafficking in Women: Problems in the Countries of Origin?

In addition to the poverty-wealth and unemployment-employment push and pull factors, two more recent developments have begun to interact with these traditional motives, amplifying their effects and thus creating an environment in which trafficking can prosper. The first development gathered momentum throughout the 1970s and 1980s and culminated in the restriction of all legal channels of migration into the EU's member states. The so-called "immigration stops" of the 1970s were initially a response to changes in national economies, in particular the phenomenon of rapidly rising unemployment following the global economic slowdown. Immigration was, after all, largely a means of recruiting labor in the face of domestic shortages and once this market began to shrink, foreign workers were no longer an essential import. There was also a less savory facet to the tightening of immigration controls in Western Europe as political and social implications of integrating large immigrant communities into the host society dominated much of the debate at this time. Furthermore, the noticeable increase in applications for asylum following the introduction of restrictive immigration policies, has led to a similar restrictive trend in asylum legislation in many of the EU's member states. In the words of one commentator, "what started as an optimal movement of labor from south to north became, in the 1970s and 1980s, a sociopolitical liability as economic growth in Western Europe and North America slowed in the aftermath of the first big postwar recession (1973–1974)".[40] Such legislative changes in the fields of immigration and asylum severely limited the opportunities for legal migration into the EU, creating a significant market for smuggling rings and traffickers.

There are also, of course, those Central and Eastern European countries (CEECs) for whose citizens a visa is no longer required for entry into the EU. Others may be able to obtain visas as "entertainers" only to find themselves involved in the less savory side of the industry. Finally, there are also women who voluntarily subject themselves to the uncertainties of being smuggled into the West: the IOM's report on trafficking reveals that 40 percent of women surveyed in the Ukraine were at risk of becoming a victim of trafficking as they wished to leave the impoverished conditions in which they were forced to live.[41] Although cases such as these certainly make a common definition of trafficking in women more difficult to substantiate, their impact on "market developments" is clear. The ability to gain legal entry as a tourist or on a visa, the rising number of women willing to travel, and the short distance to be covered between countries of origin and destination, have added to the demand for women from Central and Eastern Europe to work in the sex industry, overshadowing the traditional source countries in the developing world.

The second development, or at least perceptions of it, appears to be far more a product of the 1990s. Transnational organized crime has become a key political issue for almost all EU member states with widespread recognition of its most common manifestations. Since the early 1990s, for example, public opinion has consistently favored increased action and cooperation to combat drug trafficking, international crime, and terrorism.[42] A German appeal for a European Internal Security Union was based on the analysis that "one of the most significant threats to internal security comes from the growth of organized crime that has become apparent in recent years".[43] This perception is shared throughout the EU, and the Heads of State and Government have repeatedly emphasized the new danger presented by organized crime. The growth in transnational organized crime has, in part, resulted from the growth of certain "environmental" facilitators, two of which demand particular attention: the first being globalization and the second the collapse of the Soviet Union and the Eastern bloc.

Globalization has significantly influenced the development of organized crime. Technological advances in communications, travel, and infrastructure increase both the opportunities for criminal activities and the operational capabilities of organized crime groups. Growing economic interdependence and the development of global financial and trading systems greatly facilitate the fusing of illegal with legal business ventures, making the identification of crime and criminals increasingly difficult. The attractiveness of drugs as a global commodity and the globalization of the market economy have "transformed the production and trafficking of drugs from a small cottage industry into a vast multinational or more appropriately transnational business enterprise".[44] Alongside the more traditional trade in illegal drugs, global markets for other illicit products and commodities, including women and children, have been developed and consolidated.

In the former Soviet bloc the gradual globalizing changes to the nature of human interaction were supplanted largely *en bloc* into a relatively fragile environment. In essence, there have been developments in the social, political, and economic milieu in Russia and many CEECs, that have made the entire environment highly conducive to the consolidation of organized crime. The high levels of unemployment and extreme poverty which have accompanied economic liberalization have led to rising domestic crime and corruption. These are just some of the many factors which have made attempts to establish a credible and effective post-communist criminal justice system a difficult undertaking for some states and a near impossibility for others. In addition to domestic developments, the opening of borders between east and west has allowed an intensification of trafficking on pre-existing routes and the development of new ones,[45] ensuring that the development of organized crime has increasingly impacted upon EU member states. In the words of the IOM "the main facilitating element of trafficking in women is the existence of organized networks of traffickers and criminals who bring women from poorer countries to the West in order to exploit them".[46]

However, it is not simply the consolidation of "push factors" in Central and Eastern Europe and the existence of organized crime which deserve attention. It is also clear that the manifest growth in trafficking originating from, or organized in, these countries is linked to the high return-low risk nature of the venture. Despite the existence of a number of international conventions and declarations on the need to combat trafficking, until recently there has been insubstantial legislation in the destination countries, either to protect the women (and thus encourage them to come forward) or to punish the traffickers.[47] Alien smugglers, when charged, rarely received long sentences and the women victims are often immediately deported, leaving little evidence for cases against traffickers to be built.

From the preceding analysis of trafficking in women from east to west in Europe, it becomes clear that the phenomenon presents a complex and multifaceted problem. As a result of this complexity, attempts to address the issue of trafficking in women necessarily have to focus on developments in the countries of origin and transit as well as the problems created in the countries of final destination. This suggests a "holistic" approach that requires: measures to support and educate women in CEECs and protect those trafficked into the destination states; measures to further secure the borders to cut-off trafficking routes and prevent illegal immigration; and initiatives to combat the growth of organized crime in the CEECs and prevent the consolidation of its activities further west.

A ROLE FOR THE EUROPEAN UNION? PERCEPTIONS AND RESPONSES

The development and consolidation of EU cooperation in justice and home affairs has made some notable advances. The issue of trafficking in women and children appears to be an area where there has been significant success. Indeed the scope, nature, and intensity of cooperation point to a policy sector in which the institutional and political difficulties, which have traditionally characterized the work of the Third Pillar, have been transcended. The reasons behind this transcendence warrant further investigation, in particular as they may hold the key to the successful "management" of the immigration-crime fusion.

Trafficking in Women: Problems for the Countries of Destination?

The key implications of the trafficking phenomenon for the EU are twofold and involve both the contemporary situation and future developments. As the preceding section reveals, trafficking in women has increasingly become a movement from eastern to western Europe, with many EU member states constituting the final destination. Given the proximity of the source countries, the introduction of unrestricted travel for tourists from many of the CEECs, and the continued permeability of many land borders in the region, the trafficking phenomenon is of increasing concern for the EU's member states. In terms of future developments, the proposed enlargement of the EU to include states which are either sources of, or transit stations for, such traffic, is also viewed with anxiety in many of the EU's current member states.

Following the application of the states of Central and Eastern Europe for membership in the EU, the Commission has been involved in an ongoing evaluation of the ability of applicant states to meet the EU's body of law (the *acquis communautaire*). Despite the unusual position of justice and home affairs as a kind of halfway house between traditional intergovernmental cooperation and supranational decision making, adherence to the justice and home affairs *acquis* has been identified as a key objective in preparation for EU membership.[48] Reports issued by the Commission on the status of the applications for membership have revealed a number of worrying developments in the field of justice and home affairs, and the traffic in women and children is no exception. The Commission's opinion on the application of Poland, for example, highlights the vulnerability of Poland's borders to exploitation by criminal gangs seeking to smuggle illegal aliens. The report goes on to state that "Poland has a serious problem of trafficking in women, who are brought under duress both from Poland to the west and from the NIS to Poland. The effectiveness of Poland to tackle all forms of organized crime is hampered by institutional and resource constraints".[49] Similar conclusions have been reached *vis à vis* the other applicant states, although the severity of the problem naturally varies from country to country.

Following its involvement in an international conference on the trade in women in June 1996, the Commission published a Communication on Trafficking in Women later in the year. The communication highlighted the extent of the trafficking problem and suggested areas in which concrete progress should and could be made. In response, a number of practical programs and policy initiatives have been developed both by the Commission and by the member states. The following examination will illustrate how the many problems of cooperation and obstacles to progress in the justice and home affairs sector outlined above appear not to have seriously affected progress in the trafficking issue.

One of the biggest collective advances made by the EU came with the agreement of the Justice and Home Affairs Council on a joint action to combat trafficking in human beings and their sexual exploitation.[50] The joint action stated as its purpose "to reach a common approach in respect of the definition of offenses relating to trafficking in human beings and sexual exploitation".[51] The agreement also paved the way for simplified legal cooperation and action by the competent authorities. Two of the biggest problems facing member states in their attempts to forge cooperation against trafficking were the general lack of legislative experience in this area and the widely differing national approaches to the issue. In the joint action the member states agreed to review national legislation with a view to facilitating cooperation, particularly in the judicial realm.

On November 29, 1996, the Justice and Home Affairs Council adopted a joint action establishing an exchange program for public officials and representatives of NGOs responsible for combating the trade in human beings.[52] The STOP Program, covering the period from 1996 to 2000, aims to promote coordinated initiatives in the fight against trafficking in humans through training and information measures and the establishment of exchange programs for those involved in the fight against trafficking.[53] More recently the Commission established the DAPHNE Initiative to support NGOs combating violence against women and children. The DAPHNE initiative provided three million ECU in 1997 and 1998 to support training, information dissemination, and personnel exchanges. The Commission hopes to continue with the project through 1999.

Several related developments in the fields of policing and criminal justice have also produced positive ramifications for the development of cooperation in the fight against trafficking. In 1996 the Justice and Home Affairs Council agreed to a joint action to extend the competence of the European Drugs Unit (the precursor of Europol) to include the exchange and analysis of information and intelligence relating to, inter alia, crimes involving clandestine immigration networks, and trafficking in human beings.[54] The EU's efforts to combat the growth in international organized crime has also impacted positively upon its program of cooperation against trafficking in humans. The Commission's communication on the trafficking in women highlighted how Russian women, unable to obtain visas for entry into the EU, were selling themselves to organized crime gangs. The Russian Mafia is said to control markets in Poland and Germany with the Ukrainian Mafia dominating Hungary and Austria.[55] As a result, this element of international criminal activity has been acknowledged in the EU's programs to combat international organized crime. More importantly, despite problems of agreeing on the final text of the Europol Convention and the delays in its ratification, the Council has resorted to other legislative and policy making measures. In particular, by adopting the Action Plan on organized crime in April 1997, the Council illustrated a willingness to bypass the traditional and cumbersome intergovernmental methods of decision making.[56] The Action Plan was formulated by a high level group of national experts and presented a number of recommendations (with deadlines) to be implemented by the member states, the Commission, and Europol. Although not making direct reference to the trafficking issue, measures outlined in the report encourage progress in a number of areas which, when implemented, would have a positive impact on the fight against trafficking. Furthermore, a Multidisciplinary Group on Organized Crime, which grew out of the recommendations of the Action Plan, meets at least once a month to ensure continued momentum.

Perhaps the two most important measures in this respect are the proposals for a joint action, making it an offense in all member states to participate in a criminal organization, and for a pre-accession pact on organized crime with the applicant states of Central and Eastern Europe.[57] The target date given for the former was the end of 1998 and for the latter, the end of 1997 (although the potential for problems to arise given the different legal traditions of the member states was acknowledged). In fact, progress in both areas has been notable, with political agreement on the joint action being reached in March 1998 and the pre-accession pact being signed in May 1998.[58] The Joint Action which makes participation in a criminal organization in EU member states a criminal offense, presents the first internationally agreed definition of what constitutes a criminal organization and participation in it.[59]

> The Joint Action defines a criminal organization as meaning "a lasting, structured association of more than two persons, acting in concert with a view to committing crimes or other offenses which are punishable by deprivation of liberty or a detention order of at

least four years or a more serious penalty, whether such crimes or offenses are an end in themselves or a means of obtaining material benefits and, if necessary, of improperly influencing the operation of public authorities.

Agreement on this definition is vital for the myriad of other cooperative efforts involving judicial and law enforcement bodies across the EU. Among these measures are programs involving law enforcement communities, judiciaries, and immigration bodies. Thus, for example, an illustration of further progress made in the broad area of organized crime can be found in the Falcone Program. This program, which has a budget of ECU 10 million for the period 1998–2002, allows for exchanges, training, and cooperation for persons involved in the fight against organized crime.[60] Given the link between organized crime networks and the trafficking of women and children, initiatives such as this can only afford further momentum to the fight against trafficking. This is also true of the May 1998 Justice and Home Affairs Council decision on a Joint Action to create a European Judicial Network to strengthen cooperation among member states in their fight against organized crime, which itself strengthens the progress made by the Grotius program.[61] Alongside common agreement on the criminal offense of participating in a criminal organization, efforts such as these can only have positive consequences.

Within the realm of frontier controls and migration policy a number of similar initiatives are currently being implemented. The Sherlock Program dealing with many facets of the migration issue, in particular the use of false documents to cross frontiers, has more recently been replaced by the Odysseus Program. Odyssus will run from 1998 to 2002 with a budget of ECU 12 million and states as its objective:

> the extension and strengthening of existing cooperation – through training of officials, exchange programs, as well as studies and research activities – in the areas of asylum, immigration, crossing of external borders, and security of identity documents, and cooperation in these same areas with countries applying for accession".[62]

CONCLUSION

The central puzzle outlined in the introduction concerned the impact of the fusion of immigration and crime issues on cooperation among EU member states. Although a number of negative ramifications for both member states and individuals were detailed throughout the analysis, the inevitability of the fusion was not denied. It would, of course, be better and more productive to treat issues of immigration and asylum as separate from traditional internal security concerns. However, changes in security perceptions have themselves been influenced by significant changes in the nature of mass migration (identified by Garson as acceleration, globalization, and regionalization).[63] Consequently, the fusion of the two issues should not be identified as solely the result of political manipulation. The introduction also suggested that the fight against trafficking in women has been one area in which the fusion has not prevented progress. A number of reasons for this success were suggested throughout the subsequent analysis. In conclusion to this examination of fusion, cooperation, and trafficking, these key facilitators will be highlighted and briefly explained.

One essential characteristic of the trafficking issue which greatly facilitated efforts to develop cooperation is the issue's pertinence to both migration and crime issues. The fight against trafficking is, therefore, concerned with a sector which exhibits a clear tendency towards fusion. A comprehensive response to the issue would necessarily demand action in equal measure in both the law enforcement and immigration policy sectors. Member states' activities illustrate the extent to which this dual approach can be achieved. Separate social and security elements of the issue appear to have been recognized, accepted, and balanced.

Trafficking was also characterized as an issue area in which there was little pre-existing national legislation and few commonly accepted international definitions. Starting with what essentially amounted to a "blank slate" made progress among member states significantly easier than in areas where a substantial body of national law was already in place. Thus, it can be concluded that the fusion may prove easier to "manage" when it is not in direct competition with national interests, experiences, and traditions.

The Commission's key role was also highlighted, as was the contrast this presented in terms of its overall caution to the development of the Third Pillar. Trafficking in women has proved a key area of concern for the Commissioner for Justice and Home Affairs, Anita Gradin. As Commissioner, Gradin has been a vocal and forceful player in the European arena and much of the progress made in the area can be attributed to her success in putting trafficking on the EU's policy agenda and ensuring it stayed there.[64]

Enlargement has also been a positive element in the creation of an effective response to trafficking. As the analysis has indicated, this is an area where applicant and associated states share significant problems, and their future membership of the EU has ensured that current member states recognize their need for assistance in combating the supply side of the equation. This resulted, in May 1998, in the signing of a Pre-Accession Pact on Organized Crime by the member states of the European Union and the Applicant Countries of Central and Eastern Europe. In addition, funds are available from other EU sources to aid the consolidation of civil society, for example through the Phare and Tacis Democracy programs of the Commission. Both the Phare and Tacis programs have made significant financial contributions to initiatives to combat trafficking in women from eastern to western Europe.[65] Efforts such as these have been greatly aided by the growing involvement of non-governmental organizations, including the International Organization for Migration, STV in the Netherlands, and the Council of Europe.

Finally, trafficking in women has proved an area of significant interest and some success for cooperation between the EU and the United States. Although justice and home affairs cooperation has been high on the "Transatlantic Agenda" since 1995, a number of high profile disagreements have hampered progress in certain key areas.[66] However, efforts to combat trafficking appear not to have been affected by such differences. In December 1997 the conclusions of the EU–U.S. summit revealed that progress was being made in EU–U.S. cooperation in combating trafficking in women. In addition, the two sides were able to agree to initiate a joint information and prevention campaign in Poland and Ukraine, two countries seriously affected by trafficking in women.[67] More recently a United States-European Union Transatlantic Seminar to Prevent Trafficking in Women was held in Ukraine, providing further proof of the commitment to continue developing common strategies.

It has been the interaction of all these elements which has ensured the successful introduction of a strategy to combat trafficking in women. As problematic as it is, the fusion of immigration and crime issues appears so central to the trafficking phenomenon that a multidisciplinary response is without doubt the only appropriate solution. The EU's ability to combine the strengths of its supranational institutions and its member states to create a comprehensive program of financial, social, frontier control, and law enforcement measures testifies to the potential of justice and home affairs cooperation. The initiatives are, however, still in their relative infancy and the real proof of the successful management of the "fusion" will only surface when evidence of changes to national legislation and widespread examples of program implementation are revealed.

NOTES

1. Throughout the paper the term immigration, when related to the fusion concept, refers to both traditional immigration and asylum seeking.
2. Didier Bigo, "The European Internal Security Field: Stakes and Rivalries in a Newly Developing Area of Police Intervention", in Malcolm Anderson and Monica den Boer (eds.), *Policing Across National Boundaries* (London: Pinter, 1994), p.164.
3. Article 8a of the Single European Act.
4. The External Borders Convention has been on the EU's agenda since the late 1980s. The convention has been dogged by numerous controversies and condemned to a situation of perpetual stalemate. The importance of the convention for the creation of a common area of free movement has been stressed repeatedly by the Heads of State meeting in the context of the European Council. However, the territorial dispute between the United Kingdom and Spain (concerning the status of Gibraltar) has, in particular, proved more resilient than any resolve to move forward with agreement on the convention.
5. Sarah Collinson, *Beyond Borders: West European Migration Policy Towards the 21st Century* (London: Royal Institute for International Affairs, 1993).
6. John Benyon *et al.*, *Police Cooperation in Europe: An Investigation* (Leicester: Center for the Study of Public Order, University of Leicester, 1993), p.18.
7. House of Lords Select Committee on the European Communities 10th Report, *Europol* (London: House of Lords, 1995), p.10.
8. R. Rupprecht, M. Hellenthal and W. Weidenfeld, *Internal Security and the Single Market* (Gütersloh: Bertelsmann Foundation Publishers, 1994), p.27.
9. Malcolm Anderson, Monica den Boer, Peter Cullen, William Gilmore, Charles Raab and Neil Walker, "Policing the European Union" (Oxford: Clarendon Press, 1995).
10. "Justice and Home Affairs Council Meeting 2002", Press Release, Brussels, April 28, 1997, Document 7568/97.
11. See for example Mike King, "Policing Refugees and Asylum Seekers in 'Greater Europe': towards a reconceptualization of control", in M. Anderson and M. den Boer (eds.) *op.cit.*
12. International Organization for Migration, *Trafficking and Prostitution: The Growing Exploitation of Migrant Women from Central and Eastern Europe* (Budapest: Migration Information Program, International Organization, May 1995), p.13.
13. Including national officials, practitioners, and academic and other commentators.
14. The origin of the term Trevi is subject to some disagreement; some members claim it is the acronym for Terrorisme, Radicalisme, Extremisme et Violence Internationale. Others proffer a more simple explanation referring to the Trevi Fountain in Rome.
15. Membership of the Trevi forum was limited to the member states of the European Community, although seven "friends of Trevi" (United States, Canada, Austria, Norway, Sweden, Switzerland, and Morocco) were also involved in its work.
16. Trevi I was established in May 1977 to address the issue of terrorism. Cooperation in this

sphere has made a number of advances, of both an operational (communication and exchange of information) and a more fundamental nature (e.g. agreeing to a common definition of the term terrorism). Trevi II, again established in May 1977, advanced police cooperation in technical fields, including training, public order, and forensic science. Trevi III was introduced to address the increasingly high profile issue of international organized crime, with particular emphasis on drug trafficking and related offenses. Finally Trevi '92 was created to deliberate on the many internal security implications of achieving the full implementation of free movement.

17. Malcolm Anderson, "The Agenda for Police cooperation", in M. Anderson and M. Den Boer (eds.), *op.cit.*

18. In the late 1980s the Trevi Group played a key role in the early efforts to establish a European police agency (Europol). In response to proposals from Trevi Working Group III and following the successful establishment of Drug Liaison Officers and National Drug Intelligence Units, Trevi Ministers, in their Action Program of 1990, agreed in principle to the establishment of a European Drugs Intelligence Unit (EDIU). The EDIU, later renamed the European Drugs Unit (EDU) provided the foundation on which Europol was to be developed.

19. Immigration became a Steering Group on Immigration and Asylum within the decision making framework of the Third Pillar of the EU.

20. See for example King, *op.cit.*

21. The original Schengen Agreement (1985 Agreement Concerning the Gradual Abolition of Controls at the Common Borders) was signed by France, Germany, Belgium, the Netherlands, and Luxembourg in June 1985. Norway and Iceland are currently associate members in order for the Scandinavian states to be able to maintain the functioning of the Nordic passport free zone. The supplementary Convention (Convention implementing the Schengen Agreement of June 15, 1985 between the Governments of the States of the Benelux Economic Union, the Federal Republic of Germany, and the French Republic on the gradual abolition of checks at their common frontiers) was signed in June 1990.

22. It has become increasingly apparent that Ireland would apply for membership of Schengen were it not for the passport free zone established between the UK and Ireland and the British government's refusal to countenance any involvement in the Schengen project.

23. J. Schutte (1991), "Schengen: Its Meaning for the Free Movement of Persons in Europe", *Common Market Law Review*, Vol.28, No.3, p.555.

24. King, *op.cit*, pp.69–70.

25. The most important of which in terms of direct effect was the 1963 case Van Gend and Loos.

26. Covering immigration, asylum, crossing of external borders, visas, drugs policy, criminal and civil justice issues, customs and policing cooperation. Title VI Article 1(1–9) of the Treaty on European Union.

27. See for example Penelope Turnbull, "Understanding the 1991 Intergovernmental Conference and its Legacy: *New Institutions" and the Flaws of the Third Pillar* (Manchester: University of Manchester, European Policy Research Paper 5/98, 1998).

28. See note 25.

29. *Ibid.*

30. Hence the establishment of Statewatch in the UK: an organization which monitors levels of civil liberties and human rights throughout Europe.

31. For example the Schengen Information System (SIS) and more recently Europol's European Information System (EIS). Greece refused to sign the Schengen convention at one point because of difficulties with its provisions on data protection, and Germany's tough data protection legislation may cause difficulties with the development of the EIS.

32. Bigo, *op.cit.*, p.164

33. *Ibid.*

34. Statement by Mrs. Narcisa Escaler, Deputy Director General of the International Organization for Migration at the United States – European Union Transatlantic Seminar to Prevent Trafficking in Women. L'viv, Ukraine, July 9–10, 1998.

35. The lack of empirical data has been matched until recently with a lack of academic or public policy research. However both the IOM's report on trafficking and the Commission's Communication contain bibliographies of published and unpublished works on the issue.
36. IOM, *op.cit.*, p.7.
37. The IOM's report on trafficking identifies the first wave of women being trafficked from Asia, the second from South America, the third from Africa, and most recently from Central and Eastern Europe.
38. See for example N. Barr, "Income Transfers: Social Insurance", in *Labour Markets and Social Policy in Central and Eastern Europe, A World Bank Book* (New York: Oxford University Press, 1994).
39. Escaler, *op.cit.*
40. Wayne A. Cornelius, Philip L. Martin, and James F. Hollifield (eds.), *Controlling Immigration: a Global Perspective* (Stanford: Stanford University Press, 1994), p.7.
41. IOM, *op.cit.*
42. When asked about the desirability of key elements of the Maastricht Treaty debate, cooperation in the fight against drug trafficking and crime polled 89 percent support in December1992 and 91 percent in June 1993, Eurobarometer 38 (Dec. 1992), p.33 and Eurobarometer 39 (June 1993), p.33.
43. Rupprecht, Hellenthal, and Weidenfeld, *op.cit.*, p.10.
44. Paul B. Stares, "The Global Drug Phenomenon: Implications for Policy", in Georges Estievenart (ed.), *Policies and Strategies to Combat Drugs in Europe* (Dordrecht: Martinus Nijhoff Publishers, 1995), p.4.
45. A report on police cooperation in Europe submits that the overall decline in the enforcement of law and order in the former communist countries of central and eastern Europe, and the concomitant growth in organized crime and corruption, is allegedly leading to new routes and opportunities for drug trafficking into the European Union. John Benyon *et al.*, *op.cit.*, p.30.
46. IOM, *op.cit.*, p.13.
47. Although both the Netherlands and Belgium in particular have begun to develop new legislative measures in their fight against trafficking.
48. Although it should be noted that east-west cooperation in the justice and home affairs field got off to a very shaky start. The so-called "Structured Dialogue" in justice and home affairs cooperation was condemned as an "unstructured monologue" by representatives of Central and East European states who were disappointed by the lack of progress made. The problems with the establishment of the Structured Dialogue were twofold. First, there were (and indeed still are) concerns among EU member states as to the suitability of information sharing and exchange in areas of such sensitivity, particularly given the growth in organized crime in these states. Secondly, as the opening section of the paper has illustrated, the member states were themselves struggling to establish and consolidate cooperation with each other in the new decision making context provided by the EU. The institutional, procedural, and political difficulties of the early years provided little in the way of a stable foundation on which to build cooperation with third states.
49. Commission opinion on Poland's application for membership.
50. Joint Action 97/154/JHA. *Official Journal* L 63, Feb. 24, 1997.
51. *Ibid.*
52. Joint Action 96/700/JHA. *Official Journal* L 322, Dec. 12, 1996.
53. Other elements include the fight against the sexual exploitation of children, the disappearance of minors and the use of telecommunications for such purposes.
54. Joint Action 96/748/JHA. Official Journal L 342 (Dec. 31, 1996).
55. Commission of the European Communities, *Communication from the European Commission to the Council and the European Parliament on Trafficking in Women for the Purpose of Sexual Exploitation* (Nov. 1996).
56. *Official Journal* C 251, Aug. 15, 1997.
57. Until this point there were highly differentiated approaches to the organized crime issue

throughout the EU. The difference in the legal approaches of Germany and the United Kingdom illustrates the extent of this range. Legislative developments in Germany include the 1992 *Gesetz zur Bekämpfung des Illegalen Rauschgifthandels und anderer Erscheinungsformen der Organisierten Kriminalität* (legislation to combat the illegal trade in drugs and other forms of organized crime) and the 1993 Geldwäschegesetz (money laundering legislation). Other more recent initiatives include the *Verbrechensbekämpfungsgesetz* of 1994 (legislation to combat crime) which contained further measures to combat organized crime and a variety of reforms to rules on asylum and aliens introducing *inter alia* harsher penalties for smugglers of illegal immigrants. In the UK, by contrast, there are no legal provisions with which to designate organized crime as an offense *per se*. The Association of Chief Police Officers (ACPO) working definition of organized crime is reflective of the legal situation, concentrating more on the activity than the perpetrators.

58. Other proposals of the Action Plan on Organized Crime which have been achieved include the signing of the Naples II Convention on customs cooperation; agreement on the Falcone Program for action against organized crime; joint action establishing a mutual evaluation mechanism; joint action establishing a European judicial network; and a joint action on good practice in mutual legal assistance in criminal matters.

59. See Justice and Home Affairs Council meeting press release (Mar. 19, 1998), Brussels, Document 6889/98.

60. Joint Action 98/245/JHA. *Official Journal L 99*, Mar. 31, 1998. The Joint Action categorizes such persons as judges, public prosecutors, police and customs departments, civil servants, public tax authorities, and authorities responsible for overseeing financial establishments and public procurement contracts and for combating fraud and corruption, representatives of professional circles and academics and scientists.

61. The EU's Grotius Program was established to provide for the training of magistrates and judges to promote and facilitate judicial cooperation.

62. Justice and Home Affairs Council Meeting 2075, Press Release (Mar. 19, 1998), Document 6889/98. The Odysseus Program will also benefit from current attempts to improve the effectiveness of CIREFI and CIREA in the dissemination of their information and statistics.

63. J.-P. Garson, "International Migration: Facts, Figures, Policies", *OECD Observer*, June/July 1992, pp.18–24.

64. Interviews with national officials have revealed occasional impatience with her "obsession" with the trafficking in women issue.

65. For example 'La Strada' is a program developed and coordinated by the Dutch Foundation against Traffic in Women (STV) which seeks to promote policies to prevent trafficking in women and provide victim support where necessary and has run from 1995 onwards.

66. The International Law Enforcement Academy (ILEA) is an important case in point. Established in Hungary to retrain law enforcement officials in eastern Europe, the Academy was supposed to attract joint support from the U.S. and the EU. The opposition of the French government to the American role in the project has, however, prevented the EU from participating in ILEA thus far.

67. Press release (Dec. 5, 1997). EU-U. Summit in Washington, DC.

DOCUMENTATION

Memorandum for the Secretary of State, the Attorney General, the Administrator of the Agency for International Development, the Director of the United States Information Agency – March 11, 1998

WILLIAM J. CLINTON

SUBJECT: STEPS TO COMBAT VIOLENCE AGAINST WOMEN
AND TRAFFICKING IN WOMEN AND GIRLS

As we celebrate International Women's Day today, we highlight' the achievements of women around the world. We also acknowledge that there is much work yet to be done to ensure that women's human rights are protected and respected. The momentum generated by the United Nations Fourth World Conference on Women in Beijing in 1995 continues to encourage our government, as well as nations around the world, to fulfill our commitments to improve the lives of women and girls.

I have once again, called upon the Senate to give its advice and consent to ratification to the Convention on the Elimination of all Forms of Discrimination Against Women, thus enabling the United States to join 161 other countries in support of the Convention. This Convention is an effective tool that can be used to combat violence against women, reform unfair inheritance and property rights, and strengthen women's access to fair employment and economic opportunity. Ratification of this Convention will enhance our efforts to promote the status of women around the world. As we look at Afghanistan and the egregious human rights violations committed against women and girls at the hands of the Taliban, we recognize that this is an issue of global importance.

My Administration is working hard to eliminate violence against women in all its forms. Our efforts help to combat this human rights violation around the world and here in the United States. As part of the 1994 Crime Bill, I signed into law the Violence Against Women Act. This legislation declares certain forms of violence against women to be Federal crimes and provides for critical assistance to States, tribes, and local communities in their efforts to respond to this problem. The Department of Justice is implementing the Violence Against Women Act and working with communities across the country to promote criminal prosecution and provide services to victims. Through the Department of Health and Human Services we have established for the first time a nationwide domestic violence hotline, so that women throughout the country can call one toll-free number and be connected to a local domestic violence support center. We have come a long way since 1994, and I am proud of our efforts.

Each day recognition of the importance of this issue grows around the world. In recent years, many countries have begun to respond to calls for legislation and government programs addressing violence against women. The international community increasingly regards violence against women as a fundamental human rights violation, an impediment to a nation's development, and an obstacle to women's full participation in democracy.

Today I am directing the Secretary of State, the Attorney General, and the President's Interagency Council on Women to continue and expand their work to combat violence against women here in the United States and around the world. We have made great progress since the enactment. of the Violence Against Women Act in 1994, but there remains much to be done. We must continue to work to implement the Act fully and to restore the Act's protection for immigrant victims of domestic violence here in the United States so that they will not be forced to choose between deportation and abuse.

The problem of trafficking in women and girls, an insidious form of violence, has received a great deal of attention from the world community. This is an international problem with national implications. Here in the United States, we have seen cases of trafficking for the purposes of forced prostitution, sweatshop labor, and exploitative domestic servitude. The victims in these cases often believe they will be entering our country to secure a decent job. Instead, they are virtual prisoners, with no resources, little recourse, and no protection against violations of their human rights. My Administration is committed to combating trafficking in women and girls with a focus on the areas of prevention, victim assistance and protection, and enforcement. Our work on this issue has been enhanced by a strong partnership with nongovernmental groups and the U.S. Congress.

I am also directing the Secretary of State, the Attorney General, and the President's Interagency Council on Women to increase national and international awareness about trafficking in women and girls. I want to ensure that young women and girls are educated about this problem so that they will not fall prey to traffickers' tactics of coercion, violence, fraud, and deceit.

I also want to provide protection to victims. And finally, I want to enhance the capacity of law enforcement worldwide to prevent women and girls from being trafficked and ensure that traffickers are punished.

Therefore, I direct:

I. The Secretary of State, in coordination with the Administrator of the Agency for International Development, to strengthen and expand our efforts to combat violence against women in all its forms around the world. These efforts should be responsive to government and nongovernment requests for partnerships, expert guidance, and technical assistance to address this human rights violation.

II. The President's Interagency Council on Women to coordinate the United States Government response on trafficking in women and girls, in consultation with nongovernmental groups.

III. The Attorney General to examine current treatment of victims of trafficking including to determine ways to insure: the provision of services for victims and witnesses in settings that secure their safety; precautions for the safe return of victims and witnesses to their originating countries; witness cooperation in criminal trials against traffickers; and consideration of temporary and/or permanent legal status for victims and witnesses of trafficking who lack legal status.

IV The Attorney General to review existing U.S. criminal laws and their current use to determine if they are adequate to prevent and deter trafficking in women and girls, to recommend any appropriate legal changes to ensure that trafficking is criminalized and that the consequences of trafficking are significant, and to review current prosecution efforts against traffickers in order to identify additional intelligence sources, evidentiary needs and resource capabilities.

V   The Secretary of State to use our diplomatic presence around the world to work with source, transit, and destination countries to develop strategies for protecting and assisting victims of trafficking and to expand and enhance anti-fraud training to stop the international trafficking of women and girls.

VI.   The Secretary of State to coordinate an intergovernmental response to the Government of Ukraine's request to jointly develop and implement a comprehensive strategy to combat trafficking in women and girls from and to Ukraine. The U.S.-Ukraine cooperation will serve as a model for a multidisciplinary approach to combat trafficking that can be expanded to other countries.

VII.   The Secretary of State, in coordination with the Attorney General, to expand and strengthen assistance to the international community in developing and enacting legislation to combat trafficking in women and girls, to provide assistance to victims of trafficking, and to continue to expand efforts to train legal and law enforcement personnel worldwide.

VIII.   The Secretary of State and the Director of the United States Information Agency to expand public awareness campaigns targeted to warn potential victims of the methods used by traffickers.

IX.   The President's Interagency Council on Women to convene a gathering of government and nongovernment representatives from source transit, and destination countries and representatives from international organizations to call attention to the issue of trafficking in women and girls and to develop strategies for combating this fundamental human rights violation.

Exerpts from General Assembly Fifty-first Session Agenda Item 106, October 7, 1996

PROMOTION AND PROTECTION OF THE
RIGHTS OF CHILDREN
(Sale of children, child prostitution, and child pornography)

NOTE BY THE SECRETARY-GENERAL

In another case, in October 1997, Spanish police dissolved an international smuggling operation that transferred Chinese from the province of Fujian to destinations in Canada, the United States, and Great Britain. In short, there are multiple suppliers and multiple destinations for women and children who have become part of the global sex trade.

BRIEF REVIEW OF CONCERNS

Characteristics

There are certain characteristics that typify most commercial sexual exploitation of children, including the following:

(a) It is invisible. Children drawn into the net of prostitution are for the most part hidden from public scrutiny, either physically (they are not placed on display as are their adult counterparts), or under the guise of being of age, through the falsification of identification papers;

(b) It is mobile. The invisible nature of the phenomenon necessitates not only deviation from the usual places of operation like brothels, hotels, bars, and the like, but also frequent changes in the areas of operation;

(c) It is global. While the gravity of the situation for children may vary from region to region or from country to country, reports show that this kind of child abuse exists in practically all corners of the

218

world. The contagious nature of the phenomenon causes the blurring of lines between sending and receiving countries. Some countries that used to be considered supply countries are becoming demand countries as well. Likewise, children of countries heretofore considered to be on the demand side, are starting to be victimized either in their own country or elsewhere;

(d) It is escalating. Fear of AIDS and other sexually transmitted diseases, inter alia, leads to a greater demand for younger sexual partners. Children used to be substitutes for adult prostitutes; now, however, there is marked increase of preference for children over adults, pushing up the worth of children in the sex market.

(e) It is a highly profitable business. This is borne out by the fact that it involves not only *ad hoc* or individual "entrepreneurs", it is often conducted by international profiteers using systematic methods of recruitment within a highly organized syndicated network, which is often also involved in other criminal activities such as drug dealing.

SPECIAL FOCUS ON THE JUSTICE SYSTEM

The justice system is among the three catalysts the other two being the media and education, that the Special Rapporteur has identified as having crucial roles to play in the fight against child abuse. It is reiterated that this is not intended to exclude other sectors that have just as important an impact on the problems. This is simply the Special Rapporteur's way of tackling the issue in a more focused manner.

The justice system can be a forceful ally of children on at least two levels: on prevention of child abuse and exploitation, and on avoiding secondary victimization of children in its response processes.

LAW ENFORCEMENT

The police force, as a system, and its internal organization must change and adapt itself to the care of children. The seriousness of offenses against children must be acknowledged, both through formal policy of the force and through informal internal norms. This change has to be visible in terms of programs and in terms of the exercise of authority and power.

As it is not likely to be feasible for all police officers to be trained in handling children, special police officers should be appointed to look into cases involving children. There should be training program to sensitize and motivate them to effectively intervene in this area. Crimes against children must be addressed by adopting a victim-centred approach. Training should be institutionalized and regular, not ad hoc or sporadic activities. A police manual on procedures in handling children should be adopted to ensure avoidance of secondary victimization during the investigation process.

Where there is perceived corruption or inefficiency in the police force, powerful information campaigns should be conducted to create the groundswell of popular indignation necessary to promote reform.

Mobile units for the surveillance of the places of usual operation where children are at greater risk should be set up and made operational.

Laws aimed at protecting children should be enforced more effectively. Law enforcement officers should be provided with more incentives to improve their performance, and should be encouraged to work in coordination with, and not in opposition to, non-governmental organizations.

PROBLEMS AT THE INTERNATIONAL LEVEL

The prosecution of international crimes against children is extremely difficult, expensive, and time-consuming. Not only are the substantive and procedural issues endemic, the national concerns and priorities may also be dissimilar Differences in language and legal systems and bringing the witness(es) from abroad further complicate the issue. Some of the pressing problems on the international level are:

(a) Disparity in the laws of the different countries concerned may act as an insurmountable barrier to effective prosecution of the case. The substantive provisions may relate to the elements of the offense, the penalties imposable therefore and the prescriptive periods for prosecution. For example, the use of a real child as a subject may be one of the elements for the crime of child pornography in one country, while in another visual imagery may be sufficient to sustain a conviction. Countries adopt different strategies in the penalization of offenses involving abuse and exploitation of children.

Some classify the crimes as minor, thereby making them more susceptible to successful prosecution, whereas others classify them as serious and even heinous, thereby making them susceptible to the imposition of a grave penalty. This imposition of a grave penalty may work as a deterrent on the national level where the offender is also a citizen of the same country, but it may have an adverse effect where foreigners are involved. International cooperation is difficult to achieve where there is a serious variance between the imposable sentence of the country of the offense and the country of the offender The issue becomes even more complex when there is great difference. in the nature of the penalty, as when in lieu of or in addition to imprisonment there is mutilation inflicted;

(b) Lack of a workable arrangement between the countries where demand emanates and the countries providing the "supply" of children giving prime consideration to crimes against children where trafficking is involved;

(c) Lack of a workable arrangement between countries to ensure the protection and safety of child victims of trafficking in the process of repatriation. Where children are victims of trafficking across frontiers, victimization can start with the retrieval of the children from their employers, and continue with the referral to immigration authorities prior to their repatriation, the manner by which the children are transported, their reception by the immigration authorities of their country of origin, and even their release either to their families or to welfare organizations;

(d) Foreigners in countries where there is no extradition treaty act with impunity because of the assurance that they are beyond the reach of the law after leaving the country where the abuse has been committed;

(e) Countries where the commercial abuse of children is not perceived as a problem may not be as concerned in the search for solutions, even if its nationals are participants in child exploitation activities. Eliminating the demand is an often-forgotten facet of child protection. Attention is usually lopsided, focusing on the used rather than the user, seeking solutions addressing the source of supply without corollary measures to eliminate the demand for children;

(f) Advances in the development of modern technology pose a very serious problem to law enforcement in the field of pornography. Anonymity is available on the Internet. A user can manufacture virtually any identity and route from country A, through country B, to country C and then to country A again, where it would be impossible to determine the origin of the first message. The industry is also experiencing a rapid development in cheap, user-friendly encryption software which is employed by child pornographers. Decoding the files is often extremely difficult for law enforcement agencies. An individual may now trade and/or sell images of almost any kind from one end of the world to the other.

Even if law enforcement officials discover the image, the ability to distribute it may not be impaired. Once an image is introduced on the Internet, it can be downloaded by any number of users and can be reproduced repeatedly without any loss of quality.

RECOMMENDATIONS AT THE INTERNATIONAL LEVEL

The search for solutions cannot be in isolation within the confines of a country, especially where there is cross-border trafficking or difference in nationality between the abused and the abuser Regional and/or worldwide cooperation will often not only be desirable, but indispensable. At the same time, however we should not fall into the trap of believing that there can be a single magic formula that can work for all countries. Every country will ultimately have to determine for itself how to remedy its own situation, taking into account all the circumstances peculiar to the country, from causation, to the political, social and cultural background of its peoples, to modes of recruitment, the *modus operandi* of the abusers, the identification of other countries with which it has links, etc.

The following are some recommendations on how cooperative efforts between countries could be carried out:

(a) There must be a determination by a country of the other country or countries with which it has links, either because they are the sending country and the receiving country or because the offenders in one country are usually nationals of another country. Countries with common borders, for instance, would have need for closer coordination in order to prevent trafficking in children;

(b) Having determined the country or countries with which links exist, governments should explore the possibility of having cooperative arrangements through any of the following:

(i) Synchronization of laws on the elements of the crime against children, on the nature and length of the penalties imposable and on rules of procedure, especially in evidence-taking;

(ii) Arrangements by which abusers in a foreign country may be subject to prosecution either where the offense took place or in the country of the offender. This could be done either through extradition or expansion of jurisdiction through extraterritoriality. With respect to extradition, there should be analysis of how extradition relationships could be effectively designed between nations. We must also take note of the fact that for some States, extradition is an available alternative even without a treaty, but on the basis of the national law of both of the States concerned.

World Congress Against the Commercial Sexual Exploitation of Children – Provisional Report of the Congress

GENERAL RAPPORTEUR
PROFESSOR VITIT MUNTARBHORN

DECLARATION AND AGENDA FOR ACTION

The Declaration and Agenda for Action of the World Congress was adopted unanimously on August 28, 1996. Colombia and Cuba made declarations concerning the text subsequent to its adoption.

The Declaration and Agenda for Action are tantamount to a commitment from the global community to eliminate the commercial sexual exploitation of children. The Declaration calls for all States in cooperation with national and international organisations and civil society to:

- Accord high priority to action against the commercial sexual exploitation of children and allocate adequate resources for this purpose;

- Criminalize the commercial sexual exploitation of children as well as other forms of sexual exploitation of children, and condemn and penalize all those offenders involved, whether local or foreign, while ensuring that the child victims of this practice are not penalized;

- Enforce laws, policies and programs to protect children from commercial sexual exploitation and strengthen communication and cooperation between law enforcement authorities;

- Develop a climate through education, social mobilisation, and development activities to ensure that parents and others legally responsible for children are able to fulfill their rights, duties and responsibilities to protect children from commercial sexual exploitation;

- Enhance the role of popular participation, including that of children, in preventing and eliminating the commercial sexual exploitation of children.

The Agenda for Action is a checklist, a set of guidelines for concrete action at the local, national, regional and international levels. Its components include coordination and cooperation, prevention, protection, recovery, and reintegration and child participation to counter the commercial sexual exploitation of children. Two time frames are stated as guidance for local and national cooperation as follows:

(a) urgently strengthen comprehensive, cross-sectoral, and integrated strategies and measures, so that by the year 2000 there are national agenda(s) for action and indicators of progress, with set goals and time frame for implementation, targeted to reducing the number of children vulnerable to commercial sexual exploitation and nurturing an environment, attitudes, and practices responsive to child rights;

(b) urgently develop implementation and monitoring mechanism(s) or focal point(s) at the national and local levels, in cooperation with civil society. so that by the year 2000 there are data bases on children vulnerable to commercial sexual exploitation, and on their exploiters, with relevant research and special attention to disaggregating data by age, gender, ethnicity, indigenous status, circumstances influencing commercial sexual exploitation and respect for confidentiality of the child victims especially in regard to public disclosures.

The Declaration and Agenda for Action are particularly supportive of the 1989 Convention on the Rights of the Child and refers to this treaty and other international instruments, recommendations and targets which have bearing on children and their families.

While the message of law, implementation, enforcement, and sanctions was often heard during the Congress against both the demand and supply factors, there was also recognition that substantive laws need to be coupled with cooperative mechanisms such as extradition and mutual assistance agreements, both formal and informal, at the bilateral, regional, and multilateral levels, for evidence gathering, sharing of data, and the tracing of the sex exploiters as well as prosecution in child-friendly judicial systems. However, the legal perspective is incomplete when tested from the psychological and socio-medical angle of child sexual exploitation. The mere fact that one manages to convict an exploiter and to sentence him/her to prison does not necessarily lead to behavioral changes. Psychological and socio-medical interventions may thus be needed to treat the sex exploiter as well as to offer long-term monitoring.

The global mobilization against the commercial sexual exploitation of children and this World Congress are thus essential for complementing the existing international standards, promoting needed reform, fostering enforcement of child-friendly laws and systems and supporting stronger monitoring for transparency and reporting for accountability to key international organs working on the issue. These include, in particular, the Committee on the Rights of the Child established by the Convention on the Rights of the Child and the Special Rapporteur on the Sale of Children mandated by the UN Human Rights Commission.

INTERNATIONAL COOPERATION

"International cooperation" was voiced throughout the period of the World Congress. It is a key to the intentions of the World Congress and future action. It implies multi-levelled cooperation, inter-disciplinary, and inter-sectoral by nature, including the following:

- promotion of alliances between the international, regional, and national communities and related agencies to counter the commercial sexual exploitation of children;

- improved coordination/collaboration between government and non-government sectors, including businesses, the media, law enforcers, community leaders, politicians, parents and children, bearing in mind the call for decentralization and support for grass roots initiatives;

- bilateral, sub-regional, regional, and multilateral action and agreements (both formal and informal) to monitor against commercial sexual exploitation of children, to detect the exploiters and trace the children affected, to facilitate prosecution and other measures against the exploiters, and to assist the recovery of children;

- restructuring of international and national development and aid so as to provide more support for child/family related programs to focus on action against commercial sexual exploitation;

- promotion of technical cooperation to share knowledge/expertise on the issue;

- standardization of procedures for legal/judicial cooperation, e.g. on evidence sharing, on video-taping, and on a non-punitive response to the child victims.

Abstracts

Illegal Migration: Personal Tragedies, Social Problems, or National Security Threats? *by Margaret E. Beare*

This study surveys the issue areas and policy dilemmas related broadly to illegal migration. Like all complex issues, to understand illegal migration one must understand the context: political, economic, and social environments; motivations of the illegal migrating populations and other non-illegal migrant groups; the identity of those who exploit and/or are serviced by the illegal migrants. This essay discusses illegal migration within the wider debate over "security threats" which result as a consequence of transnational crimes. It concludes that if "human security" is seen to be distinct from a more traditional focus on "national security", and if human security is responded to in a manner that is not reliant on the police and the military, then the broader human security terminology can legitimately be applied to illegal migration. A predominantly law enforcement or military response is argued to be seldom appropriate for the diverse issues that fall under illegal migration.

Capitalizing on Transition Economies: The Role of the Russian Mafiya in Trafficking Women for Forced Prostitution *by Gillian Caldwell, Steven R. Galster, Jyothi Kanics, and Nadia Steinzor*

This essay explores the issue of child pornography as it has been transformed by new technologies. Following a discussion of definitional issues, it provides an overview of contemporary manifestations of child pornography, particularly the transnational dimension. It then reviews some of the counter-measures which are being mobilized, and indicates what the most appropriate configuration of these counter-measures might entail, in both domestic and transnational contexts.

Trafficking in People in Thailand *by Pasuk Phongpaichit*

Thailand is a major center for human trafficking. This piece presents a description of the main flows, and a calculation of the profits (value-added) earned from the trade in 1994–95. Thai workers and sex-workers are trafficked to Japan, Taiwan, Germany, and elsewhere. Cheap labor is trafficked into Thailand from Burma and other neighboring countries. The estimated profit earned in Thailand from agents' fees was 5–7 billion baht, equivalent to US $200–280 million at the current exchange rate. The traffic of Thai women as sex-workers to Japan, in particular, is a system of indenture or slavery. Profits from trafficking arise because governments refuse to acknowledge the reality of labor markets. Trafficked sex-workers are often doubly illegal and hence vulnerable to exploitation. These problems should be tackled by more realistic government-to-government agreements on labor flows and the treatment of migrant labor, and by the de-criminalization of adult prostitution.

Organized Crime and Trafficking in Women from Eastern Europe in the Netherlands *by Gerben J.N. Bruisma and Guus Meershoek*

The prostitution sector is becoming more international. After the fall of the Iron Curtain the number of prostitutes from eastern and central Europe in the Netherlands increased rapidly. This contribution presents the results of an empirical study on trafficking in women from central and eastern Europe, conducted by researchers of the University of Twente in close cooperation with a team of policemen and crime analysts of a special inter-regional criminal investigation department on organized crime from East Europe and Turkey. Based on empirical data from 1994 to 1996, police sources, information from local police units concerned with supervising prostitution, and interviews with victims and with persons involved in the prostitution business, special attention is given to the *modus operandi* and nature of the criminal groups involved. Although most of the women leave their country voluntarily, once in the Netherlands they have to work under bad conditions, are more or less imprisoned, and earn only a very small fraction of the amount of money they were promised in their home country. Not all arrested offenders for trafficking in women are members of organized crime groups. A more differentiated picture emerges from the data. The Dutch police files show small, loosely organized cliques of professionals as well as larger organized crime groups having their center in eastern and central Europe or in the Netherlands.

Prostitution and the Mafia: The Involvement or Organized Crime in the Global Sex Trade by Sarah Shannon

Organized criminal syndicates specialize in such illicit behaviors as drug trafficking, arms smuggling, gambling and extortion. A lesser-known phenomenon is organized crime's involvement in forced prostitution and other forms of commercial sexual exploitation, which together create the multibillion-dollar industry known as the global sex trade. The functions that criminal organizations perform in this unlawful enterprise are numerous and vary by global region and criminal group. However, the incredibly lucrative nature of the sex business ensures organized crime's increasing participation. This study highlights various facets of the sex trade and examines the scope and nature of organized crime's involvement in what is a burgeoning global industry.

Trafficking in Women and Children: A Market Perspective by Phil Williams

The markets in women and children for commercial sex are similar in their essentials to any other illicit market. This essay attempts to understand the phenomenon by applying a market analysis. It sets out a market framework for trafficking in women and children: its size and scale, its profitability, the dynamics of supply and demand, and the market actors. It then considers the measures governments and law enforcement agencies can take in order to create market barriers. It concludes that the scale of the problem requires a concerted domestic and international program to attack the market in all its dimensions.

Child Pornography in the Digital Age by Anna Grant, Fiona David, and Peter Grabosky

Among the most significant developments in the world today are those brought about by the convergence of computing and communications. For all the positive opportunities they have brought, these new technologies have also been exploited for criminal purposes. In particular, child pornography and its distribution have been significantly transformed in the digital age. This essay explores how new technologies have greatly facilitated the production, reproduction, and dissemination of child pornography. Following a discussion of definitional issues, the article looks at contemporary manifestations of child pornography,

230

particularly its transnational dimension, and the degree of organization which its distribution can entail. Noting that the application of new technologies to child pornography presents significant new challenges for law enforcement, the study then reviews some of the counter-measures that are being mobilized against child pornography in the digital age, and indicates what the most appropriate configuration of these counter-measures might entail, in both domestic and transnational contexts.

The Fusion of Immigration and Crime in the European Union: Problems of Cooperation and the Fight against the Trafficking in Women *by Penelope Turnbull*

Since the early 1990s the member states of the European Union (EU) have been engaged in an attempt to create and consolidate an essentially unique institutional architecture to address contemporary challenges to internal security in Europe. The fusing of immigration and crime issues into an "internal security continuum" has been a notable tendency in discursive developments and has since become a defining element in both institution building and substantive policy responses. This essay is concerned with the process of fusion, in particular its implications for the development of European cooperation. It will be argued that it has created significant institutional and political barriers to improved cooperation and has obscured the human rights and civil liberties dimensions of many migration issues. Despite these difficulties however, it would appear that in the case of the trafficking in women there has been a concerted effort to advance cooperation. The study analyzes the position of this issue on the EU's internal security agenda and its implications for the EU's enlargement. The nature of the EU's response to the trafficking issue is examined with a view to establishing whether political rhetoric has been matched by policy practice.

Notes on Contributors

Margaret E. Beare combines academic teaching with research and policy development. She worked in the area of police research for eleven years within the Department of the Solicitor General Canada, and served two years as Director of Police Policy and Research. She is presently Associate Professor in the Sociology Department at York University and is the Director of the Nathanson Centre for the Study of Organized Crime and Corruption, at Osgoode Hall Law School. Her previous research includes two volumes on legalized gaming, police powers, an assessment of the RICO Statute, and a report on money laundering. Her book *Criminal Conspiracies: Organized Crime in Canada* was published in 1996 by Nelson Canada.

Gerben J.N. Bruinsma is Professor of Criminology and Director of the International Police Institute Twente at the Faculty of Public Administration and Public Policy of the University of Twente in the Netherlands. He was recently appointed Director of the Netherlands Institute for the Study of Criminality and Law Enforcement (NISCALR) at Leiden and Professor of Criminology at the Law Faculty of the University of Leiden. He has published a number of books and articles on organized crime and the police.

Gillian B. Caldwell is an attorney with a background in international human rights, civil rights, family law, and filmmaking. She is the Director of the WITNESS project at the Lawyers' Committee for Human Rights, which uses video and technology to advance human rights. She is currently working to produce a documentary film on trafficking and the associated exploitation of immigrants in New York City sweatshops. Ms. Caldwell was previously Co-Director of the Global Survival Network (GSN), where she was the project director for a three-year investigation into and campaign to combat the international trafficking of women. At GSN, Gillian produced and directed "Bought & Sold", a highly publicized documentary on GSN's exposé of the an mafia's trafficking of women for forced prostitution.

Fiona David is a Research Analyst at the Australian Institute of Criminology in Canberra, Australia. A former tutor in the Faculty of Law at the Australian National University, her current areas of specialty include laws relating to sexual offences, the sex industry, and criminal injuries compensation. She is currently engaged in a national stocktake of legislation and policy on services to crime victims in Australia, and in research on the prevention and control of sexual assault.

Steven R. Galster is Executive Director of the Global Survival Network (GSN), which he co-founded in 1995. He has led international investigations and remedial campaigns related to the illegal trade in wildlife, people, and arms. While in the Russian Far East, he started a two-year undercover investigation into the trafficking of women and girls from the former Soviet Union to Asia, Europe, and North America. He led GSN's research efforts by developing a dummy company and, working with Russian assistants, documenting, on hidden camera, a long series of business discussions with traffickers in Russia, Japan, Germany, United States, Macau, and Hong Kong. Information and film derived from this investigation were used to create a written report, "Crime & Servitude", and a video documentary, "Bought & Sold". Using these informational tools, GSN led an international campaign to raise governmental and grass-roots awareness of the phenomenon of trafficking, and to tackle it with education, economic reform, and enforcement. He is currently helping to coordinate GSN's research efforts into sweat shops, forced prostitution and domestic servitude in Asia, Eurasia and the United States.

Peter Grabosky is Director of Research at the Australian Institute of Criminology in Canberra, Australia, and President of the Australian and New Zealand Society of Criminology. He has written or co-written numerous books and articles on white collar crime, regulatory enforcement, and violence. His current area of specialization is complex criminal activity and high technology crime, and he has recently written, with Russell G. Smith, *Crime in the Digital Age: Controlling Telecommunications and Cyberspace Illegalities* (Sydney: the Federation Press and New Brunswick: Transaction Publishers, 1998). He is currently collaborating on a book about Internet-related theft.

Anna Grant is a Research Analyst at the Australian Institute of

Criminology in Canberra, Australia, where she currently specializes in research on correctional issues, including sex offender treatment. She has recently completed papers on such issues as the establishment of a new correctional facility, community correctional programs, prisoner management issues, treatment programs, and the management of elderly prisoners. With her co-authors of the study published in this volume, she recently completed a major report to the Australian Government on the commercial sexual exploitation of children.

Jyothi Kanics is Co-Director of the Human Trafficking Program at the Global Survival Network. She is currently responsible for facilitating GSN's electronic mailing list STOP-TRAFFIC and drafting educational materials for the Open Society Institute's Network Women's Program in Central and Eastern Europe and the Newly Independent States. She has spoken about trafficking to many audiences including the United Nations and international conferences sponsored by the European Union and United States Government. Ms. Kanics has taught English in the United States and as a Foundation for Civil Society fellow in Slovakia. Since 1995, when she interned with their OnLine Project, she has collaborated actively with the Nework of East-West Women.

Guus J. Meershoek is a historian and researcher at the International Police Institute Twente at the Faculty of Public Administration and Public Policy of the University of Twente. He recently finished a study on Russian organized crime in the Netherlands and is completing his doctorate on the role of the Amsterdam police during the Second World War.

Pasuk Phongpaichit is Associate Professor in the Faculty of Economics, Chulalongkorn University, Bangkok. She has published widely on the Thai economy, Japanese investment, labor issues, prostitution, corruption, and the illegal economy. With Chris Baker, she has written *Thailand: Economy and Politics* (Oxford University Press, 1995), which won a national research prize and is currently being translated into Japanese, and *Thailand's Boom and Bust* (Silkworm Books, 1998). She recently won the National Research Excellence award.

Sarah Shannon is a former student of the Matthew B. Ridgway Center of International Security Studies in the Graduate School of Public and

International Affairs (GSPIA), University of Pittsburgh. She is currently pursuing a joint degree (Master's of Business / Master's of Public and International Affairs) from GSPIA in the University of Pittsburgh's Katz Graduate School of Business.

Penelope Turnbull is a doctoral candidate at the Institute for German Studies in the UK. Her main areas of interest are the development of justice and home affairs cooperation in the European Union, Europe's new internal security agenda and the internationalization of internal security issues in Britain and Germany. She has published work on the creation of the EU's Third Pillar, the Europeanization of migration policy in Germany and Britain, Germany's asylum crisis and the European policy of the British Labour Party.

Phil Williams, Director of the Ridgway Center for International Security Studies and Professor of the Graduate School of Public and International Affairs, University of Pittsburgh, has published extensively in the field of international security and has co-edited books on security in Korea and crisis prevention in the Third World, as well as on the Carter, Reagan, and Bush presidencies. During the last seven years his research has focused on transnational organized crime and drug trafficking. He has written many articles on these subjects and is managing editor of the journal *Transnational Organized Crime*.

Index

Abella, Manolo, 23
Ad Hoc Group on Immigration, 193
Africa
  child exploitation, 137, 160
AIDS, 126, 132, 161, 162
air travel
  human smuggling, 30–1
Albanians
  in Italy, 138
Alderdice, Gary, 57–8
Asia
  child prostitutes, 3, 160
  migration flows, 75
  organized crime, 129–32
  sex tourism, 3, 82, 125, 130, 163
  trafficking of women, 2
Australia
  child pornography legislation, 174
  cost of illegal entry, 33
  prostitutes, 29
Austria
  trafficking, 18, 151–2
Axworthy, Lloyd, 13–14

balkanization, 26
Baytler, Gregory, 59–60
Bertelsmann Foundation, 191
Beyer, Dorianne, 135–6
Bigo, Didier, 190, 191, 198
Blair, Tony, 11
Bolivia
  sexual exploitation, 124
Bond, Jeff, 57
Brazil
  child prostitution, 136, 160
bribery, 31
Burma
  migrants to Thailand, 74, 89–92, 93–4,
    98–9

Cali, 135
Canada
  child pornography legislation, 174–5
  Chinese Triads, 129
  counter-measures, 18, 38

Hong Kong women, 126–7
case studies
  Thai prostitutes in Japan, 100–2
child pornography, 3–4, 8, 171–88
  counter-measures, 179–86
child prostitution
  counter-measures, 164–9
  Latin America, 135–7, 160
  market for, 159–64
  sex tourism, 3, 162, 163
  United States, 139
children
  global sex industry, 120
  sale by family, 122, 127–8
  trafficking of, 3–4, 48–9, 128, 131–2,
    136–7, 159–69
China
  affluent migrants, 20–1
  guanxi networks, 27
  illegal immigrants in United States, 1–2,
    126–7
  push-pull factors, 21
  'snake-heads', 1, 30, 31
  Triads, 38, 126, 127–8, 139–40
citizenship
  buying and selling, 23–4
Clinton, President, 9, 11, 17, 156–7, 214–17
Coffman, Douglas, 127
computer networks
  child pornography, 3–4, 162, 175–7
contracts
  signed by prostitutes, 63–4, 122
corruption, 4, 31, 34–6, 67–9, 94, 125, 134
counter-measures
  child pornography, 179–86
  child prostitution, 164–9
  European Union, 8–9, 18, 157, 189–213
  illegal migration, 17–18, 38–9
  trafficking, 8–9, 96–8, 156–9
criminal investigations
  child pornography, 183–6
Czech Republic
  trafficking to Netherlands, 110, 111

DAPHNE Initiative, 205

237